Positive Work Ways

L.S. Thomas

Copyright © 2025 L Thomas

All rights reserved.

ISBN 9798316380954:

Author's note

'There comes a point in your life when you need to stop reading other people's books and write your own.'
— unknown

I never set out to write a book. But after years of working with organisations, supporting wellbeing, performance, safety, and leadership, I reached a point where the same patterns kept showing up - and so did the same missed opportunities.

This book is my response. A way of bringing together the principles I've seen work in therapy and the workplace - and offering something practical, preventative, and genuinely useful. Not theory for theory's sake, but tools and ways of thinking that help people work, lead, and connect more effectively, starting with how the brain works under pressure.

Whether you're keen to explore ways to get more from your business or you want to do more to support your people proactively before things break down, this book is for you.

Note on sources and approach.

This book simplifies complex ideas from neuroscience, psychology, and solutions-focused practice into plain language and everyday examples. It's not an academic text, and it doesn't try to be. Instead, it aims to make science relatable and usable for busy professionals who want to understand what's going on underneath workplace behaviour - and how to influence it.

A short list of further reading is provided at the end of the book for those interested in exploring the underlying ideas in more detail.

Foreword

In many organisations, the signs are familiar. Teams under pressure. Communication slipping. Good intentions getting lost in reactive patterns. Whether it's labelled as a culture issue, a performance gap, or a leadership challenge, at the core it's often the same thing: people caught in the wrong state of mind for the situation they're in.

This book came from a simple belief: that workplaces can do more, and be more, than they perhaps realise, and even small changes in the ways we all communicate, work, and lead each day can start to change things for the better.

Positive Work Ways isn't built on a single theory or programme. It's a practical and relatable framework, shaped by professional experience and a long-standing interest in how the brain influences behaviour. It draws from established ideas in psychology and neuroscience, but it doesn't claim to have all the answers.

What it offers is a way to notice what's going on underneath, to ask better questions, and to create the kind of culture where people can think more clearly and work more effectively together.

I believe that when we get this right, the impact will go far beyond the workplace - not only improving the performance, resilience, wellbeing, and safety of individuals, teams, and organisations, but also wider society.

That's why I've focused on bringing proactive, preventative thinking into the workplace. And if this book helps start that shift - or supports the one you're already making - then that's exactly what it's here to do.

Contents

Author's note V
Note on sources and approach. VII
Foreword IX
Contents XI
Quick Start: Understanding Positive Work Ways XV

PART ONE: UNDERSTANDING YOUR BRAIN 1

Introduction 2
1: Decision-Making 5
2: The Push and Pull of Brain Dynamics 9
3: The Power and Pitfalls of Pattern Matching 13
4: The Default Mode Network – The Brain's Reflection Zone 17
5: Neurotransmitters and Neuroplasticity – How the Brain Talks and Grows 21
6: Downward and Upward Spirals 26
7: Communication 31
8: Culture – The Invisible Force 36
9: Perception – The Stories We Tell Ourselves 40
10: Individual Differences 44
Summary and Recap of Part 1 46

PART TWO: ENGAGING THE INTELLECTUAL MIND 49

Introduction 50
1. Active Visualisation 54
2. The Miracle Question 57
3. What Does Good Look Like? 60
4. Solutions-Focused Inquiry 62
5. Scaling 64
6. Challenging Negative Beliefs 68
7. Positive Self-Talk 71
8. Affirmations 74
9. Optimism 76
10. Empathy 78
11. Authenticity 80
12. Curiosity 82
13. Gratitude 84
14. Humour 86
15. Breathing Practices 88
16. Smiling 91
PART 2 REFLECTION 93

PART THREE: STRATEGIC INTERVENTION 95

Introduction 96
1: Strategic Vision 98
2: Strategic Goal Setting 101
3: Engaging Leaders 104
4: Communication – Building a Culture of Connection 107
5: Leadership and Workforce Development 111
6: Safety as a Brain State 114
7: Addressing Key Business Functions 117
8: External Well-being Providers: Maximising Impact 120
9: General Supply Chain – Beyond Your Organisation 123
10: Measurement 126
11: Support Resources: Bringing It All Together 129
Part 3 Summary 133
Conclusion 135

PART 4: WORKBOOK 137

Introduction 138
Activity 1: Active Visualisation 141
Activity 2: The Miracle Question 146
Activity 3: What Does Good Look Like? 150
Activity 4: Solutions-Focused Inquiry 154
Activity 5: Scaling 158
Activity 6: Reframing Limiting Beliefs 161
Activity 7: Positive Self-Talk 164
Activity 8: Affirmations 168
Activity 9: Empathy 172
Activity 10: Authenticity 176
Activity 11: Curiosity 180
Activity 12: Gratitude 183
Activity 13: Humour 187
Activity 14: Breathing Practices 190
Activity 15: Smiling 193
Workbook Section 2 196
Exercise 1: Reflection 197
Exercise 2: If… Then Mental Preparation 199
Exercise 3: Personalised Crib Sheets 201
Exercise 4: Active Visualisation – 'Imagining Success' 204
Exercise 5: Solutions-Focused Team Conversations 206
Exercise 6: Solutions-Focused Goal-Setting 209
Exercise 7: Introduction to Scaling 210
Exercise 8: Team Challenge 212
Workbook Section 3 214
Application 1: Difficult Conversations 216
Application 2: Shaping Corporate Voice 221

APPLICATION 3: GOAL SETTING WITH SCALING	226
APPLICATION 4: ENGAGEMENT & COLLABORATION ACROSS TEAMS	230
APPLICATION 5: DEVELOPING A FRAMEWORK FOR INTEGRATION	236
WORKBOOK REFLECTION: PROGRESS AND INSIGHTS	242
INTRODUCTION TO ORGANISATIONAL INTEGRATION	244
MODULE 1: ALIGNING STRATEGIC VISION	246
MODULE 2: STRATEGIC GOAL SETTING	252
MODULE 3: ENGAGING LEADERS WITH POSITIVE WORK WAYS	259
MODULE 4: STRATEGIC COMMUNICATIONS WITH POSITIVE WORK WAYS	265
MODULE 5: INCORPORATION OF POSITIVE WORK WAYS INTO L&D PROGRAMMES	271
MODULE 6: ALIGNING SAFETY STRATEGY WITH POSITIVE WORK WAYS	277
MODULE 7: FUNCTIONAL ALIGNMENT	282
MODULE 8: LEVERAGING EXTERNAL WELL-BEING PROVIDERS	287
MODULE 9: RETHINKING MEASUREMENT	292
MODULE 10: SUPPORT RESOURCES – BRINGING IT ALL TOGETHER	298
FINAL SUMMARY	304
TEMPLATES SECTION	**307**
UNIVERSAL TEMPLATE	308
SOLUTIONS-FOCUSED QUESTION BANK	311
REFRAMING RESPONSE BANK	315
SCALING FOR SUCCESS TEMPLATE	317
FURTHER READING	321
ACKNOWLEDGEMENTS	323
CONCLUSION	325
ABOUT THE AUTHOR	327
CONTACT & FURTHER SUPPORT	329

Quick Start: Understanding Positive Work Ways

This section gives you a fast, practical introduction to the Positive Work Ways framework - a straightforward approach that combines brain-based insights with practical techniques to encourage positive workplace change.

You don't need a background in science, just a few clear concepts that help make sense of what's going on underneath, so you can work with it more effectively.

Because every interaction has an impact. And once you can see what's shaping it, you're in a better position to influence what happens next: in yourself, your team, and the culture around you.

What is Positive Work Ways?

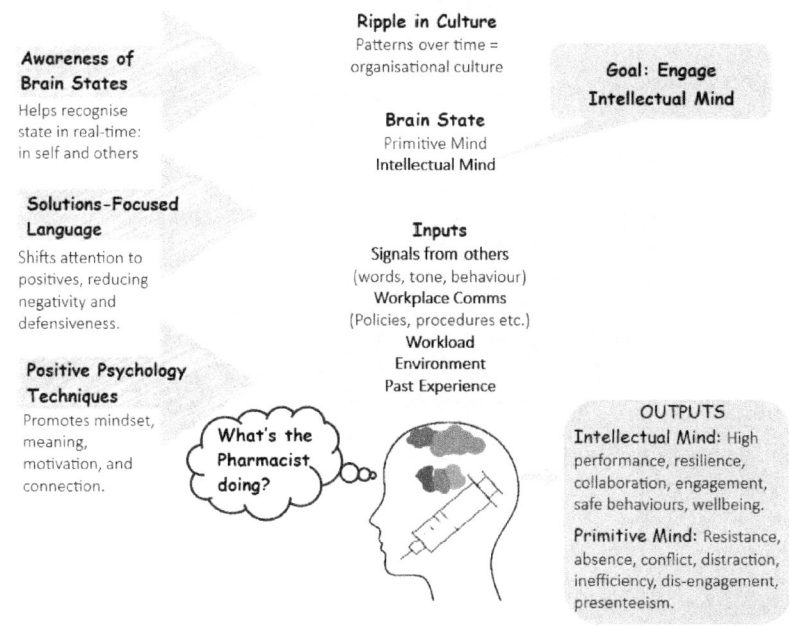

Positive Work Ways offers a practical approach to improving culture, performance, and well-being. It uses simple, well-known brain metaphors as a relatable way to explain some complex brain processes and pairs them with practical ways to turn insight into action. It's built on three layers:

Awareness of brain states

Understanding the difference between two very different brain states that we refer to as the Primitive and Intellectual Mind, and recognising which one you (or those around you) are in at any given time.

A guiding question: What's the Pharmacist doing?

This question prompts you to pause and check in. Are you calm or triggered? Thinking clearly or reacting? What is your internal state doing to your behaviour?

Tools to influence brain state

Once you've noticed the state, Positive Work Ways draws on proven techniques from positive psychology, solutions-focused thinking, and neuroscience to help you make a shift, for yourself and others.

It's not about being perfect. It's about small, consistent changes that help people feel safer, think better, and perform more sustainably. Over time, the way people work and interact starts to change - and culture follows.

A Simple Analogy

Your brain is working in the background all day long. It's not just thinking - it's constantly scanning, storing, retrieving, comparing, and reacting - often before you're even aware of it. Positive Work Ways uses a simple analogy built around two core elements:

The brain team: comprised of 3 key internal players, continually working behind the scenes and influencing your reactions.

Two brain 'states': the overall mindset you're in at any given moment. Together, they shape how you think, feel, behave, and how you interact with others.

The Team

The Radar (amygdala)

Your early warning system, continually scanning for anything that might signal a threat, such as sights, sounds, facial expressions or even a tone of voice.

Fundamental to our survival, it always assumes it's better to be safe than sorry – reacting super-fast and without conscious input. However, it's not always accurate.

The Filing Cabinet (hippocampus)

Your memory store. When the Radar spots something, it checks in with the Filing Cabinet: Have we seen this before? What happened last time? The brain forms an almost instantaneous interpretation of what's happening and whether action is needed.

The Pharmacist (hypothalamus)

Once the decision is made, the Pharmacist responds by releasing brain chemicals that, in turn, influence how you feel and act.

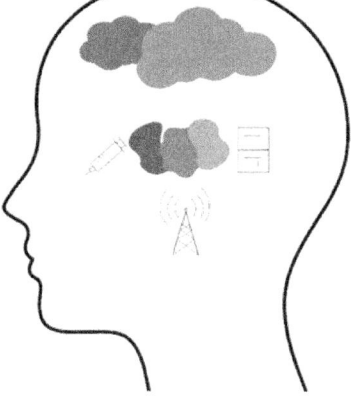

If the Radar senses danger, it might trigger cortisol or adrenaline, and if things feel safe and positive, it might release dopamine or serotonin.

These chemicals shift your internal state and shape your outward behaviour - often without you even noticing. This internal team is working in the background - all day, every day - influencing your thoughts, actions, and how you respond to the people around you.

The Two Brain States

Positive Work Ways draws on a common analogy: your brain operates in two distinct states, shifting between them depending on how safe, supported, or under pressure it feels.

The Primitive Mind

This is your survival state. It kicks in when the Radar senses danger, threat, or stress and prioritises speed over logic. You might feel defensive, anxious, withdrawn, angry, or stuck. You may want to act fast - or freeze altogether.

The Intellectual Mind

This is your 'thinking' state. It's where logic, empathy, creativity, and perspective-taking live. When you're in this state, you think clearly, solve problems, manage emotions, and connect with others.

These states aren't permanent, we all move between them throughout the day. But which one you're in makes a big difference to what happens next.

Inputs and Outputs: Brain State Outcomes

Your brain doesn't shift states at random. It reacts to inputs - both external and internal.

- An unclear message,
- A loaded email,
- An unsupportive tone,
- A raised eyebrow,
- A memory that pops into your head.

The Radar picks up those signals. The Filing Cabinet adds context. The Pharmacist acts on the result. That combination determines your brain state, and your brain state drives your outputs.

When you're in the **Primitive Mind**, you're more likely to:

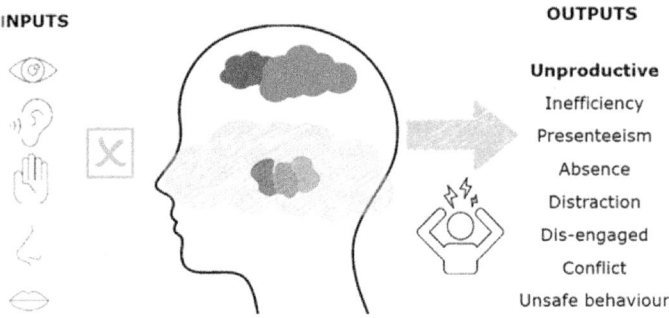

- **React** emotionally or defensively.
- **Avoid** problems or get stuck in short-term thinking.
- **Withdraw**, snap, or shut down.
- **Experience** conflict and low morale.

When you're in the **Intellectual Mind**, you're more likely to:

- **Communicate** calmly and clearly.
- **Solve problems** and make sound decisions.
- **Show empathy**, ownership, and resilience.
- **Contribute** to innovation, safety, inclusion, and well-being.

INTELLECTUAL MIND

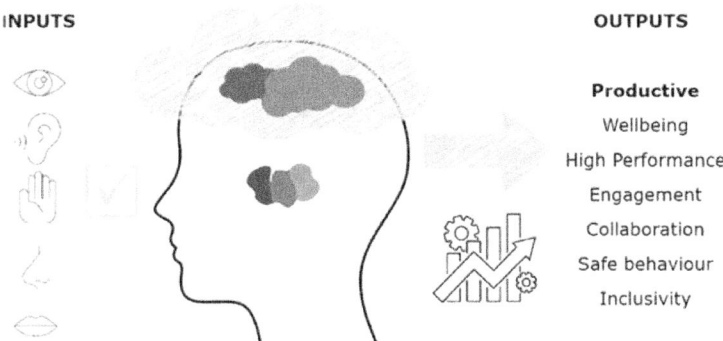

INPUTS

OUTPUTS

Productive
Wellbeing
High Performance
Engagement
Collaboration
Safe behaviour
Inclusivity

You can't be in both states at once. And over time, staying stuck in the Primitive Mind takes a toll - on health, performance, and workplace culture.

But the goal isn't to eliminate stress completely. Sometimes, the Primitive Mind gives us what we need to act quickly or push through something tough. The key is knowing which state you're in and learning how to shift if it's not the right one for the situation.

That's what Positive Work Ways helps you do - for yourself, and across your workplace.

Why This Matters

When you understand how the brain states work, and what triggers them, you can start to:

- **Recognise** your own state in the moment.
- **Notice** the impact of your actions on others.
- **Shift** your state when needed.
- **Support** and facilitate a shift in others.
- **Change** how you communicate and interact - for better outcomes.

It helps you step back from blame and start asking more constructive questions, such as:

- What's really going on underneath that reaction?
- What signals am I sending out?
- **What's my Pharmacist doing right now?**
- **How are my words and actions influencing the Pharmacist in others?**

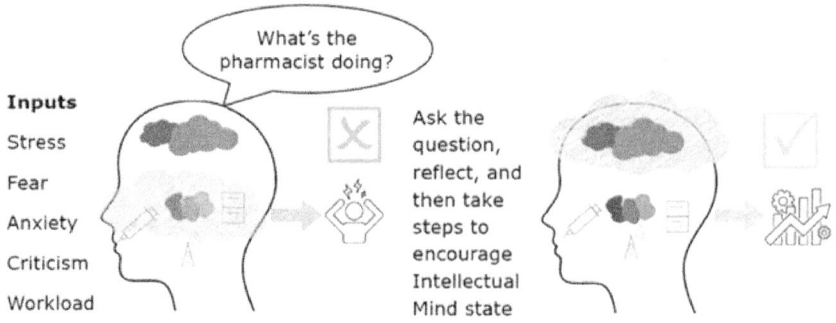

What's the Pharmacist Doing?

Those last two questions lie at the heart of Positive Work Ways.

Continually questioning what your Pharmacist is doing, or how your actions might influence someone else's pharmacist, can start to change the way you communicate, lead, and collaborate.

Culture as Collective Brain State

So far, we've looked at individual brains. But what happens when we scale that up? Imagine entire teams, departments, or organisations operating from either the Primitive or the Intellectual Mind.

Culture can feel vague or abstract, but it's just repeated patterns of behaviour, communication, and interaction. In other words, **culture can be viewed as brain state at scale.**

When the Intellectual Mind is dominant, culture is more likely to feel positive:

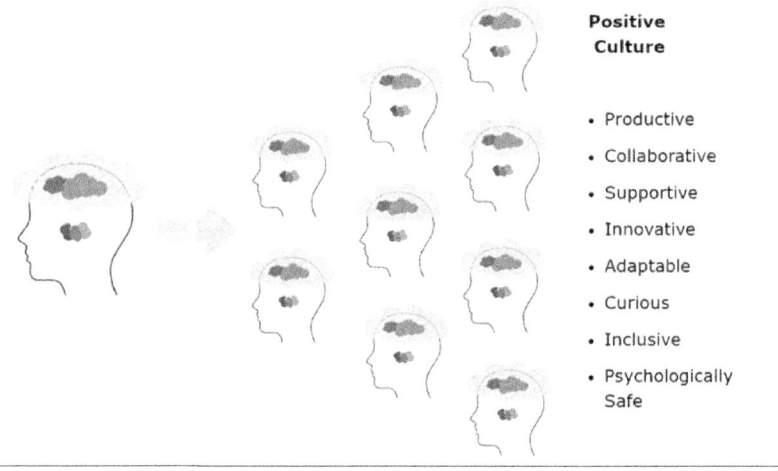

Quick Start Guide

When the Primitive Mind dominates, the culture is more likely to be negative.

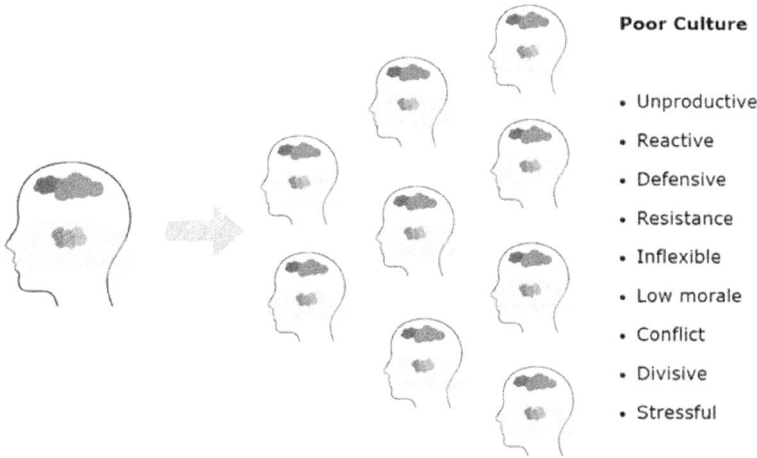

Poor Culture

- Unproductive
- Reactive
- Defensive
- Resistance
- Inflexible
- Low morale
- Conflict
- Divisive
- Stressful

Leaders influence this significantly, often without realising it. Your tone, timing, tension, or even silence? That's someone else's input. Your mindset and language ripple into someone else's Pharmacist.

This is why brain state matters far beyond the individual level. If we want to shift culture, we don't start with posters or campaigns. We start with awareness, behaviour, and communication shaped by brain-friendly principles and built into the way people work.

Your Starting Challenge: Spend a Day with Your Pharmacist

To start building your awareness, try this:

- Spend one whole working day asking yourself: **What's my Pharmacist doing right now'**
- Check in a few times. What thoughts, tone of voice, or interactions are shifting your state?
- Is that email triggering a Primitive Mind reaction?
- Is your tone helping others feel safe, or adding pressure?
- How are my words and actions affecting the Pharmacist in others?

It's not about fixing everything. It's about starting to notice. And once you notice, you can start to influence what happens next.

In Summary

Positive Work Ways is about more than personal awareness, it's about creating conditions that influence brain state across teams, organisations, and beyond.

- It helps you recognise the patterns shaping behaviour
- It helps you influence them, in yourself and others
- It starts with noticing - but it doesn't end there

By applying this thinking throughout everyday work, you don't just improve outcomes - you change the way your organisation feels to be part of.

Part One: Understanding Your Brain

Introduction

> *'Would you tell me, please, which way I ought to go from here?'*
> *'That depends a good deal on where you want to get to,' said the Cat.* – Lewis Carroll, Alice in Wonderland

When things feel stuck or uncertain, it's easy to assume we need more information, more time, or a new strategy. But often, the biggest shift comes from seeing what's already happening underneath the surface.

We talk about leadership, communication, performance, and culture every day. But what if the way we think, decide, and behave isn't just shaped by skill or experience… but by something even more fundamental - our brain state?

The Brain's Role in Leadership

Whether you're leading a conversation, a project, or a business, your brain is constantly shaping how you show up. It affects

- The decisions you make.
- The tone you set.
- The way you handle pressure.
- How you interpret others, and how they interpret you.

Understanding how your brain works doesn't mean ignoring gut instinct or experience. It means working with them and building on them. Even a small insight into what's driving your reactions can help you lead with more clarity, confidence, and connection.

Think of it like this: a pilot with years of flying experience still needs to understand the aircraft they're in. That knowledge doesn't replace experience - it enhances it, especially under pressure. Leadership is no different.

Why This Knowledge Matters

This part of the book doesn't aim to turn you into a neuroscientist, and it doesn't need to. But it will introduce some key concepts that can help you:

- Make sense of your own leadership patterns
- Recognise what's influencing others
- Change how you respond, especially in high-pressure moments

Understanding how your brain responds to stress, uncertainty, and interactions gives you an extra edge, especially when the stakes are high. And when more people in an organisation have that insight, culture starts to shift too.

What Part One Explores

In the chapters ahead, you'll start to build a practical understanding of the brain's role in leadership, and how small changes in brain state can drive much bigger shifts in behaviour and culture.

You'll explore:

- The brain's internal team, and how it works behind the scenes.
- What happens to your thinking under pressure.
- A practical analogy to help make sense of it all.
- How communication, tone, and leadership style affect brain state.
- Why this matters - not just to individuals, but to entire teams and organisations.

This section builds the foundation for everything that follows.

Reflect and Act

Before we dive in, take a moment to check in:

- How often do you think about how your brain affects your leadership?
- What's one thing you'd like to change about how you respond under pressure?
- What would change if you understood what was going on underneath your own reactions, and other people's, too?

You don't need to know everything about the brain to lead well. But knowing a little more, especially about what drives behaviour, might just change the way you lead for good.

Let's meet your team.

1: Decision-Making

'The leader is one who, out of the clutter, brings simplicity... out of discord, harmony... and out of difficulty, opportunity.' Albert Einstein

The average adult makes tens of thousands of decisions every single day. Continually shaped and reshaped by habits and past experiences, your brain makes most of those decisions without your conscious awareness - from deciding what to eat to handling essential meetings.

Every decision that you make relies on communication between the parts of your brain that help you think, react, and lead. Each part plays a different role, and how effectively they all work together affects your success. An understanding of this decision-making process can provide you with a greater sense of control and help you to lead more effectively. Let's meet the team.

Your Brain's Leadership Team

Think of your brain as a team, each with a different role:

The CEO (Prefrontal Cortex): Plans ahead, makes decisions, and keeps things objective.

The Radar (Amygdala): Scans for threats - it protects you but sometimes overreacts.

The Filing Cabinet (Hippocampus): Key role in memory retrieval and learning.

The Pharmacist (Hypothalamus): Releases brain chemicals that influence your energy, mood, and emotions.

Throughout Part 1, we will explore the role these different members play and how they interact with each other to influence our in-the-moment brain state.

Two Brain States: Primitive Mind vs. Intellectual Mind

The brain is the most complex organ in the human body. So, to keep things simple, we are going to be working with the analogy of two leading brain states that direct how you think, feel, and act:

The Primitive Mind: Reacts immediately and instinctively, perfect for survival.

The Intellectual Mind: Acts calmly and strategically - great for leadership.

Both states are equally important. The Primitive Mind steps in to protect our survival when there is no time to stop and think, while the Intellectual Mind navigates us through our daily lives in a calmer, more objective manner. Simply becoming aware of which state is in play at any time builds resilience and helps you make better decisions.

How Brain State Affects Leadership

Any perceived threat from our environment triggers the Radar (Amygdala) and brings the Primitive Mind into play. The Primitive Mind is there for our survival. It is quicker and more powerful than our Intellectual Mind – it has to be, in order to keep us alive. Because the language of the Primitive Mind is reactive, once this part of your brain takes control, it can lead to:

- Rapid, emotional decisions.
- Tense team dynamics.
- A narrower focus, obscuring the bigger picture.

However, once the threat passes and the Intellectual Mind - led by the CEO – is able to regain control, things are very different with:

- Thoughtful and well-balanced decisions.
- Productive and collaborative team dynamics.
- Objective consideration of the whole picture enabling practical, strategic thinking.

Imagine you're in a meeting, and someone disagrees with you. If the Primitive Mind is in play, you are likely to feel defensive and respond quickly without thought. If, however, the Intellectual Mind is leading, you are more likely to pause and think before responding more constructively.

The Ripple Effect

You're stressed, and your Primitive Mind takes over. In the heat of the moment, you bang out an email using negative language and apportioning blame. After sending it, you don't feel any better, and you walk away from your laptop.

But it doesn't stop there. The hostile tone of the email causes the recipient's brain to detect a threat, activating their Primitive Mind. The ripple then continues throughout the team, leading to misunderstandings, low morale, and reduced performance.

Stress-driven decisions affect more than you—they can cascade rapidly through your team and beyond. Recognising your brain state in these moments and taking a few simple steps to intervene can very quickly lead to better outcomes - for you, your team, and your organisation.

Practical Exercise

Take a few minutes to reflect on a recent challenge (e.g., resolving a conflict, friction in a meeting, sending a frustrated email, making a tough decision under pressure).

Goal: Identify which part of your brain was in play during key moments.

Steps:

Ask yourself:

1. Did the Radar (Amygdala) trigger?

2. Did the Primitive Mind come into play?

3. How did this influence your thoughts, feelings, and actions?

4. How did the Intellectual Mind regain control?

Reflection:

Reflect on how these dynamics shaped your behaviour and the outcome.

Chapter 1 Recap

- Your brain's leadership team guides your decisions and emotions.
- Stress can activate the Primitive Mind.
- When the Primitive Mind is in play, this can lead to impulsive and reactive decisions.
- When the Intellectual Mind is in play, you think more calmly and strategically.
- Being aware of which part of your brain is in play can help you make better choices.

Key Leadership Takeaway

Your brain's leadership team is your ultimate toolkit for making precise, thoughtful decisions, even under pressure. How these parts respond to our environment affects our brain state.

By noticing whether your Primitive Mind or Intellectual Mind is in control, you can improve your decisions, build trust, and inspire confidence in your team.

Reflect and Act

Think about a recent decision:

- Did you pause to think, or did the Primitive Mind take over?
- Before making your next decision, pause for five seconds.
- Take a couple of deep breaths.
- Notice how it changes your thinking.

Meeting your brain's leadership team is just the start of our journey. In the next chapter, we'll explore a little more about how your brain manages the constant push and pull between instinctive reactions and strategic thinking.

2: The Push and Pull of Brain Dynamics

'Your mind is a powerful thing. When you filter it with positive thoughts, your life will start to change.' ~ *Gautama Buddha*

The Primitive Mind: Quick and Reactive

Within the brain team, the Radar (Amygdala) is continually scanning your environment for threats. Once a threat is detected, it immediately steps to the rescue. By the time the Intellectual Mind has had a chance to catch up, the Primitive Mind has already taken action - working closely with the Filing Cabinet (Hippocampus) to determine what action to take (we cover more on this later in Part 1) and sending a signal to the Pharmacist (Hypothalamus) to release brain chemicals like cortisol and adrenaline to prepare your body to respond.

This fast and powerful response can save your life in real emergencies, but unfortunately, in the modern world, what our Radar perceives as a threat often doesn't merit the force of response that is initiated.

The Primitive Mind is reactive and survival-driven, meaning that the language it responds with is always a survival response—either anger, anxiety, or withdrawal (think fight, flight, freeze). Anger makes us stronger to fight, anxiety gets us ready to flee, and depression causes us to withdraw.

These are great responses when your survival is at stake, but they are not so helpful when you have to make an important decision quickly under high pressure. The Primitive Mind can be like a runaway train - fast and hard to control.

Imagine you're in an important meeting, and someone uses a sharp and slightly aggressive tone. Your Radar instantly detects it and triggers a stress response. Your heart races, and you feel the urge to react quickly. With your Primitive Mind in play and your Intellectual Mind sidelined:

- You struggle to think objectively.
- Your speech becomes rapid and jittery.
- You become either defensive, overly assertive, or completely withdrawn.
- You start jumping to conclusions or overreact.

Once you calm down and your Intellectual Mind comes back into play, you may be surprised or even embarrassed by your response. Welcome to the Primitive Mind!

The Intellectual Mind: Calm and Strategic

The Intellectual Mind, led by the CEO (Prefrontal Cortex), works very differently. It, too, works alongside the Radar (Amygdala), Filing Cabinet (Hippocampus), and Pharmacist. Still, the process is a little different, allowing it to do what it does best – think creatively, consider options, and make balanced decisions.

In contrast with the Primitive Mind, the language of the Intellectual Mind is focused on logic, reason, and solutions. Let's revisit the same meeting to see how things would play out if you are able to prevent your Primitive Mind from jumping in and instead keep your Intellectual Mind in play.

The Intellectual Mind listens and then pauses while it quickly accesses and considers any relevant past experiences (thanks to the Filing Cabinet), calms your emotions (with help from the Pharmacist), and then tries to find a solution that works for everyone. With your Intellectual Mind in play, you can:

- Stay calm under pressure.
- Think creatively and solve problems.
- Build trust and work well with others.

The Intellectual Mind is like a GPS-guided car—steady, adaptable, and focused on the best path forward.

Practical Exercise

Objective: Raise awareness of when Primitive and Intellectual Minds are in charge.

Steps

Over the next week, notice when you feel stressed or reactive (e.g., getting negative feedback, friction with a colleague or team member, or handling an urgent request).

For each moment, ask yourself:

1. Was this my Primitive Mind reacting quickly?

2. What clues (like feeling tense or upset) told me that?

3. How could I have paused and re-engaged my Intellectual Mind?

Try taking a couple of deep breaths or counting to five before responding in similar situations – see if it changes things.

Reflection Questions
- What signals tell you that your Primitive Mind is in play?
- How does pausing before reacting change the outcome?
- What helps you engage your Intellectual Mind when you're under pressure?

How Leadership Shapes Culture

The dynamics between your Primitive and Intellectual Minds don't just affect you - they influence your team and everyone else around you.

When the Primitive Mind is in play, you are far more likely to make impulsive and unpredictable decisions, creating a team culture of anxiety and mistrust. However, by taking steps to keep the Intellectual Mind in play, you make considered, objective choices that encourage a healthier team culture of collaboration and productivity.

Think again about the example of a leader sending an email in a stressful situation. Once the Primitive Mind comes into play, the response is more likely to include hasty decisions and a negative tone - resulting in tension and confusion quickly spreading throughout the team.

This is a stark contrast to a calmer and more considered response generated by the Intellectual Mind that reassures, motivates, and builds trust. Either response creates the ripple effect we discussed in Chapter 1, and the brain state from which the response is sent can be enough to influence whether that ripple is negative or positive.

Setting the Stage for Growth

Understanding these two brain states is a step to better leadership. When you notice your Primitive Mind coming into play, you can pause, refocus, and let your Intellectual Mind regain control. This doesn't just improve your decisions - it creates an environment where your team can thrive. In Part 2, we explore lots of different ways to encourage you to spend more time in the Intellectual Mind and to gain control back quickly and efficiently when the Primitive Mind starts knocking.

Chapter 2 Recap: The Push and Pull of Brain Dynamics

- The Primitive Mind reacts quickly to stress, which can lead to impulsive decisions.
- The Intellectual Mind slows things down, allowing for thoughtful responses.
- Great leadership balances these two brain states to make better decisions and to foster trust and collaboration in their teams.
- Recognising when stress takes over helps you pause, shift gears, and make choices that inspire confidence.

Key Leadership Takeaway

Balancing your Primitive and Intellectual Minds helps you move from reacting to leading. This balance improves your decisions and shapes a positive team culture.

Reflect and Act

- Think about a time when your Primitive Mind took over. What happened?
- How can you shift to your Intellectual Mind when you feel stressed?
- This week, notice one moment when you can pause and lead with your Intellectual Mind.

The tug-of-war between brain states shapes how we lead, but what happens when your brain uses past experiences to guide quick decisions? In the next chapter, we'll look at pattern matching and how it can help you make decisions faster.

3: The Power and Pitfalls of Pattern Matching

'All that we are is the result of what we have thought.'
— Buddha.

Think of situations when you know what to do without conscious thought. That's your brain's pattern-matching system at work - using past experiences to guide your decisions in the present moment. But what happens when those patterns don't match the situation?

We all rely on pattern matching when making decisions, spotting trends, or solving problems. It's also a key method our brain deploys to process vast volumes of information efficiently, enabling us to react and respond quickly to our surroundings.

But sometimes, it can also lead to mistakes. In this chapter, we'll look at how pattern matching works, why it's helpful, what problems it can cause, and how it can affect your decisions, your team, and your workplace.

What Is Pattern Matching?

Pattern matching is when your brain links a current situation and something similar that has occurred in your life before, relying on memories to help you decide what to do next. It's a quick way for your brain to connect the dots.

Here's how it works in day-to-day life when things are just ticking nicely along:

The Radar (Amygdala) scans for threats and detects nothing of concern.

The Filing Cabinet (Hippocampus) pulls out a memory that feels similar.

The CEO (Prefrontal Cortex) decides how to respond.

However, if the Radar detects what it perceives as an 'immediate' threat to our safety - for example, an angry or aggressive voice or facial expression - then things work a little differently:

The Radar (Amygdala) detects the aggressive tone of voice or facial expression.

The Filing Cabinet (Hippocampus) still pulls out a memory that feels similar, but instead of the CEO being engaged to make the decision, a stress response is triggered.

The Pharmacist (Hypothalamus) responds to the perceived threat by releasing brain chemicals that prepare us to fight, take flight, or withdraw.

Now, imagine getting an email from your manager. It's short, feels abrupt, and is worded rather negatively. Your brain pulls out memories of past emails that were critical, and you assume there's a problem. But in reality, your manager might simply be busy or having a bad day.

The Benefits of Pattern Matching

Pattern matching is beneficial most of the time. It aids with:

Quick Decisions: It saves time by using what you already know.
Example: A leader sees signs of team burnout, remembers similar situations, and takes action.

Spotting Trends: It helps you notice patterns in data or behaviour.
Example: A sales manager spots a change in customer habits and updates the sales strategy accordingly.

Building Confidence: Familiar situations feel more manageable, and outcomes feel more predictable, helping you to act with more certainty.
Example: Each time a team repeat an activity with positive outcomes, confidence continues to grow.

The Risks of Pattern Matching

Sometimes, though, pattern matching can lead you in the wrong direction. Pattern matching relies heavily on memories, but unfortunately, those memories are not always accurate, or they are applied out of context. Here are some problems it can cause:

Overgeneralising: Thinking that what worked before will always work again.
Example: Under pressure, an employee automatically responds to a situation by applying a previous solution when the current situation is actually very different and requires a different response.

Bias: Memories can cause unfair judgments.

Example: A hiring manager may be more drawn to candidates who remind them of past employees, entirely missing fresh talent.

Tunnel Vision: Focusing too much on past patterns can block new ideas.

Example: Repeatedly sticking to the same methods instead of trying something new, even when the outcomes are potentially sub-optimal.

Emotional Reactions: Stressful memories can also make you act defensively.

Example: Avoiding risks because of a past mistake or missing opportunities.

How Pattern Matching Affects Teams

Pattern matching doesn't just affect one person - it influences entire teams.

Hiring: Leaders might choose people who seem familiar, which reduces diversity.

Change: Someone might resist new ideas, sticking to what they know.

Team Dynamics: Misunderstandings and jumping to conclusions can hurt relationships, for example, thinking someone is uninterested or inattentive just because they're quiet.

Recognising and questioning some of these patterns can raise self-awareness, lead to fairer decisions, and encourage creativity and inclusion.

Finding Balance

As we have explored above, in the face of perceived threats, pattern-matching can pull you into your Primitive Mind, where decisions are fast but reactive. The problem is that these reactive decisions are not always rational or logical – and sometimes, they can even be inappropriate. To engage your Intellectual Mind and get back on track, sometimes you need to intervene consciously.

Example

An individual gets some feedback that feels critical. The Radar flags it as a threat, and the Filing Cabinet pulls out memories of past criticism. If the manager reacts defensively, it may lead to an instinctive, perhaps even poor, response. However, they may be able to pause and take active steps to re-engage their intellectual mind. In that case, they are far more likely to be able to reframe the feedback more positively and experience better outcomes.

Practical Exercise

Objective: Notice and question assumptions based on past experiences.

Steps:

Think of a recent time you made a quick judgment about an individual or a situation. Ask yourself:

- Was my reaction based on a memory?
- Could I have misunderstood?
- What other ways could it have been interpreted?

Next time, try to pause for a moment and take a few breaths to encourage your intellectual mind to re-engage.

Try asking questions that open up and explore the situation, for example: 'What would a good outcome be here?' or 'Could you share your thoughts?'

Chapter 3 Recap

- Pattern matching helps your brain link situations to past experiences, aiding quicker decision-making.
- Although it can be beneficial most of the time, it can sometimes lead to errors such as bias, tunnel vision, or emotional reactions.
- Becoming more aware of and questioning these patterns can lead to better decisions and encourage more productivity, fairness, and innovation in teams.

Key Leadership Takeaway

Understanding how your brain uses pattern matching is a key step to making better choices. Raise your awareness, challenge your assumptions, stay curious, and create space for new ideas.

Reflect and Act

- Think about when pattern matching helped - or misled - you.
- What's one pattern you could reassess this week?

In the next chapter, we'll explore how quiet moments of reflection activate your brain's Default Mode Network, opening the door to more creativity and insight.

4: The Default Mode Network – The Brain's Reflection Zone

'Sometimes I sits and thinks, and sometimes I just sits.'
– A.A. Milne, Winnie the Pooh

With technology woven into almost every aspect of our daily lives, it can feel like we're constantly glued to a screen - whether answering emails, attending online meetings, mulling over spreadsheets, or drafting reports.

The more recent trend in remote and hybrid working has brought with it increasing pressure to be constantly online and available. Taking time away from screens and devices to sit and 'think' or work offline can be misinterpreted as unproductive or even 'skiving.'

Yet, sitting at a laptop for hours on end with a constant influx of data can, at the least, prove distracting - and at worst, mentally exhausting. So, could stepping away and taking a break be precisely what your brain actually needs? Let's learn about the Default Mode Network (DMN) and why it matters.

What Is the Default Mode Network?

Imagine you're sitting, sipping a coffee, gazing out the window and lost in thought. You're roused suddenly by your phone pinging as another email arrives - instantly grabbing your attention and bringing your entire focus back to the room. You look at the time and realise you've been totally lost in thought for over ten minutes.

You chastise yourself for losing focus and turn your attention back to the report you were writing. However, far from being unproductive during your time out, your brain has been constantly working hard in the background the entire time - connecting ideas, thinking about the past, and imagining the future.

This is the Default Mode Network (DMN), your brain's 'reflection zone.' The

Default Mode Network works quietly away behind the scenes, activating whenever your attention isn't focused on a specific task to assist with things like:

Self-Reflection: Thinking about your actions and feelings.

Social Understanding: Reflecting on others' emotions or what they might do.

Planning: Looking back at past events or thinking about the future.

Have you ever had a brilliant idea in the shower or while going for a walk? That's your DMN at work!

Why the Default Mode Network Matters for Leaders

The Default Mode Network is essential for leadership because it helps you think beyond what's happening right now.

Imagine you're on a bus to work, sitting quietly and not focusing on anything specific, when a solution to a tricky dilemma that's been bothering you for weeks pops into your mind – seemingly from nowhere.

That's the Default Mode Network at play, linking past experiences with future possibilities to come up with a creative new solution. Here's how the Default Mode Network supports you as a leader:

Self-Awareness: Quiet moments allow the mental space needed to reflect more objectively.

Empathy: Reflecting on how others may feel nurtures stronger relationships with your team and others around you.

Creativity: Creative and innovative reframing and connection of ideas.

Resilience: Reflection and reframing of challenges and exploration of potential solutions strengthen resilience.

The Double-Edged Sword of the DMN

The Default Mode Network is mighty, and most of the time, it is a positive and beneficial tool in your brain toolkit. However, just like other brain processes, it can cause problems in times of doubt or stress, leading to:

Overthinking: Rumination may arise if too much time is spent worrying about past mistakes or potential future events.

Self-Criticism: Self-esteem may become damaged if too much focus is repeatedly placed on perceived weaknesses.

False Assumptions: Friction and poor decisions may arise through misinterpretation of others' words and actions.

Example

When something goes wrong, brooding for too long on any mistakes we feel we made can draw us into rumination, leading to increased self-doubt and less favourable future outcomes. However, when reflection is positive and paired with positive action, it has the opposite effect and instead becomes a powerful vehicle for personal growth.

Practical Exercise

Steps

Take a break and let your mind gently wander.

1. Reflect on a recent challenge or opportunity.
2. Notice any ideas or patterns that come up, trying not to judge them.
3. Write down your thoughts - how could you start turning them into actions?

Reflection Questions

- What ideas came to you during your reflection?
- How did taking time out to reflect change the way you view certain things?
- How can you make space for reflective moments in your daily life?
- How can you encourage reflection time among your teams?

Balancing Reflection and Action

The Default Mode Network springs to life during our quieter moments. The reflective process it initiates can lead us to uncover and explore some great ideas, but action is still required to turn those ideas into reality.

The art comes in acquiring the skill to switch between reflection and decision-making to get the best outcomes. Achieving this paves the way for a balance between reflection and action that supports more effective strategies and successful outcomes.

Chapter 4 Recap: The Default Mode Network

- Active during rest, the DMN is your brain's reflection zone.
- It helps to fuel new ideas, supporting creative problem-solving and decision-making.
- It helps raise self-awareness and strengthen empathy.
- When used effectively, it can enhance leadership and create more positive team cultures.
- Although reflection is powerful, it requires action to follow through.
- It can be used consciously to drive personal growth as well as team success.

Key Leadership Takeaway

Reflection isn't wasted time - it's when your brain connects ideas and generates creativity. By making time for quiet moments throughout your day, you'll improve your leadership and inspire your team.

Reflect and Act

- Reflect on times you've had your best ideas - what were you doing when the eureka moment struck?
- This week, make a point of taking two 10-minute reflection breaks and allow your mind to wander.
- Make a note of your ideas.

Quiet reflection fuels creativity, but what helps your brain grow and adapt to challenges? In Chapter 5, we'll take a look at the role of neurotransmitters and neuroplasticity, and how you can use this knowledge to become a more effective leader.

5: Neurotransmitters and Neuroplasticity – How the Brain Talks and Grows

> *'We are what we repeatedly do. Excellence, then, is not an act, but a habit.'*
> *– Aristotle.*

Similar to the changing environment in a forest, your brain is continually evolving throughout your lifetime. Nutrients (chemical messengers) nourish and enrich the soil, and animal tracks (pathways of thought) appear and disappear depending on how often they are used. Your brain is continuously responding and adapting in a similar way, strengthening well-travelled neural pathways and allowing redundant ones to diminish.

In this chapter, we'll examine two key brain processes that facilitate these changes: neurotransmitters—the chemical signals that keep everything in balance—and neuroplasticity, the process that enables your brain to evolve and adapt over time.

What Are Neurotransmitters?

Neurotransmitters are chemicals that carry messages between brain cells. They affect how you feel and act. Let's look at a couple of the key players - and how they impact leadership:

Dopamine: Motivation and Reward

- Each time a goal is accomplished, the brain releases dopamine, which makes you feel good and motivates you to do more.
- Inspiring and motivating people in the workplace engages their dopamine reward systems, encouraging higher performance.
- Even small wins can boost dopamine levels that help to keep teams motivated.

Cortisol: The Stress Alarm

- Cortisol is a key player in the stress response necessary for our survival. At the appropriate levels, it can help respond effectively to stress.
- Chronic stress can lead to excessive levels of cortisol in your body - elevated levels over a more extended period can be harmful to your health.
- Managing stress effectively keeps cortisol levels in check, safeguards mental health and avoids burnout.

Oxytocin: The Trust Builder

- Oxytocin encourages social bonding – it helps people feel connected and valued.
- Simple acts, such as showing kindness and gratitude, release oxytocin, creating a more supportive atmosphere.
- A simple (authentic) 'Thank you for your hard work' after a meeting may be all your team needs to feel appreciated.

Serotonin: The Mood Booster

- At the correct levels, serotonin regulates mood and aids memory.
- Serotonin helps you stay calm and confident, even during more challenging times.
- When a leader stays steady under pressure, it can help to reassure the team and keep things balanced.

Practical Exercise

Goal: Integrate ways to motivate and support your team into daily activities.

Steps

1. Choose one action to try with your team this week:
   - Celebrate a small win or progress.
   - Show gratitude or encourage teamwork.
   - Create space for a break or a calm moment.
2. Use this action during a team interaction (e.g. praising someone's effort or offering support during a stressful time).
3. Notice how it affects the team's mood and energy.

Reflection Questions
- How did your action change the team's mood or teamwork?
- How can you do this regularly to keep the team motivated?

What Is Neuroplasticity?

Neuroplasticity is your brain's capacity to adapt and rewire throughout your life, building new neural pathways every time you learn something new. With each repetition, these new pathways strengthen, becoming increasingly quicker and more efficient, whilst pathways that are no longer required weaken and slowly fade away.

Neural pathways shape how you think, learn, and respond to the world around you - strong pathways are faster and more efficient. For leaders, this is excellent news, it means you can:

- Build positive habits by repeating good behaviours to reinforce existing pathways.
- Help your team grow by encouraging them to try new things to build new pathways.

Example: A leader who encourages learning creates a team that's open to new ideas. This helps everyone become more creative and adaptable.

Practical Exercise

Goal: Strengthen your brain and your team's growth.

Steps

Pick a new skill you'd like to develop this month.

1. Plan when and how you will practice it – set reminders if necessary.
2. Repetition is key, so be sure to practice it regularly – no skipping!
3. Notice how quickly this skill becomes easier.

How This Helps Leaders

A tiny bit of knowledge about neurotransmitters and neuroplasticity is enough to help you start creating a more positive and motivated workplace. Here's how:

Motivation and Energy
Setting realistic goals and celebrating even small successes boosts dopamine.

Stress and Calm

Managing stress more effectively can lower cortisol and other chemicals released during the stress response, helping your team remain calm and focused.

Trust and Connection

Displaying authentic gratitude releases oxytocin, which builds trust and strengthens relationships with those around you.

Learning and Growth

Learning new skills builds and strengthens neural pathways, helping your team adapt and become more agile.

Why This Matters for Teams

Even just a superficial insight into how the brain grows and adapts enables you to use this knowledge to build a high-performing, flourishing team. When you focus on working with the brain rather than continually fighting against it, you create a robust foundation for productivity and growth.

Example

A leader who shows empathy, encourages learning, and finds ways to work in more brain-friendly ways inspires creativity and resilience in their team.

On the other hand, ignoring stress or failing to show empathy can lead to burnout and disengagement.

Chapter 5 Recap: Neurotransmitters and Neuroplasticity

- Neurotransmitters directly influence how you and your team feel, think, and act.

- Neuroplasticity means your brain is constantly learning and adapting by building new neural pathways, whereas pathways that aren't used fade over time.

- Leaders who apply this knowledge to themselves and their teams can create a motivated, happy, and resilient team.

Key Leadership Takeaway

You don't need an in-depth knowledge of all the different chemicals and brain processes – just an essential awareness is sufficient to enable you to influence your team's energy, motivation, trust, culture, and resilience.

Reflect and Act

- How do your actions influence the brain chemicals of yourself and those around you – is it positive, or is there room for improvement?

- How could you use this knowledge to optimise your team?

- This week, pick one positive habit, like giving feedback or encouraging learning, and make it part of your routine.

Understanding these few basic brain concepts is powerful knowledge in its own right. In the next chapter, we'll explore how your actions create ripple effects - both positive and negative - and how you can use these to build a stronger, more connected team.

6: Downward and Upward Spirals

'What we achieve inwardly will change outer reality.'
– Plutarch.

Patterns shape every organisation—repeated ways of thinking, working, and interacting that either fuel progress or reinforce barriers. Influencing individuals, teams, and leadership, these same patterns shape everything from daily decision-making to long-term strategy.

Some patterns build momentum toward confidence, engagement, and growth, while others pull people into cycles of stress, avoidance, or disengagement. In this chapter, we'll explore two ways in which these patterns develop:

Ripples – The way our actions, attitudes, and behaviours spread outward and influence those around us.

Spirals – Self-reinforcing cycles that propel our feelings, thoughts, and behaviours in either a positive or negative direction.

Understanding how these forces work—and how to influence them—can transform an organisation from the inside out.

What are Ripples?

The way we think, act, and communicate doesn't just remain with us—it extends outward, also influencing those around us. Every interaction, no matter how small, creates a ripple effect that, in turn, shapes the thoughts, emotions, and behaviours of others

Ripples can be positive or negative, and they can either set the tone for collaboration, engagement, and trust - or trigger tension, doubt, and disengagement. They happen automatically, without conscious effort. A leader's enthusiasm about a project can energise a whole team, just as an offhand negative comment can drain motivation. The brain is wired to detect and respond to these cues—often before we even realise it—creating a chain reaction that influences how people feel, behave, and make decisions.

The cumulative effect of these ripples can define workplace culture. When positive ripples dominate, teams are far more likely to feel engaged, resilient, and open to any challenges that arise. However, when negative ripples start to creep in, stress, friction, and miscommunication can quickly spread.

A raised awareness of the ripples we transmit and receive can help us take greater control over how they influence our own actions, as well as those of our teams and organisations.

How the Intellectual and Primitive Mind Influence Ripples

Our brain constantly scans. It interprets and responds to every expression, tone of voice, or change in body language to determine whether an environment is safe or threatening before we consciously process what's happening.

- **When a signal is perceived as positive**, the brain responds from the Intellectual Mind.
- **When a signal is perceived as negative**, the Primitive Mind is more likely to be triggered.

Our brain state directly influences our behaviour, meaning that our interpretation of our environment determines our reaction, which in turn also sends a ripple outward:

So, if I sense frustration in you, I might tense up or become defensive. My reaction, in turn, becomes a new signal for those around me, who, in turn, will respond accordingly.

And so, the ripple spreads—one shift in brain state influencing the next, until the entire dynamic of a team, meeting, or even organisation is shaped by it.

What Are Spirals?

Spirals are self-reinforcing cycles that can be either positive or negative:

Upward Spirals – Where positive experiences, thoughts, and actions build on each other, strengthening engagement, creativity, and resilience.

Downward Spirals – Where negative experiences, thoughts, and actions build on each other, diminishing engagement, creativity, and resilience.

Spirals and the Intellectual and Primitive Mind

The Primitive Mind focuses on our survival, which can lead to negative behaviours and responses that can quickly ripple out to others. If this negativity continues to build, a downward spiral can start to develop, pulling us into a cycle of rumination that potentially exacerbates any issues we face even further.

A team consistently operating from their Primitive Minds creates more individual and collective negative spirals, leading to unhelpful behaviours and actions that reflect the language of the Primitive Mind, such as increased anxiety, friction, withdrawal, etc.

The Intellectual Mind, on the other hand, supports rational thinking and measured responses that make us more open to listening, adapting, and finding solutions. As we spend more time in the Intellectual Mind, it becomes easier to remain there as the positive thoughts and emotions continue to build and strengthen - and so a positive spiral develops.

A team consistently operating from the Intellectual Mind creates more individual and collective positive spirals, driving a positive momentum that leads to rational and considered behaviours and actions.

The Role of Neuroplasticity

As covered in the previous chapter, neuroplasticity is the ability of our brains to rewire themselves. Each repetition of a thought or behaviour builds and strengthens the neural pathways required to sustain it, making it more likely to happen again.

Neuroplasticity is one of the reasons that negative spirals can feel so difficult to escape from—the more time we spend in a repeated pattern of negative thought, the more our brains become conditioned to expect failure, frustration, or conflict.

The good news is that we can all utilise neuroplasticity to intentionally influence positive spirals, replacing habits that might be keeping us stuck with ones that drive growth and success instead.

Influencing Spirals in the Workplace

Ripples and spirals continually occur and develop in response to our environment. Raising awareness of these patterns as they form and taking deliberate action to influence them enables us to initiate and maintain more upward spirals and interrupt and halt downward ones.

Some ways to redirect a downward spiral and initiate positive momentum:

Reframe the narrative. When you start to dwell on a problem, intentionally forcing the focus onto possibilities, 'This won't work' to 'What could work?'

Introduce small wins. Even a minor success can sometimes be sufficient to break a negative cycle. Take some time to reflect and focus on things that have gone well or worked.

Change the environment. If you sense a downward spiral starting, step away—whether that means shifting the conversation, introducing a lighter activity, or taking a break.

Reinforce what's working. Focusing on strengths and progress helps to redirect energy away from setbacks and toward solutions.

Create emotional shifts. Even small doses of encouragement, humour, or appreciation can interrupt negative cycles and change direction.

Practical Exercise

Reflect on a recent team meeting and identify when a ripple occurred.

1. Reflect on how it started and evolved.
2. How did it affect the mood or energy of the team?
3. How did it influence engagement, motivation, and behaviour?

Identify a current spiral happening in your team or organisation.

1. Is it upward or downward?
2. What behaviours or interactions are reinforcing it?
3. What might shift the direction of this spiral?

Choose one small action you could take to shift or reinforce a spiral.

- If it's positive, how can you amplify it?
- If it's negative, what simple intervention might begin reversing it?

The aim of this exercise isn't to fix everything at once—it's to become more aware of the ripples and spirals around you and understand how small, deliberate changes can redirect momentum.

Chapter 6 Recap

We are all continually sending out ripples and initiating spirals that don't just impact ourselves - they also impact those around us. As a leader, your words, your tone, and your actions are continually influencing how your teams think, feel, and perform.

Understanding this isn't about control—it's about raising awareness to create positive change. Recognising the significant impact our words and actions can have on others enables us to create ripples and spirals that benefit everyone.

Key Leadership Takeaway

If your reactions lead to stress-based responses, those around you will be more likely to operate from their Primitive Mind, leading to short-term thinking, resistance, and disengagement. If your responses support Intellectual Mind thinking, you're far more likely to see effective problem-solving, creativity, and resilience in your teams.

Reflect & Act

- What small actions do you take each day that send ripples into your team?
- Are those ripples leading to an upward or downward spiral?
- What is one thing you could change today to start shifting momentum in a positive direction?

7: Communication

'You don't spell it, you feel it.'
— *Winnie the Pooh*

Imagine building a bridge to connect two islands. In leadership, communication is that bridge—connecting ideas, solving problems, and developing trust. How you communicate with those around you each day influences whether the bridge consistently strengthens or weakens and eventually falls apart.

In this chapter, we'll explore how the brain responds to communication, exploring how even minor changes in communication could improve leadership and enhance outcomes for you and your team.

How the Brain Reacts to Communication

Let's start by taking a look at what happens with your brain team when you communicate:

Radar (Amygdala): Scans for facial expressions, body language, and tone of voice. Detection of anything perceived as a threat—such as an aggressive facial expression or tone of voice—can activate the stress response and bring the Primitive Mind into play.

Intellectual Mind: The Intellectual Mind (led by the CEO) becomes progressively less effective as the stress response strengthens and the Primitive Mind takes greater control.

Filing Cabinet (Hippocampus): This area aids the pattern-matching process by recalling memories of past communications, directly influencing the action your brain takes in the moment.

Pharmacist (Hypothalamus): If the communication is perceived as positive, the Pharmacist releases feel-good chemicals that keep the Intellectual Mind in play. However, if the Radar is triggered and the Primitive Mind takes over control, stress chemicals are released instead.

Clear, positive communication keeps the Radar calm and allows the Intellectual Mind to remain in control. Unclear or overly negative messages can trigger a stress response, causing confusion and tension and bringing the Primitive Mind into play.

The Power of Tone and Words

Imagine receiving these two emails:

1. 'This is wrong. Fix it immediately.'
2. 'I noticed an issue and thought you'd want to know. Could you look into it when you have time?'

The first email is worded in a way that could easily trigger the recipient's Radar and cause them to react defensively. The second email has a softer tone that is likely to have a far more positive and productive impact. Words matter—kind, respectful language reduces stress and helps to build and reinforce trust.

Practical Exercise

After your next meeting, reflect on one moment when your words or tone shaped the outcome. Did they help or hurt the conversation?

Why Communication Breaks Down

Communication often suffers in busy or stressful environments. Emails become more negative, tones become sharper, people start to 'look' stressed, and conflict and misunderstandings increasingly arise. Here's why this happens:

The Radar Reacts Too Fast: The more you are surrounded by stress and negativity, the more your brain starts to anticipate it. Eventually, even a neutral comment may be perceived as criticism.

The Filing Cabinet Pulls Negative Files: Locked in a negative state, the pattern-matching process repeatedly recalls past conflicts and challenges, directly influencing how you interpret messages in the present.

The CEO Gets Overwhelmed: As the negative cycle continues, the rising stress response makes it increasingly difficult to think and respond calmly and rationally.

Example

A rushed email written during a stressful day might unwittingly reflect frustration and negativity, and if composed under time pressure, it may also sound abrupt. If the recipient is in a great place, then they may be able to brush it off and bounce back more quickly, especially if it is an isolated event.

However, if the recipient is already having a bad day or week, then their resilience is already lowered, and so the communication will have a more negative impact. Now consider repeated harmful communications over a day, a week, or a month—even the most resilient will start to struggle.

The Impact on Teams

Poor communication doesn't just affect individuals; it affects the whole team:

- **Trust Breaks Down**: Harsh or unclear messages make people feel unappreciated.
- **Conflict Increases**: Misunderstandings cause tension and frustration.
- **Morale Drops**: Teams feel disengaged and unsupported.

Positive communication does the opposite:

- **Trust Grows**: Clear, kind messages build respect.
- **Collaboration Improves**: Teams work better when they feel heard and valued.
- **Creativity Rises**: A calm, positive environment encourages new ideas, raises performance, and improves productivity.

Leaders who communicate well don't just solve problems - they build stronger teams that are more resilient, innovative, and productive.

Small Changes, Big Impact

Imagine responding to a team member's mistake with encouragement instead of frustration. A simple shift in tone to one that is supportive rather than threatening prevents them from sinking further into a stress response and instead helps build trust. Rather than fuelling a downward spiral, you are encouraging their Intellectual Mind back into play.

Here's how small changes can make a difference:

Pause Before Responding: Taking a moment before responding calms your

Radar and allows your Intellectual Mind to maintain control.

Language: Use respectful and constructive language and consider the impact on the recipient's Pharmacist—will it elicit a positive or negative response?

Appreciation: A simple 'thank you' releases oxytocin, helping strengthen relationships and build trust.

Tone: Adopting an open and warm tone can transform how a message is received.

Practical Exercise

Goal: Mindful communications.

Steps

Before sending an email, pause to reflect:

1. Is my tone clear and respectful?
2. Is my language simple and solutions-focused?
3. How might the other person interpret my words?
4. What impact might my words have on the recipient's Pharmacist?
5. Make minor adjustments to ensure your message fits your goal.

Deliver the message and observe the response.

Reflection Questions

- How did pausing to reflect change things?
- What feedback did you receive?
- How might you make this reflective pause a regular habit?

Dealing with Tough Conversations

Challenging situations, such as addressing performance issues or navigating conflicts, can often induce a stress response in one or both parties that results in defensive or overly emotional reactions. At times like these, we need to work harder to keep the Intellectual Mind actively engaged, instilling calmness, objectivity, and empathy in the situation.

A Solutions-Focused Twist

This is where a 'Solutions-Focused' approach can shine. Solutions-focused techniques provide a simple and effective way to encourage the Intellectual

Mind into play. Part Two provides an overview of some of the main techniques, which we will also weave throughout Part Three to illustrate the potential such an approach offers for organisations.

In Part 4, there is also a step-by-step guide to navigating difficult conversations, covering planning and preparation, asking the right questions, and identifying realistic next steps.

Chapter 7 Recap: Communication

- Communication builds trust, motivates, and strengthens collaboration.
- Every communication and interaction you have with others affects how they feel and how they perform.
- Clear, kind, and respectful communication calms the Radar and engages the Intellectual Mind, leading to better decision-making and encouraging positive upward spirals.
- Positive communication underpins a positive culture.

Key Leadership Takeaway

The Intellectual Mind is where people engage, collaborate, and perform at their best. Viewing workplace communication through the lens of brain states enables leaders to use their communications more powerfully in order to elicit more Intellectual Mind time in their teams.

Reflect and Act

- How do your words and tone affect your team?
- Reflect on a misunderstanding - how could tone or clarity have improved it?
- Pause before your next key message and adjust to build trust and collaboration.

While communication shapes immediate interactions, culture is the invisible force that guides how teams think, feel, and work. In Chapter 8, we'll explore how leadership behaviours create a thriving culture and how to sustain it for lasting success.

8: Culture – The Invisible Force

"The whole is greater than the sum of its parts." – Aristotle

Culture is often described as 'the way we do things around here.' It can be likened to the air around you—invisible but essential for survival. An organisation's culture directly influences how the people within it think, feel, and act each day – so let's explore culture through the lens of brain states.

Culture Through the Lens of Brain States

In previous chapters, we've explored how your brain responds to both positive and negative inputs. We have looked at how this shapes your decisions and actions as a leader, as well as how it influences the decisions and actions of the teams that you lead. But what happens when we expand this thinking beyond individuals and teams to consider organisational culture as a whole?

An organisation is the sum of its parts. In large businesses, this can mean tens or even hundreds of thousands of individual brains, each playing a role in shaping the culture, with the decisions and actions taken each day dictating final business outcomes. So, it is no surprise that when we apply the concept of brain states at an organisational level, a fascinating pattern emerges.

The Primitive Mind is reactive. As we covered in earlier chapters, its language is one of fear, impulsivity, conflict, and stress. When these traits dominate a workplace culture, what do we see? Heightened tension, siloed thinking, disengagement, and a workforce operating in survival mode. People are more focused on self-preservation and firefighting than they are on collaboration or innovation.

In contrast, the Intellectual Mind, led by the CEO (Prefrontal cortex), leads with logic, objectivity, and solutions-focused thinking. Organisations with thriving cultures in which employees are engaged, creative, and motivated mirror these qualities. A workplace that fosters Intellectual Mind states is one where trust, innovation, and strategic thinking naturally flourish.

How Culture Affects the Brain

The above perspective provides an alternative, practical way to assess organisational culture. Rather than viewing culture as an abstract concept, we can use brain states as a gauge: Are your people spending too much time in their Primitive Minds?

Or is your environment actively encouraging your people to spend more time in their Intellectual Minds? Without too much effort, a simple and honest reflection on your organisation's present culture will give you the answer.

Viewing the organisation this way and recognising the brain states at play provides a simple yet powerful insight into the real drivers of your organisation's culture. Electing to work with this simple concept actively enables you to shape environments that bring out the best in leaders, teams, and businesses as a whole.

Positive Culture
The Pharmacist (Hypothalamus) releases those feel-good chemicals, meaning that people are more likely to feel psychologically safe, engaged, and motivated.

Without unnecessary stress chemicals getting in the way, the Intellectual Mind (led by the CEO) can work more effectively, enabling higher levels of productivity, resilience, and collaboration.

Negative Culture
A negative culture is not an easy place to be - it triggers stress and fear. The Radar (Amygdala) goes on high alert, and as things decline, the Pharmacist releases more stress chemicals.

The more stress rises, the less effectively the CEO is able to function, leading to quick, reactive, and sometimes inappropriate decisions across the business.

Leaders Shape Culture

As a leader, culture starts with you because your actions set the tone for your team. Your words and actions tell your team what's necessary and expected. They can drive high performance and build resilience, or they can lead to disengagement and high turnover.

Consistent leadership, delivered by leaders who operate from a positive brain state, is essential in nurturing a more positive organisational culture.

Remember

Support Builds Trust: Actions such as providing positive feedback, focusing on strengths, and celebrating success strengthen bonds and increase motivation and productivity.

Criticism Creates Fear: Actions such as providing harsh feedback, focusing on weaknesses, and apportioning blame can trigger defensiveness, conflict, and anxiety.

By changing your leadership style, you can start creating a culture where your team feels psychologically safe and delivers consistently high performance.

Practical Exercise

Goal: Show the behaviours you want in your team.

Steps

Choose one cultural value that you would like to strengthen.

1. Identify one behaviour you could adopt that would clearly convey this value (jump ahead and check out Part 2 for ideas if you are stuck).
2. Practice this behaviour for 2 weeks (set daily reminders to keep you on track).
3. Observe your team dynamics (or ask your team for feedback).
4. What difference has it made?

Reflection Questions

- Did the change to your behaviour change how the team worked together?
- How can you build on this progress?

The Ripple Effect of Culture

Culture spreads through your team and organisation. A positive culture builds trust, collaboration, and resilience, while a negative culture spreads stress and disengagement.

Remember

- In a positive culture, teams share ideas, solve problems, and feel motivated.
- In a hostile culture, teams feel overwhelmed, avoid risks, and make more mistakes.

- Leaders influence these ripples. One supportive action can inspire others to do the same.

Practical Exercise

Ask your team to describe the culture in three words. Compare their answers to your vision. Use this feedback to identify gaps and make changes.

Chapter 8 Recap

- Culture is the foundation of trust, collaboration, and innovation.
- Positive cultures create safety and connection, helping teams thrive.
- Negative cultures increase stress, leading to poor decisions and low morale.
- Leaders shape culture through their actions, decisions, and communication.

Key Leadership Takeaway

Your actions shape the culture of your team. By showing trust, openness, and collaboration, you can create an environment where people feel safe and motivated.

Reflect and Act

- What three words describe your team's culture now?
- Which of your actions help the culture, and which have the potential to harm the culture?
- Choose one behaviour this week to align your culture with your vision.

Culture is the invisible force behind every successful team. While this chapter introduces the basics, we'll explore tools to measure and strengthen culture later in the book.

9: Perception – The Stories We Tell Ourselves

> *"An open mind leaves a chance for someone to drop a worthwhile thought in it."*
> *— Mark Twain*

Recall a time you were out walking alone at night, heard a sound, and instantly assumed it was something threatening - only to discover it was merely the wind rustling the leaves. That's your brain working, as it does continuously, to keep you safe. It draws on your knowledge, emotions, and experience in order to decide what's happening and what action to take.

But what if the sound really was something harmful? Your brain's capacity to respond to what you think to be true - whether that is real or imagined, aids your survival. As a leader, an understanding of how perception operates can help you make smarter decisions and strengthen your understanding of – and connection with - your team.

What Is Perception?

Perception is the way your brain makes sense of the world around you. All the various inputs from your external and internal environments - such as sights, sounds, thoughts, and feelings – are continually being processed and combined to form an interpretation of your reality. It is perhaps no wonder that each of us perceives things so very differently.

And here's the tricky bit to comprehend: your brain isn't able to clearly distinguish the difference between what is imagined and what is real. So, if you vividly imagine something happening, then your brain responds by releasing the same brain chemicals - and initiating the same responses - it would if the event were actually occurring. Don't believe it? Try closing your eyes and imagine sucking a lemon - see how your mouth responds!

Perception is complex and influenced by many different factors, including:

Genetics: the hereditary traits with which you were born.

Past Experiences: Life experiences influence how you see future events.

Habits: Repetition of thoughts and actions builds new 'paths' in your brain throughout your life.

Emotions: Your emotional state influences what you notice and how you respond.

This means two individuals may witness or experience the same event yet interpret it in entirely distinct and different ways. For example, one person might interpret critical feedback as helpful and an opportunity to improve, while another might interpret it as unfair and disengage from the discussion.

Your Perception Isn't Neutral

Your brain filters everything through your past experiences and current feelings—it is part of being human. This means that your perception is always biased, no matter how 'neutral' you think you are. And so, unsurprisingly, it can sometimes lead to mistakes.

Common perception biases in Leadership include:

Assuming Intent: Thinking you know why someone acted a certain way. For example, believing a colleague ignored your email because they're upset when they might just be busy or distracted.

Confirmation Bias: Only noticing things that prove what you already believe and remaining blind to those that don't. For example, thinking a team member isn't committed even though they are reliable, and instead only focusing on their mistakes.

Negativity Bias: Paying more attention to negative things than positive ones. For example, remembering a missed deadline but forgetting the great work leading up to it.

How to Question Your Perception

Remember your brain's ability to build new neural pathways that we covered in earlier chapters? Thanks to this ability, it is possible to improve your perception by teaching your brain to take a couple of quick and simple steps.

Pause Before Reacting: Ask yourself, 'Am I seeing the whole picture?' and consider how others may see it differently.

Ask Questions: Before responding, take steps first to understand the other person's perspective. Just a simple 'What do you think?' may be enough to start seeing things a little differently.

Challenge Assumptions: Look for evidence that your first thought might be wrong.

If applied consistently, these steps will become habits—you will take them automatically without any conscious effort.

Perception and Leadership

In leadership, perception affects how you view and understand your team, how you make decisions, and even how you build trust. If you hold too tightly to your view of things without consciously staying open to the opinions of others, you risk:

- Misjudging others' actions or motives.
- Missing out on good ideas because they don't match your way of thinking.
- Creating tension and disengagement by repeatedly being dismissive of other perspectives.

For example, if a team member disagrees with you, you might see them as problematic. However, their point of view is highly valid, and it may improve your outcome. When you stay open to other views, you:

- Build trust by showing respect for others' ideas.
- Encourage teamwork by valuing everyone's input.
- Make better decisions by seeing the bigger picture.

Diverse perspectives lead to stronger teams. Effective leadership recognises this, continually questioning and trying to understand others' views.

Practical Exercise

Goal: Practice looking at situations from a different perspective.

Steps

Think about a recent misunderstanding or disagreement.

1. Write down your first thoughts about what happened.
2. Imagine what the other person might have been thinking or feeling.

3. Get creative and see how many different perspectives it is possible to generate for just one situation.
4. Reflect on how this new perspective changes your view of the situation.

Reflection

- What assumptions shaped your first reaction?
- How did imagining another perspective change your understanding?
- How will you question your perceptions in the future?

Chapter 9 Recap: Perception

- Perception is how your brain interprets the world. Your past shapes it, along with your feelings and your habits.
- Your perception is never neutral - it's always filtered through your brain's biases.
- Questioning your perception helps you avoid mistakes and build better connections.
- Great leaders seek to understand different viewpoints, improving trust and teamwork.

Key Leadership Takeaway

Your perception may be your reality, but it is not the reality of others. Continually questioning your assumptions and consciously remaining curious and open to other perspectives enables you to lead with greater understanding and precision.

Reflect and Act

- Think about a recent situation where your perception influenced your response. How might the other person's perspective differ?
- Choose one conversation this week where you will actively listen and ask questions to understand the other person's view. Notice the impact on your understanding and connection.

10: Individual Differences

'We must not only learn to tolerate our differences. We must welcome them as the richness and diversity which can lead to true intelligence.' ~ Albert Einstein

As we finish Part One, it's essential to look at how leadership and brain science work for everyone. While the ideas of Primitive and Intellectual Minds give us a straightforward way to understand decisions, emotions, and behaviour, the way these ideas manifest can vary.

Although individual differences such as neurodiversity, age, gender, and disability may affect how our brain responds, everyone can benefit from spending more time in their Intellectual Mind.

The Brain's Common Ground

Although individual experiences add extra layers, the principles behind the brain's leadership team, and the dynamic between the Primitive and Intellectual Minds, work for everyone.

We all have a Primitive Mind that reacts quickly to any threat that's detected and an Intellectual Mind that enables us to think more calmly, rationally, and creatively.

Neurodiversity: People with conditions like autism or ADHD react more strongly to stress, and for some, engaging their intellectual mind might take more effort or specific strategies - but the steps outlined in this book are still helpful.

Age: As we age, some parts of the brain may work a bit slower. However, activities that keep the brain active can help slow down this process.

Disability or Mental Health: Some conditions can make the Primitive Mind more sensitive and/or active. Using strategies to strengthen the Intellectual Mind can help balance these responses over time.

Adapting the Analogy

A leader with a neurodiverse team might observe how different pressures affect team members, creating a supportive environment that helps reduce triggers for the Primitive Mind.

A young professional might easily use their Intellectual Mind during calm times but struggle when deadlines are tight.

Someone managing mental health challenges might need more tools or support.

Even with these differences, the main steps are the same:

1. Spot your triggers.
2. Become aware of which brain state you're in.
3. Take steps to spend more time in the Intellectual Mind.

These ideas work for virtually everyone, no matter their circumstances.

The Universal Path Forward

You might wonder, 'Can these ideas really work for me, given my challenges?' The answer is yes. Although it may prove a little more challenging for some people than others, the benefits remain largely the same for most of us.

Reducing the influence of the Primitive Mind by taking steps to train your brain to spend more time in the Intellectual Mind helps you make better decisions, build stronger relationships, and lead with empathy. This applies to everyone, no matter the starting position.

Embracing Differences, Pursuing Excellence

Every brain is unique, and applying the concepts and tools in this book will help you harness this uniqueness to enhance your leadership even further. Great leadership capitalises on uniqueness to build a successful organisation.

Whether it's providing the right tools, demonstrating greater patience, or responding more dynamically to different team needs, adapting the way you lead to work with, rather than against, the brain can help you create a healthier and more successful team.

Learning about the brain—even at a superficial level through the basic analogies and concepts presented in this book—is important because it empowers you to take steps to improve your leadership and, in turn, help your team succeed.

Summary and Recap of Part 1

We started Part 1 by exploring a simple analogy of two distinct brain states – the Intellectual Mind and the Primitive Mind. We then continued our journey with superficial overviews of just a few of the key brain processes responsible for switching between these states.

Part 1 provides the knowledge needed to recognise and manage your brain state more easily and to become an even more effective leader.

Connecting the Dots: How It All Fits Together

Each chapter in Part 1 builds on the last, showing how your brain influences leadership and teamwork. Here's the big picture:

1. **The Brain's Leadership Team:** Guides your actions, emotions, and decisions.
2. **Primitive vs. Intellectual Mind:** Helps you shift from reactive to strategic thinking.
3. **Pattern Matching:** Raises awareness of snap decisions.
4. **Reflection (Default Mode Network):** Unlocks creativity, innovation, and problem-solving.
5. **Brain Chemistry and Adaptability:** Supports learning, motivation, and resilience.
6. **Downward and Upward Spirals:** Too much negativity can lead to downward spirals, whereas positivity encourages upward spirals.
7. **Communication:** Shapes trust and collaboration.
8. **Culture:** Builds an environment where teams can thrive.
9. **Perception & Bias:** Everyone experiences things differently.
10. **Individual Differences:** Highlights the importance of understanding unique needs while applying universal principles.

Part 1 Reflection

Looking Back
What is the most useful thing you discovered about how the Primitive Mind and Intellectual Mind impact your everyday decisions?

Personal Check-In
Recall a time recently when you felt reactive or stressed - how might this new understanding of your brain state have helped you respond more positively?

Key Takeaway
Which concept from Part 1 feels most relevant to your current leadership challenges?

Small Step Forward
Identify one action you can implement right now: it could be a brief breathing exercise before tough meetings or a short reflection when you feel tension rising.

Prep for Part 2

Part 2 will provide an overview of interventions taken from the fields of Solutions Focus and Positive Psychology that can be used to capitalise on the knowledge in Part 1 and help you manage your own – and your team's – brain state more effectively.

Part Two: Engaging the Intellectual Mind

Introduction

In Part One, we explored two very different brain states: the Primitive Mind, which reacts instantaneously to any perceived threat, and the Intellectual Mind, where we make rational decisions, are more collaborative, and solve problems creatively. This is a powerful analogy to work with because it highlights ways in which we can influence it for our benefit.

How we make sense of the world around us directly influences how we respond. This understanding is key because it can help us become more adaptable and flexible in our thinking. It can also make the transition between these two states easier to control, from the turmoil and reactivity of the Primitive Mind to the calmness and rationality of the Intellectual Mind.

The great news is that a few quick and simple techniques and practices can facilitate the transition between these two states even more readily.

The Brain Benefits of Positive Practices

The brain thrives on repetition and consistency—it supports the development and reinforcement of the neural pathways we discussed in Part 1. You can use this knowledge to your advantage by applying techniques and undertaking practices that encourage your brain to build and strengthen pathways that build your resilience and, over time, 'rewire' your responses to be more constructive.

These techniques and practices have the potential to transform how you experience and respond to the world around you. When woven through the different aspects of your professional and personal lives, they will all work in harmony, intensifying their effects.

The more consistent and interwoven your approach, the greater the impact and the further the ripple effect will extend. This will help you and your teams build a workplace that thrives consistently under pressure and delivers sustained high performance.

Revisiting Perception

Perception is powerful and extremely personal, and it can change over time. It's the lens through which we interpret the world around us, continually being shaped and defined by our individual experiences, emotions, and beliefs.

No two people will experience the same situation in precisely the same way, and this can mean that where one person sees a fantastic opportunity, another may only see an insurmountable challenge. While such diverse perspectives can introduce misunderstanding, friction, or even conflict in a workplace, they also drive creativity and innovation.

Introducing the Approaches

Two evidence-based approaches—solutions focus and positive psychology—underpin all the strategies in this book. They complement each other seamlessly within an organisational setting and offer ways for leaders and teams to access the Intellectual Mind more consistently and effectively.

The analogy covered in Part One provides a useful means for understanding why the techniques and practices in this section are so effective. Applying the concepts of Primitive and Intellectual Minds, how neural pathways are formed, and the role of perception equips leaders – and their teams – to communicate and manage pressure more effectively, sharpen focus, and enhance decision-making.

Solutions Focus
A forward-thinking mindset that explores – and then works toward – a preferred future or outcome by adopting techniques that shift attention from problems and challenges to solutions and opportunities. Solutions-focused Inquiry, Scaling, and Reframing help identify strengths and possible solutions.

Unlike conventional problem-solving, which draws attention to what's wrong, solutions-focused approaches instead place the spotlight on success and the small, actionable steps required to achieve it.

Positive Psychology
Positive Psychology is based on three pillars: positive experiences, positive traits, and positive institutions. Each pillar emphasises the cultivation of strengths, positive emotion, and resilience. It builds and fortifies individual and collective resilience by consistently shifting the brain's natural negativity bias (its tendency to focus on threats) toward a more constructive and helpful perspective.

Complimentary Interventions

The interventions in this section help you, your teams, and your organisation spend more time in the Intellectual Mind. Applying and combining these interventions creates a robust framework for lasting, brain-friendly change throughout your organisation.

Solutions Focus: Shapes organisational communication and culture by directing attention to strengths and solutions, embedding constructive communication and sustainable habits.

Positive Psychology: Builds emotional and cognitive resilience, supporting individuals and teams to flourish – for sustained performance, even under pressure.

These approaches align strategic goals with personal and team well-being and reinforce behaviours that improve collaboration, innovation, and resilience.

The Role of Imagination in Creating Change

Imagination is a core element of many of the interventions explored in Part Two. It is a proven technique used in a wide range of applications—from therapy to education to Olympian athletes.

When we imagine positive outcomes—whether a thriving team, a resolved conflict, or a personal achievement—we do more than calm the stress response; we engage the Intellectual Mind and prime the brain to begin constructing new neural pathways.

Like perception, imagination is personal – we all experience it differently. Some people may visualise clear pictures, while others may experience thoughts, feelings, or sounds. The interventions in this section allow for these differences, offering flexible approaches to suit the various styles of engagement.

What to Expect

The chapters ahead introduce practical ways to help you and your teams spend more time in the Intellectual Mind.

Here's what you'll explore:

- **Active Visualisation** to mentally prepare for success and boost confidence.
- **Solutions Focus techniques** to shift thinking from problems to

possibilities.

- **Positive Psychology Interventions** (PPIs) for cultivating optimism, resilience, and emotional well-being.
- **Practical strategies** for managing stress and maintaining focus in high-pressure situations.
- Each intervention includes 'Reflect and Act' exercises to help you explore their potential for enhancing leadership, teams, and organisations.

For those ready to dive deeper, Part Four includes a comprehensive workbook with ready-to-use activities that provide practical applications for individuals, teams, and organisational integration.

Whether you're a Senior Leader, HR leader, team manager, or seeking personal growth, the Part Four workbook equips you with practical templates to embed these interventions into your workplace. Using this book alongside the workbook will give you the knowledge and tools to create a thriving, brain-friendly workplace.

1. Active Visualisation

Introduction

Imagine you're delivering an important presentation to a key client or a team of senior leaders, and you are giving the best presentation you could possibly envisage. Include as much detail as you can and observe yourself in action—dressed in clothes that make you feel great, speaking clearly with confident body language, fully engaging your audience, and receiving great feedback.

How does it look and feel when you're confident, calm, and in control? When you undertake this exercise, you're not simply daydreaming; your brain is already getting to work by rehearsing it, in turn, gearing you for success. That's the magic of Active Visualisation—a simple yet powerful intervention that boosts confidence and composure and prepares you for the actual event.

When you mentally explore and rehearse future scenarios, you're not simply preparing ahead of the event, though—your brain starts building and reinforcing the neural pathways to help make it real. Every repetition develops and reinforces these pathways further, improving your ability to handle similar situations in the future with calm, focus, and confidence.

The prospect of conjuring up – and vividly imagining – positive outcomes may feel a little overwhelming at first, particularly if your Primitive Mind keeps trying to direct your focus to everything that could go wrong. Just like any new skill, Active Visualisation takes a little time and effort to develop – but the more you practice, the easier and more natural it becomes.

Starting small—perhaps with something that has gone well in the past—and simply imagining it happening again can be a great way to get started. You may be pleasantly surprised at how quickly those first small steps build the confidence and familiarity needed to move on to bigger things.

Active Visualisation and the Brain

Stress can make it more challenging to think clearly, but consciously focusing on – and mentally rehearsing – positive outcomes reassures your Primitive Mind that it's safe. This makes it easier to get your Intellectual Mind back in play.

When you imagine yourself succeeding - whether nailing a presentation or navigating a challenging conversation - the same networks activate in your brain as if it were actually happening.

With each repetition, these pathways strengthen, making it easier and more natural to approach similar future situations with optimism and confidence.

Why It Matters

For You: Imagine if each day began with the excitement of possibilities rather than anxiety and worry. How much lighter does that feel?

For Your Team: A collective focus on the same positive outcomes builds alignment, energy, and motivation toward achieving shared goals.

For Your Organisation: Active Visualisation can inspire a culture of innovation and growth.

Dream It, Build It

Think of Active Visualisation as your personal rehearsal space for success. By actively visualising successful outcomes – and building as much detail as possible – you train your brain to believe they're feasible. This isn't just wishful thinking; it's mental preparation. Whether you're preparing for a difficult conversation or leading your team to a big win, Active Visualisation helps you set the stage for success.

Reflect and Act

Think about a challenge you're facing right now and take a few moments to visualise yourself navigating it successfully.

- **Build detail** – use all your senses to create a detailed mental rehearsal that primes your brain for success.

- **Mentally explore** all the different possibilities and then take a few moments to reflect.

- **What's one small step** you could take to start aligning with this vision? Where are you? Imagine the setting in detail – what can you see, hear, or even smell?

Key Leadership Takeaway

Active Visualisation is a great way to start shifting your brain state and getting the Intellectual Mind back in play. Each time you actively visualise successful outcomes, you encourage new neural pathways that guide you toward that future, even under pressure.

2. The Miracle Question

Introduction

Imagine walking into work tomorrow morning and a problem you've been struggling with for months is completely gone. Everything is working exactly as it should. What's different? What do you notice, see, hear, or feel that would signal the problem is resolved?

The Miracle Question is a deceptively simple-yet-powerful tool for shifting focus from what's wrong to what's possible. Placing all the focus on a preferred – or even perfect – outcome helps your brain bypass any mental blocks that may be preventing you from getting there.

The Miracle Question disrupts the brain's natural negativity bias by shifting our focus directly onto an end goal, cutting out any obstacles that may be getting in our way. This helps engage the Intellectual Mind and build momentum by determining achievable actions we can take to progress toward our goal.

Whether setting a personal goal, aligning and motivating a team, or conducting a strategic organisation-wide review, the Miracle Question inspires big-picture thinking while keeping progress grounded in small, achievable steps.

In the workplace, it can provide a quick and engaging way for leaders and teams to break free from the constraints of a problem-focused mindset by defining a clear and precise vision of what 'better' looks like.

This activity isn't about dismissing challenges – it's about helping you and your team develop, envision, and then explore in detail the best possible outcome. When you imagine an ideal or preferred future, your brain naturally starts to explore steps that could begin to make it a reality.

The Miracle Question and the Brain

Building a mental image of a future where obstacles are already overcome helps to calm the stress response, reducing any negative impact the Primitive Mind may be having.

Building a mental image engages the Intellectual Mind, leading to more effective, objective, and creative problem-solving.

Developing and exploring a detailed mental image builds and strengthens neural pathways that support and start turning that vision into reality.

Why It Matters

For You: Shifting the focus to and mentally exploring a future where obstacles are already overcome helps build a clear vision that feels tangible and motivating.

For Your Team: When used with teams, the Miracle Question introduces an engaging way to inspire big-picture thinking and creative solutions while also aligning everyone around a shared vision or goal.

For Your Organisation: The Miracle Question is highly flexible. Whether used for strategic planning or introducing an element of strategic light-heartedness into daily routine, it offers a quick and simple means to inspire greater creativity and innovation.

How it Differs

You might be asking, 'Didn't we just do the same thing with Active Visualisation?' Both tools encourage you to imagine a more positive future, so there is undoubtedly some overlap; however, they serve slightly different purposes:

Active Visualisation focuses more on preparing for a future scenario by mentally rehearsing the actions and behaviours that will prime your brain for success. It builds confidence and helps create a detailed mental blueprint for what you'll do and how you will respond in the moment.

The **Miracle Question** takes a broader and more general approach. It uses imagination to conjure up a world where a problem is already wholly solved with a perfect solution in place. This helps to build a clear vision of what success looks like without getting caught up in obstacles.

Together, they're like two sides of the same coin – one helps you build a clear vision of the end goal, and the other helps you prepare for action to get there.

Reflect and Act

Take a few moments to reflect on a current challenge or problem that's been on your mind. Now, ask yourself:

- **If a miracle happened** overnight and I woke up in the morning to find this problem had vanished entirely, what would be different?
- **Focus on the whole picture** – what would a successful outcome look and feel like?
- **What small but specific changes** would you notice in yourself, your environment, and those around you?

Write down one specific action or insight from this activity.

Key Leadership Takeaway

The Miracle Question can be a fun, powerful way to help shift the focus from problems to possibilities. Imagining a world without obstacles makes it easier to generate new ideas, inspire others, and create great solutions.

3. What Does Good Look Like?

Introduction

The Miracle Question invited you to imagine and explore high-level aspirations. Asking, 'What does good look like?' brings the spotlight back onto the here and now. It cuts through ambiguity and targets specific behaviours, actions, outcomes, and milestones that represent success.

You can no doubt recall meetings and conversations where the atmosphere was draining, and the energy in the room seemed fixated entirely on problems. Given our brain's natural tendency to fixate on what's going wrong, this is perhaps hardly surprising—but it is nonetheless a little counterproductive given that focusing on negatives can cause us to lose sight of solutions!

Whether developing strategic goals, navigating a difficult conversation, resolving conflict, or planning the next steps in a project or team meeting, pausing to ask, 'What does good look like?' provides a quick, simple, and effective way to generate positive energy and facilitate a more constructive dialogue.

'What does good look like' and the Brain.

When you ask, 'What does good look like?' you disrupt your brain's inherent tendency to fixate on problems.

Focusing on 'what good looks like' engages our Intellectual Mind, which in turn encourages more constructive and helpful behaviours and decisions.

Building a detailed mental image of 'what good looks like' encourages your brain to develop and reinforce neural pathways to help to make it happen.

Why It Matters

For You: Shifting focus to what you want helps reduce overwhelm and lower stress, enabling you to think more clearly and constructively and establish a more positive way forward.

For Your Team: When used with teams, this question can help transform reactive, problem-centred discussions and meetings into proactive, solution-focused planning sessions.

For Your Organisation: 'What does good look like?' is a highly versatile question that's effective in virtually any organisational context—from strategic planning to incidental conversation.

Practical Examples

1. 'What does good look like?' is a simple, impactful tool to have in your workplace toolkit:
2. Ask participants, 'What would a good outcome from this meeting be?' before starting to set meetings off on a positive track.
3. In group discussions, ask each participant, 'What does good look like for you here?' and use individual perspectives to improve understanding and develop a shared vision.
4. Add it to performance reviews or virtually any one-to-one discussion to help clarify expectations and determine goals.
5. Adding it to protocols for project reviews provides a useful means to secure and maintain alignment between parties.

Questions to Explore

- What does success look like here?
- What outcomes will we have achieved?
- How will we know we've made progress – what signals will tell us we're on the right track?

Reflect and Act

Reflect on a current challenge or project.

- **Ask yourself**: 'What does good look like here?'
- **Write down** three individual outcomes or behaviours that would signal success.

Take ideas from the above and try incorporating this question in your next team meeting or planning session. Notice how it influences the conversation and strengthens alignment.

Key Leadership Takeaway

Asking, 'What does good look like?' directs the focus away from problems and onto possibilities. It's a straightforward yet transformative tool that can be used in almost any situation or context to provide clarity and encourage alignment.

4. Solutions-Focused Inquiry

Introduction

Solutions-focused inquiry is not only about imagining what's possible – it is about identifying what is already working in the here and now and then doing more of it. Think of it as tending a garden – instead of focusing on what isn't growing, you place your attention on nurturing the areas that are already thriving to encourage even more growth.

Solutions-focused Inquiry is a flexible technique that uses positively framed, open-ended questions to uncover existing strengths and potential opportunities to explore. It also drives progress and builds momentum by asking questions that identify small, actionable steps. Like the previous techniques, it can be applied in virtually any context or scenario.

The more you use Solutions-Focused Inquiry, the easier and more naturally you will find that it flows, over time becoming ingrained into your everyday communications. You may be surprised at how easily and effectively this technique shifts the tone of just about any interaction.

Whether it is strategy and goal formation, team or planning meetings, coaching sessions, performance management, or one-to-one discussions, this technique is invaluable for creating a more productive and healthy work environment. Its adaptability is why it features so extensively in later sections, where we explore how positive work ways can be strategically integrated into every layer and function of an organisation.

The Power of Positive Questions

Instead of reinforcing stress and negativity in the way that problem-focused questions do, solutions-focused questions:

- **Encourage the intellectual mind** back into play, for more constructive thinking.
- **Reduce defensiveness**, shifting focus off blame and back onto solutions and progress.

- **Encourage optimism**, build resilience, and help teams to see more opportunities.
- **Develop and strengthen neural pathways** that support and actively encourage a solutions-oriented mindset – even in challenging situations.

Why Solutions-Focused Inquiry Matters

For You: Shifting focus from 'fixing problems' to exploring opportunities reduces overwhelm, lowers stress and engages the Intellectual Mind.

For Your Team: When used with teams, solutions-focused questions can help transform reactive, problem-centred discussions and meetings into proactive, solution-focused planning sessions.

For Your Organisation: Solutions-focused language offers a highly versatile and influential approach that's effective in virtually any organisational context—from strategic planning to incidental conversation.

Applying Solutions-Focused Inquiry

Build on strengths: Identify existing strengths and successes by asking, 'What's already going well, and how can we build on it?'

Explore opportunities: Encourage exploration of opportunities by asking, 'How could we do this differently?'

Identify Small, Actionable Steps: Focus on realistic and achievable actions by asking, 'What's the smallest change that could have the most significant impact?'

Reflect and Act

Reflect on a current challenge and try out the above questions.

- **Write down** one small step you could take to move forward.
- **Experiment with** using these questions in your conversations and meetings.
- **Notice how** they influence the dialogue.

Key Leadership Takeaway

Solutions-focused inquiry unlocks hidden potential by shifting focus from problems to progress. Asking the right questions and adding a little creativity, helps start shifting mindsets and inspires positive action that leads to lasting change.

5. Scaling

Introduction

You've defined a clear vision for success using a tool such as the Miracle Question. You can see the destination clearly – be it a completed project, a thriving team, or the resolution of a significant challenge.

But how do you bridge the gap between where you are and where you want to be? How do you navigate changes along the way? Solutions Focus Inquiry gets you asking the right questions that inspire and motivate progress – but what when the gap seems too huge? What else can we do to help get us there?

Think of setting the SatNav in your car before driving a long journey. At the start, it determines the 'best' route and displays it on a map, and off you go. But as you drive and traffic situations change, the route is continually adapted and updated to keep the journey as smooth and fast as possible. Let's take a look at Scaling – a simple and practical approach to determining actions and tracking progress.

When we are working toward a big goal, we often approach it by planning out the entire journey at once, usually resulting in long lists of actions and complex spreadsheets that we anticipate will get us to our goal. But as we progress, just like a car journey, the landscape is continually changing. With each action we take, new opportunities – ones that we previously had no sight of – open up to us, and ones we previously thought would work well are no longer so impactful.

Scaling supports the Solutions Focus approach of taking small steps while providing structure to keep things on track. Although it may feel a little uncomfortable at first, especially for list and spreadsheet fans, scaling is a structured yet flexible tool that keeps the spotlight on progress while continually surveying the landscape for new opportunities.

Whether applied to personal goals, team development, or organisational change, scaling encourages a flexible and adaptable approach that saves time by continually re-assessing the best way forward.

Scaling and the Brain

Scaling engages the brain's decision-making centre, helping you prioritise, problem-solve, and stay focused on your goals.

Breaking down big goals into smaller steps reduces cognitive load and calms the stress response, making it easier to think clearly and act confidently.

Each small success triggers a release of the brain's reward chemical, helping to keep you motivated and energised to take the next step.

Continuously reflecting and adjusting strengthens neural pathways that encourage adaptability, creativity, and resilience.

Why Scaling Matters

For You: Breaking goals into small and more manageable steps avoids overwhelm.

For Your Team: Progress is more visible, whilst continually scanning for new ideas throughout the steps keeps people motivated and engaged.

For Your Organisation: Scaling actively supports a culture of continuous improvement, where small wins build confidence and drive long-term success.

Putting Scaling into Action

Step 1: Start with Your Preferred Future

Use the Miracle Question – or one of the other tools – to define your vision.

- Where do you want to be?
- What does success look like?

Step 2: Assess Where You Are Now

Working with a scale of 1 to 10, where 10 represents the goal being met in full, where are you currently in relation to that vision?

- What puts you at that point?
- What got you to where you are?
- What's working well already?

Step 3: Identify the Next Step

Suppose you currently score a 3 on the scale – ask yourself:

- What's one small thing I can do to move from a 3 to a 4?

- What's the simplest action I can take that would have most significant impact?

Step 4: Act, Reflect, and Adjust

Take the step, then pause to reflect:

- What changed as a result?
- What new opportunities do I see now?
- What's the next step from here?

Step 5: Celebrate Progress:

- Acknowledge every step forward, no matter how small.
- Celebrating wins reinforces your motivation and builds momentum.

This iterative process ensures you remain flexible and responsive while keeping the long-term goal in sight.

Examples in Action

Personal Leadership

Preferred Future: 'I want to feel more confident handling difficult conversations.'

Next Step: Identify one upcoming conversation to prepare for and rehearse key points in advance.

Team Development

Preferred Future: 'We want to improve collaboration between departments.'

Next Step: Schedule a joint meeting to share successes and brainstorm opportunities for greater alignment.

Organisational Change

Preferred Future: 'We want a culture that prioritises innovation.'

Next Step: Launch a small pilot initiative encouraging employees to propose new ideas.

Reflect and Act

Reflect on a current challenge or goal.

- **On a scale** of 1 to 10, where are you now?
- **What's one small step** you can take to move up just one point?

- **After taking that step**, reflect: What worked? What changed?
- **What's the next small action** you can take?

Key Leadership Takeaway

Scaling is about turning big goals into achievable steps. By targeting small, consistent actions, you can maintain momentum, build confidence, and create lasting progress individually, as a team, and across your organisation.

6. Challenging Negative Beliefs

Introduction

Have you ever found yourself thinking, 'I can't do this' or 'This will never work'? It's a natural tendency—our brains are wired to detect and focus on potential threats and problems as a survival mechanism.

But although our negativity bias serves to protect us when we are in danger, it can sometimes prove more of a hindrance than a help in our day-to-day life. Without a little attention and some timely, considered, intervention, negative beliefs can really start to get in our way—both in the workplace and in our personal lives.

The good news Is that negative beliefs aren't permanent—we aren't born with them. Becoming more aware of them as and when they arise – and taking steps to challenge and reframe them – initiates a shift toward a more constructive and helpful narrative.

A healthier and more positive perspective, in turn, eases stress and allows more opportunities for growth to emerge. Reframing isn't about ignoring the challenges or problems we encounter in our lives—it's about gently encouraging your mindset to adopt an alternative and more helpful perspective—one that enables you to navigate a more straightforward path forward.

Challenging Negative Beliefs and the Brain

Negative beliefs trigger the brain's stress response, releasing the associated brain chemicals that can exacerbate the situation.

Reframing promotes the release of the brain chemicals that support a more balanced outlook.

Consistently challenging and reframing negative beliefs strengthens neural pathways, building resilience and creating an upward spiral.

Why Negative Beliefs Matter

For You: Reframing to a more positive perspective keeps the Intellectual Mind in play, boosts confidence and increases optimism.

For Your Team: Reframing can shift a team's outlook from pessimism toward optimism, increasing motivation, and building resilience.

For Your Organisation: Reframing can encourage a more positive and confident corporate voice and tone that, in turn, supports the development of a more resilient culture.

Practical Steps to Reframe

1. Build awareness

- Take a few moments to reflect on any underlying negative beliefs.
- For example, 'This is too hard,' or 'I'm not good at this.'

2. Challenge validity

- Is this belief based on facts or assumptions?
- What evidence exists that contradicts this belief? What are the exceptions?
- How could this situation be perceived differently?

3. Reframe

- Reframe the negative belief to present an opportunity instead.
- Negative: 'I've never done this before, so I'll only fail.'
- Reframed: 'I've never done this before, so this is a great opportunity to learn something new.'

3. Repetition

- Identify one small step you can take to align with the new perspective.
- Repeated action helps to instil and reinforce the reframed perspective, building confidence and resilience.

Examples

Individuals

Negative Belief: 'I'm no good at presenting – this is going to go badly.'

Reframe: 'Every presentation I do is an opportunity to improve.'

Teams

Negative Belief: 'We'll never meet this deadline.'

Reframe: 'We've met tight deadlines before – it will be hard work, but we can do this'

Organisational

Negative Belief: 'We're stuck in outdated practices, and they're far too ingrained to change.'

Reframe: 'We've made other changes across the business before – we just need to find the right way'

Reflect and Act

Reflect on a current challenge. Identify a negative belief that may be holding you back.

- How could the negative belief be reframed into an opportunity?
- During your next team meeting, identify a current challenge and carry out a collective team reframe.

Key Leadership Takeaway

Reframing limiting beliefs unlocks hidden potential by shifting perspective from one of self-doubt to self-assurance. By challenging negative beliefs, you build confidence and resilience in yourself and your teams, inspiring positive action that leads to lasting change.

7. Positive Self-Talk

Introduction

Self-talk is the internal dialogue we all have running constantly in the background – sometimes playing quietly and at other times becoming louder and more difficult to ignore. Just as the volume fluctuates, so too does the tone: it can be reassuring, encouraging, and supportive, assisting us through our day, but it can also be the harshest critic imaginable.

As it changes to mirror our mental and emotional state, it continually influences and redefines how we perceive the world around us, including difficulties, opportunities, other people, and ourselves. It is possibly one of the most impactful inputs our brain receives, and it can propel us toward achievement or trap us in insecurity and pessimism.

The good news is that with a bit of awareness and regular practice, our self-talk can be transformed. This little voice in our minds is truly one of the most powerful resources accessible to us all; leveraging it effectively can assist us in changing our outlook, alleviating stress, and building confidence and resilience.

Positive Self-Talk and the Brain

Negative self-talk quickly leads to rumination; positive self-talk disrupts this cycle.

Strengthens neural pathways that support self-belief and build resilience.

Reduces the stress response and helps to get the Intellectual Mind back in play.

Why Positive Self-Talk Matters

For You: Builds confidence and self-esteem, reduces stress, enhances mood, and sharpens focus.

For Your Team: A positive team self-talk develops a supportive team dynamic and builds collective resilience.

For Your Organisation: Nurturing a more positive and inclusive organisational narrative that everyone feels part of provides a robust foundation for a great culture.

Examples of Positive Self-Talk

Instead of: 'I'm terrible at public speaking.'

Switch to: 'I've prepared thoroughly, and if I'm nervous, people will understand—I can do this, it will be okay.'

Instead of: 'I can't handle this project.'

Switch to: 'This is challenging, but I have the skills to figure it out step by step—I can do this, and it will be okay.'

Instead of: 'This will never work.'

Switch to: 'It's ok – I've got this. What can I do to start heading the right way?'

Making Positive Self-Talk a Habit

1. Notice Your Inner Dialogue:

Be mindful of your thoughts. Are they assisting or obstructing you? Self-talk begins with awareness, which is the initial step toward change.

2. Reframe Negative Thoughts:

When you catch your self-talk drifting into a negative narrative, challenge it by asking:

- Is this thought really true?
- What's a more constructive way to view this situation?

3. Practice Daily:

Begin your day by establishing a positive tone with an affirmation, and then turn it into your mantra for the day, reciting it to yourself frequently:

- 'I'm capable of handling whatever challenges arise for me today.'
- 'I have the ability and determination to face difficulties.'

4. Use Visual and Verbal Cues:

Choose the method that suits you best, for example:

- placing reminders in your workspace
- setting notifications on your phone or laptop,
- using an app to receive daily affirmations on your device.

Discover ways that fit with your schedule and prompt constructive self-talk during your day.

5. Reflect and Reinforce:
- At the end of each day, spend a few minutes contemplating your day.
- Notice how quickly your self-talk changes when you bring attention to it.

Integrating Positive Self-Talk into Leadership

Model It for Your Team

As a leader, your inner dialogue influences how you show up for others. Practising positive self-talk can help you maintain composure, clarity, and optimism, even under pressure.

Encourage a Culture of Positive Language

Use self-talk creatively with your team —encourage the use of constructive language in meetings and collaborations or inject a little fun by working together on building more positive team self-talk.

Support Growth and Build Resilience

When team members face setbacks, encourage them to redirect attention to their strengths and progress.

Reflect and Act

Reflect on your self-talk.

- **How could you reframe** it into a more positive and supportive narrative?
- **Write a more supportive** version and then break it down into individual statements.
- **Use these as your mantras**, repeating them to yourself regularly throughout the day.

What changes do you notice over the next few days and weeks?

Key Leadership Takeaway

Positive self-talk boosts confidence and builds resilience. By raising awareness and intentionally choosing to communicate with yourself more kindly and with greater encouragement, you cultivate a more hopeful, confident, and optimistic mindset: for yourself, your team, and your organisation.

8. Affirmations

Introduction

Whereas self-talk is the continual narrative that plays naturally in the background as we respond to life's experiences, affirmations are short, intentional, proactive statements. When pressure builds and negative self-talk kicks in, affirmations can be a quick, simple, and effective way to stop it in its tracks.

But in addition to being a useful in-the-moment technique to encourage the Intellectual Mind back in play when the Primitive Mind starts knocking, when used regularly, affirmations can also help shift more generalised and persistent negative self-talk narratives to something more positive and helpful.

Affirmations aren't complicated, and they don't require a big-time investment – but they do need to be consistent and repeated regularly to work at their best. Think of affirmations as a way to program your brain to focus on what's possible, turning self-doubt into self-belief and determination.

Affirmations and the Brain

Concentrating attention on positive attributes and strengths helps lower stress, allowing the Intellectual Mind to return to play.

Affirmations can help disrupt negative thought patterns, self-talk, or rumination.

Affirmations build new neural connections that strengthen with each repetition, making it progressively easier for your brain to adopt a more positive narrative.

Why Affirmations Matter

For You: Builds self-confidence and self-esteem, reduces stress, and sharpens focus.

For Your Team: Positive affirmations develop a supportive and confident team dynamic, building collective resilience.

For Your Organisation: Positive affirmations offer a simple and practical way to reinforce collective belief.

Examples of Affirmations

- 'I have the resilience to overcome any challenge.'
- 'I am confident in my ability to succeed.'
- 'Each step I take brings me closer to my goal.'
- 'I am capable of doing this.'
- 'I learn and grow from every experience.'

Reflect and Act

Reflect on a current challenge or niggling self-doubt and develop three affirmations that directly counter it.

- **Repeat them daily** for the next week, setting prompts throughout the day to encourage regular repetition.
- **Notice** the ways in which your perspective starts to shift.

Key Leadership Takeaway

Affirmations are a simple, effective, and practical way to instil and anchor positive thoughts and beliefs. Used regularly, they can enhance one's ability to lead and face future challenges with greater confidence by instilling a more self-assured and optimistic mindset and building resilience.

9. Optimism

Introduction

People with optimistic outlooks can be great people to have around, especially when the going gets a little challenging. Their presence alone can be enough to calm our minds and reassure us that things are going to be okay. That's because, like the other interventions here, optimism helps to counteract the brain's tendency to fixate on negatives, making it easier for the Intellectual Mind to stay in control.

Optimism isn't about ignoring problems or painting an overly rosy picture – if taken to extremes, it can prove more harmful than helpful. Healthy optimism is about believing that the challenge we are facing can realistically be overcome and that feasible solutions are within our reach. An optimistic mindset in a leader sends a ripple out through their team, instilling a sense of reassurance that helps everyone approach difficulties with more confidence.

Optimism and the Brain

Engaging the Intellectual Mind keeps attention on ways to move forward.

Calming the Primitive Mind lowers stress and reduces anxiety.

Brain chemicals are released that boost confidence and motivation.

Why Optimism Matters

For You: Helps you to remain calmer and more focused – even in demanding situations.

For Your Team: An optimistic team works better together and solves problems more efficiently and effectively.

For Your Organisation: An optimistic workplace is one where people feel good about their work and are always open and ready to find new ideas.

Practical Ways to Encourage Optimism

1. Search for Opportunity:
Pause to ask yourself, 'What's the opportunity here?' next time you're facing a challenge.

2. Focus on Strengths:

Take time to reflect on what's already working well, and then contemplate ways in which you may be able to build on it further

3. Future-Focused Thinking:

Actively direct your attention to positive outcomes to help reinforce the belief that goals will be achieved successfully.

Reflect and Act

Reflect on a current setback or challenge. What might a positive outcome look like? What could you learn from it?

- **During your next team meeting**, try encouraging a more optimistic perspective by highlighting possibilities and emphasising what's already going well.
- **Get into a habit** of asking, 'What's the best that could happen?' to start reframing challenges and encouraging your team to adopt a more optimistic approach.

Key Leadership Takeaway

A healthy dose of optimism benefits you and also ripples out to those around you. It is a powerful tool that can instil a sense of reassurance in others, help build team resilience and provide a platform for creativity and productivity.

10. Empathy

Introduction

Empathy has attracted considerable attention over recent years, especially in the realm of leadership. And justifiably so—far from merely being another leadership buzzword, empathy serves as the cornerstone of trust, connection, and collaboration, without which no organisation will succeed.

In leadership, empathy involves displaying genuine interest in the people you lead. It's not merely a case of posing superficial questions regarding others' viewpoints or providing opportunities for others to share thoughts—in an environment overshadowed by a hostile culture where fear prevails, will anyone genuinely be truthful with you?

Empathy involves genuinely listening to others and creating an environment where they feel acknowledged, understood, and appreciated—secure enough to express themselves openly and share their true opinions without any fear of reprisal.

Empathy and the Brain

Empathy activates parts of our brain that enable us to 'mirror' how another person is feeling, aiding mutual understanding, and helping us relate to one another more easily.

Empathy promotes psychological safety and helps to engage the Intellectual Mind, in turn enabling us to make more considered decisions

Empathy helps instil trust and strengthen interpersonal connections, thanks to the release of oxytocin, often referred to as the 'bonding hormone.'

Why Empathy Matters

For You: Empathy aids emotional regulation and helps us to create and maintain stronger relationships with others.

For Your Team: Providing a working environment where individuals feel safe, understood, and valued encourages openness and improves collaboration.

For Your Organisation: Empathy ensures everyone feels heard and valued, easing tensions and friction, improving communication, and building resilience.

Practical Ways to Demonstrate Empathy

Reflective listening

Help others feel heard, valued, and understood by using reflective listening to confirm your understanding and reassure them that their views and feelings are important.

Framing questions

Encourage others to share more openly and honestly by using open-ended questions that invite them to express their true views and perspectives.

Validating emotions

Reduce defensiveness in others and create an environment in which they feel psychologically safe by validating their emotions without any judgment or criticism.

Leading by example

Build trust and strengthen your relationships with others by sharing some of your own experiences and challenges, appropriately, to demonstrate a little vulnerability.

Reflect and Act

- Reflect on a recent discussion in which someone shared a challenge they were facing with you – how do you think they may have been feeling?
- How heard and valued do you feel your behaviours and responses may have made them feel?
- How might you have supported them better?

Key Leadership Takeaway

Great leadership and high-performing teams are impossible without empathy as a foundation. Promoting compassion throughout our personal and professional lives – be it in daily interactions with others, encouraging it within your teams, and finding ways to embed empathy into your organisation's culture develops an environment where trust, psychological safety, and collaboration flourish.

11. Authenticity

Introduction

Authenticity is about aligning our words and actions with our values. It means being transparent about our intentions and showing up as our genuine selves. Humans have a surprising ability to detect authenticity in others, so when we are our authentic selves, it shows, and those around us quickly pick up on it.

Authentic people tend to be more consistent, have higher integrity, and show more willingness to be vulnerable. So, it's perhaps no surprise that being around an authentic person makes us feel safer and more at ease, meaning that we are more likely to feel comfortable being our authentic selves, too. Authenticity builds more substantial and meaningful relationships across all areas of our personal and working lives.

Authenticity and the Brain

When people perceive you as genuine, it lowers their stress response and increases brain chemicals that foster positive connections with others.

Consistency between words and actions signals to others that they are safe to express themselves authentically, too, without fear of judgment or retribution.

Authenticity reduces internal conflict: when you are not being your authentic self, it doesn't just make others uncomfortable – it makes you feel uneasy, too.

Why Authenticity Matters

For You: Acting authentically helps you lead with openness, integrity, and consistency.

For Your Team: Authenticity builds trust, which is essential for healthy team dynamics.

For Your Organisation: Authentic leadership creates a culture of transparency, trust, and shared purpose.

Practical Ways to Lead Authentically

Clarify Your Values: Reflect on your core values and actively use them as strengths to guide your decisions and behaviours.

Be Consistent: Align your actions with your words – always necessary, but especially in more challenging situations when authenticity can be difficult to maintain.

Show Vulnerability: Only as appropriate, of course. Share challenges or uncertainties you feel comfortable with—it humanises you and builds trust.

Encourage Openness: Be as open and honest as you can with those around you. Fostering a culture where team members feel safe being themselves by modelling authenticity will help others be their authentic selves, too.

Reflect and Act

Reflect on how often your actions align with your core values.

- **Identify one area** where you feel you could be more authentic.
- **What's one step** you could take to show up more authentically?

Check out the exercises in Part 4 for ideas on ways to bring more authenticity to your team.

Key Leadership Takeaway

When you lead with integrity, align your actions with your values, and show up as your authentic self, you build trust, inspire confidence, and nurture a more resilient culture.

12. Curiosity

Introduction

Think about a time when you spent ages trying to solve a problem – and then, completely out of the blue, someone stepped in, asked a simple question, and hey presto, the solution appeared. That's the power of curiosity. Curiosity opens up our thinking beyond the immediately obvious and brings possibilities into view that always existed – we just couldn't see them.

Using curiosity to explore alternative possibilities can help an organisation challenge any underlying assumptions that may be obstructing current progress. From team projects to strategic planning, curiosity generates the creative thought necessary to develop more efficient and effective ways of working.

As stress rises, so too does the influence of the Primitive Mind, in turn narrowing our thinking. Asking questions such as 'What if?' or 'I wonder...' can be a useful way to help disrupt any associated fixed thinking patterns and get the Intellectual Mind back into play. This also makes curiosity a quick and simple means of shifting our brain state.

Curiosity and the Brain

Asking questions and exploring opportunities engages the Intellectual Mind.

Being curious lowers stress levels.

Curiosity activates the reward centre in our brain.

Why Curiosity Matters

For You: Curiosity is beneficial for well-being—it makes us more positive, strengthens relationships and builds resilience.

For Your Team: Curiosity drives solutions-finding. Curious teams ask more open questions, which naturally leads to the exploration of more creative ideas and new opportunities.

For Your Organisation: Empowering people to be curious without apprehension leads to a more creative, flexible, and open-minded workforce.

Questions to explore

Individuals

What assumptions could I be making here?

What would a different view be?

Teams

How might someone else view this situation?

What haven't we explored yet?

Organisational

How would this process be different if it were more effective?

What small change could we test out?

Reflect and Act

- **What potential benefits** could introducing more curiosity bring to your team?
- **Use open-ended questions** at your next team meeting to get the curiosity going.
- **Notice how curiosity influences** the team atmosphere as well as the outcomes.

Key Leadership Takeaway

Curiosity provides leaders with a simple and effective technique to broaden thinking, improve cognitive flexibility, and inspire greater creativity among their teams.

13. Gratitude

Introduction

While it may initially sound a bit 'fluffy' or appear trivial, gratitude is, in fact, a remarkably powerful emotion—and one supported by substantial research. Gratitude has a whole array of physical and psychological health benefits, and it is a great way to engage the Intellectual Mind.

Our brain's natural negativity bias directs our attention to what's wrong, at times, causing us to become fixated on problems and difficulties and to lose sight of the positive aspects of our lives. Gratitude helps us regain a more balanced perspective by recognising and contemplating the good in our lives – and then expanding on it, both emotionally and mentally. Gratitude practice is about more than simply overlooking difficulties and highlighting positives—it structurally changes the brain.

A quick 'thank you' can be pleasant for anyone to receive, but to create lasting change, gratitude must be sincere and meaningful. Specifying what you are thankful for and its impact on you and others is key. A lengthy explanation isn't necessary—just a line or two is enough.

Gratitude and the Brain

Practising gratitude lowers the stress response, allowing the Intellectual Mind back into play.

Gratitude activates the brain's reward system, releasing feel-good chemicals that boost mood and motivation.

Regular practice builds and reinforces beneficial neural pathways.

Why Gratitude Matters

For You: Contemplating the positives in your life helps to maintain a healthy, balanced perspective.

For Your Team: Showing appreciation for those around you builds trust and improves morale, leading to a more motivated and engaged team.

For Your Organisation: Promoting gratitude throughout a business creates a healthier and more resilient workforce and culture.

Practical Ways to Cultivate Gratitude

Personal Reflection: Start or end your day by listing three things you're grateful for. They don't have to be big – small wins count too.

Team Recognition: Start meetings off by expressing gratitude for something they have accomplished or supported you with.

Gratitude in Action: Thank someone who has made a difference in your day—even a small gesture can have a lasting impact.

Reflect and Act

Take a moment to reflect: What's one thing in your life that you're grateful for?

- **Express gratitude to your team** for their good work at your next team meeting.
- **Explain why you are grateful**, for example, the aspects of their work that stood out.
- **Share the positive difference** it made for you and others.

Gratitude brings attention to the positive aspects of life. Cultivate the practice of identifying one thing to appreciate each day and then spend a few moments contemplating it.

Key Leadership Takeaway

Gratitude changes your perspective by focusing on the positive aspects of your life, your team, and your organisation. Weaving gratitude into your everyday routine helps establish a basis for clear thinking, strong connections, and improved leadership skills.

14. Humour

Introduction

Humour provides a wide range of both personal and workplace benefits. Think back over times when you have shared a genuine laugh with colleagues – how quickly and effortlessly did it boost moods, cut through any tension, and help conversations flow more easily?

Humour supports happier work environments that provide people with a greater sense of belonging and improved job satisfaction that in turn translates to greater productivity. Humour also accelerates social bonding, key to successful networking and building effective professional relationships.

When applied appropriately, humour in the workplace can deepen trust and lead to a greater sense of relatability between leaders and teams. It's not about being a joker; it's about introducing a lightness that reduces pressure sufficiently to allow everyone to perform at their peak.

Humour and the Brain

Laughter releases brain chemicals that make you feel good, lower stress and help you to think more clearly.

People feel closer to each other, building trust that makes working together easier.

Helps people think outside the box – when you laugh, your brain is more open to new ideas, helping you solve problems more efficiently.

Why Humour Matters

For You: Humour lifts your mood, helping you stay calm under pressure and think more clearly – even when things get tough.

For Your Team: Like authenticity, humour helps a team bond and feel safe and open. A team that laughs together works well together and supports each other during challenging times.

For Your Organisation: Organisations that embrace—rather than frown on—humour create a great culture where people feel good about their work, which means people perform well and solve problems creatively.

Practical Tips

Create a positive atmosphere for meetings by starting with a touch of light-heartedness or an appropriate anecdote.

Increase engagement and alleviate stress and pressure by exploring opportunities to introduce a little more humour with your teams.

Model Positivity and create a greater sense of psychological safety among your team by showing that it's okay sometimes to see the lighter side of minor mistakes or challenges.

Reflect and Act

Reflect on a situation where humour eased friction and improved communication among your team.

- **How could** the targeted use of humour help to avoid future friction before it escalates?
- **How might** providing a more relaxed and open environment by introducing a little more humour enhance the wider culture in your organisation?

Key Leadership Takeaway

In the workplace, humour helps to develop and strengthen interpersonal relationships. As well as improving collaboration and easing friction, it can help alleviate stress, and lead to more resilient and productive teams.

15. Breathing Practices

Introduction

The popularity of breathing practices such as meditation and mindfulness has grown significantly over recent years, raising awareness of their benefits. Breathing is something we all do—from the moment we're born to the moment we die—and we mostly do it without any conscious thought.

When stress hits, the sympathetic nervous system activates in preparation for a fight-or-flight response. As a result, our breathing becomes shallow and quick, fuelling the stress response even further. Bringing attention to our breath and consciously taking control interrupts this process, calming our mind and bringing our attention back to the present.

Slow, deliberate breathing activates the parasympathetic nervous system—the part of the brain that promotes relaxation and recovery—stopping the stress response in its tracks. It's a quick and reliable way to regain composure in stressful moments so that we can think more clearly.

However, this simple intervention offers benefits beyond a quick way to calm a stress response and regain control in moments of panic. There is a reason it plays such a pivotal role in meditation and many other practices—it boasts many health benefits for body and mind alike.

Breathwork helps us feel more grounded, encourages time in our Intellectual Mind, and creates the mental space that enables us to reflect and think clearly and to respond effectively. Furthermore, just a few minutes a day is sufficient to start developing and reinforcing the neural pathways that build future resilience.

Breathing Practices and the Brain

Calm breathing reduces the activation of the stress response.

Slow, deep breaths activate the parasympathetic nervous system, helping to relax the body and reduce physical signs of stress, such as a racing heart.

Allows the intellectual mind to get back in play, enabling you to regain control over your thoughts and actions.

Why It Matters

For You: Even quick and straightforward breathing interventions can help you stay calmer and more focused, especially under pressure.

For Your Team: It can be a practical, quick way to lower stress levels among teams during high-pressure situations. Introducing it into daily activities can help bring a sense of composure and help teams stay grounded.

For Your Organisation: Finding creative ways to integrate breathing practices into workplace culture can help build resilience and sharpen focus, particularly during high-stress situations.

Practical Breathing Techniques

Box Breathing

- Inhale for 4 seconds.
- Hold your breath for 4 seconds.
- Exhale for 4 seconds.
- Hold again for 4 seconds.
- Continue until you feel calmer and more focused.

Simple Deep Breathing

- Take a deep breath in.
- Exhale slowly and fully.
- Repeat until you feel calmer and more relaxed.

If you are ready to explore these practices a little further, the workbook session in Part 4 includes more exercises, including a 2-minute meditation, to reap even more breathing benefits for you and your team.

Reflect and Act

Sit quietly and explore how your body responds to quickening your breathing for a few moments.

- **Slow your breathing** down by taking 3 deep, steady breaths.
- **What do you notice** – how does your body respond?
- **Continue taking** calm, steady, relaxed breaths for 2 minutes.
- **What do you notice?** How do you feel?

Key Leadership Takeaway

Practices that introduce breathwork are accessible, evidence-based ways for managing stress and enhancing focus that are quick and simple for anyone to use. In addition to being useful in the moment, they have many health benefits when used on a more regular basis.

16. Smiling

Introduction

Whether we're the one smiling or the one being smiled at, a smile can have a significant impact on our thoughts, our emotions, and our interactions with those around us. Have you ever heard the expression 'fake it 'til you make it'? Well, smiling doesn't just express happiness, it generates it too. When we smile brain chemicals are released that enhance our mood, alleviate stress, and even improve our relationships with others.

A word of caution, though: To weave its true magic, a smile needs to be authentic, and an authentic smile is potent stuff—and infectious, too. When you smile, those around you are more inclined to smile, too, creating a ripple of happiness throughout your environment that enhances communication, instils trust, and strengthens relationships—all vital components of a thriving and effective organisation.

Smiling and the Brain

Releases brain chemicals that make us feel happier and more relaxed.

Smiling hijacks the stress response, helping us calm down and think more clearly.

Releases brain chemicals that increase mood and promote social bonding and strengthen connections.

Why Smiling Matters

For You: Smiling is a straightforward and effortless way to shift yourself from feeling overwhelmed by stress to feeling calmer and more confident.

For Your Team: When you smile, you signal a safe, open atmosphere for your team that builds trust, reduces defensiveness, and enhances team dynamics.

For Your Organisation: An organisation in which people are going about their day smiling signals an organisation with a great culture!

Practical Tips

When you're getting ready in the morning, set a positive tone for the day by taking a moment to smile at yourself in the mirror.

An authentic, relaxed smile encourages open and positive communication with others.

Finding something to smile about in stressful situations can relieve stress and provide reassurance to others.

Reflect and Act

- **Stand or sit in front of a mirror** and gently smile.
- **It may feel** a little uncomfortable at first but stay with it.
- **What subtle shifts** do you notice in your mood?

Key Leadership Takeaway

Beyond making you feel better in the moment, smiling ripples out to those around you. Far more than a superficial gesture, smiling instils trust, reduces stress, and strengthens collaboration.

PART 2 REFLECTION

Reflect on Techniques

- Which technique resonated the most? Why do you think that is?
- What changes did you notice when you tried these activities in your workplace?

Identify Challenges

- What potential obstacles (e.g., time pressure, team scepticism, or your own negativity bias) might block you from using these techniques effectively?
- How could the different techniques help you to uncover solutions?

Collaborate and Grow

- How might you start introducing these techniques in your working life?
- Could you build confidence by practising with a colleague or team member?
- Check out the workbook sections in Part 4 for ideas and ready-to-go exercises.
- Consider how you might introduce one technique to your team to test its impact.
- **Have fun and explore!**

Prepare for Part 3

- Think of a process, project, or a part of your organisation that you'd like to transform.
- Keep that example in mind as you move forward.

For those who want to explore more profound applications of these tools, Part 4 offers a structured workbook with activities tailored for individuals, teams, and organisational integration. These exercises provide ready-to-use frameworks for embedding the techniques effectively in your organisation.

Part Three: Strategic Intervention

Introduction

Imagine a future where the workplace is more than a place where people come to work—it is somewhere they grow and thrive. A workplace where people leave each day better equipped to contribute to a stronger, more positive future and a healthier, more resilient society.

So far, we've examined the concepts behind positive work ways. In Part One, we explored an analogy of two very different brain states before moving on to Part Two to look at how techniques from the fields of Solutions Focus and Positive Psychology can be used to influence those states positively.

Now, it's time to take a step further as we combine and transform those principles from stand-alone initiatives into a strategic framework for your organisation—one that offers the capability to positively influence the way things are done and actively drive and embed change throughout your entire business.

Part three explores strategic organisational integration as a means of ensuring that positive work ways influence decision-making, workplace culture, and business outcomes at every level to create lasting change.

What to Expect

The chapters ahead will build your vision of how positive work ways would integrate into your organisation, exploring

1. **Strategic Vision**
2. **Goal Setting**
3. **Engaging Leaders**
4. **Communication**
5. **Leadership and Workforce Development**
6. **Safety as a Brain State**
7. **Key Business Functions**

8. External Well-being Providers

9. General Supply Chain

10. Measurement

11. Support Resources – Bringing it all Together.

By the end of this section, you will have built a clear vision of how positive work ways would look embedded into the core of your organisation. Let's get started.

1: Strategic Vision

Introduction

Let's take a moment to take a step back and take a look at the bigger picture. Think about your organisation's current strategic vision. What does success look and feel like to you? How clear is the existing vision? Does it set a strong and clear direction that consistently influences day-to-day decisions, behaviours, and priorities across your business? Or does it feel either partially or wholly disconnected from the day-to-day reality?

Is the focus on ticking off individual goals and securing one target at a time, without seeing the bigger picture? Or are you already actively creating a workplace where people flourish, ideas flow, and high performance feels second nature?

Exploring organisations through the lens of brain states provides a useful means by which to connect different functions and activities. Whether it's productivity, culture, performance, safety, or engagement, they all rely on the same simple and practical concept - a positive brain state.

Many organisations treat these areas separately, setting goals in isolation. But what if there was a way to bring them together, creating a more connected, effective, and sustainable approach to success?

Why Strategic Vision Matters

A clear strategic vision serves as the guiding light that unites every aspect of a business - it's what keeps leaders, teams and individuals aligned. A strong, compelling vision actively propels progress toward successful business outcomes. It builds resilience and growth, increases engagement and accountability, strengthens collaboration, and provides a business with a competitive edge. Without one, decision-making becomes disjointed, reactive, and confused, and friction and misalignment take hold.

In what ways could the successful realisation of your organisation's strategic vision be supported and strengthened by introducing positive work ways? Could it lead to improved business outcomes by improving alignment and consistency, and enhancing communication? How might easing areas of friction or instilling greater cooperation and collaboration change things for your organisation?

Setting the Vision

Every organisation is unique. What does success look like for your business? How could a solutions-focused approach help to encourage and support the exploration of possibilities and define what 'good' looks like to develop a clear and inspiring vision?

Start by asking:

- What does good look like for your organisation?
- How would positive work ways look and feel across different teams and functions?

Consider the level of impact and timeframes you're aiming for, and how you might introduce positive work ways:

- Are you aiming for complete, transformative change across all functions and business areas simultaneously?
- Or would a gradual, organic approach that steadily increases alignment over time feel more realistic and achievable?

Practical Steps

Define Your Vision

If positive work ways were effectively introduced, what would success look like in 12 months, three years, or five years?

Stakeholder Engagement

What role could your stakeholders play in defining and bringing this strategic vision to life? How might engaging them earlier encourage greater collaboration and help build momentum?

Develop a Roadmap

What steps could offer the potential to create an immediate impact but also set the stage for longer-term success? Could a phased approach, with small actions and quick wins, help to build confidence and secure commitment?

Reflect and Act

Define your vision of how things would be if positive work ways were integrated throughout your business. What does 'good' look like?

- **Where and how** could aligning your existing strategic vision with positive work ways produce better outcomes? Which areas would benefit the most or have the greatest impact?

- **Identify one small, tangible step** you could take today to move closer to this vision.

Closing Thoughts

It all begins with a clear and bold strategic vision. By reflecting on positive work ways and aligning your strategy, you're starting a journey to improved outcomes by transforming how your organisation operates. What possibilities could be opened up for your organisation by taking the first step?

2: Strategic Goal Setting

Introduction

Whereas strategic vision defines the long-term aspiration and sets out the road map, goals provide the clear, specific, tangible steps that drive progress and maintain the focus to get there. Effective goals are aligned yet adaptable, instil accountability, and track progress throughout every level. But what if goal setting wasn't just a routine activity?

Imagine a truly transformative goal-setting process – one that continuously questioned, aligned, engaged, and motivated and also opened the door to – and actively sought out - new opportunities.

Consider a goal-setting process that drives high performance whilst producing innovative and creative solutions - bringing clarity and focus, encouraging engagement and building momentum. Developing goals that inspire teams to aim higher whilst building organisational resilience and individual well-being.

Rather than simply measuring performance, what difference would goals that actively shape the way people work, think, and collaborate make for your organisation?

Exploring Opportunities

How effective are your organisation's existing goals? How aligned are they with your strategic vision, and how well do they work together in actively driving progress? How accurately do goals cascade throughout the business and keep everyone on a common path toward that vision?

How effectively do goals seek out opportunity or drive high performance? What opportunity is there to get more from your goal-setting process? What would greater alignment of goals across the organisation achieve in supporting progress toward your vision?

Where might a quick and simple reframing improve engagement as well as the effectiveness and impact of existing goals? For example, instead of aiming to 'reduce absenteeism,' what if the goal were to 'build resilience so teams can flourish'?

On the surface, this small shift may sound like nothing more than a superficial and insignificant change in wording. Still, it is deceptively powerful—it represents a reimagined way of thinking that encourages optimism, curiosity, and focus.

Questions to Explore

- How could your current goal-setting processes better support the realisation of your vision and strategy?
- What positive changes could introducing positive work ways bring to your existing goal-setting process?
- Could reframing existing goals offer a quick and simple way to help drive improved outcomes? Could this seemingly small action change the way goals are perceived and make them more motivating and engaging?

Bridging Vision to Practical Action

With a vision of what's possible, the next step is to explore how these ideas might take shape in your organisation. What exactly does 'good' look like when it comes to goal setting, and how do you get there?

This isn't about overhauling everything at once—it begins by exploring what aligns most naturally with your organisation's strengths and then using those insights to guide incremental, meaningful change. To support this chapter, the Part 4 workbook includes an accompanying exercise using the Universal Template at the end of the book.

Practical Steps

What does 'good' look like?

What would be happening differently if goals were more aligned: engaging, inspiring, and motivating teams across your business? In what ways would success show up in different areas, such as leadership, communication, process interfaces, personal interactions, culture, and business outcomes?

Evaluation of existing goals

Evaluation of existing goals: How could existing strategic goals - like performance, engagement, or safety - be reframed, and how might that lead to enhanced business outcomes? Could a quick and simple reframing offer a starting point for your business in introducing positive work ways?

Where are the opportunities?

Where could reframing goals to focus on growth, collaboration, and creativity have the biggest impact? What would it take to make this shift in one area as a pilot?

What existing strengths could you build on?

What's already working in your current goal-setting practices? How might you amplify these strengths to make goal setting more engaging and impactful?

What's the first step?

If you could explore one small change today, such as reframing a single goal or introducing a collaborative goal-setting session, what would it be?

Reflect and Act

How might reframing goals to emphasise growth, creativity, and resilience change the way your teams perceive and support them?

- What small changes could you make to your process to start the journey toward integrating positive work ways?
- How might this be rolled out over time across the organisation?

Closing Thoughts

If every goal engaged its target audience, drove progress, and inspired creativity, imagine what your organisation could achieve. Aligning and supporting a powerful strategic vision with powerful strategic goals generates more than milestones—it creates a catalyst for organisational transformation.

3: Engaging Leaders

Introduction

Leadership is the driving force that unites strategic vision and goals and translates them into action. In the absence of effective leadership, even the most persuasive vision and meticulously designed strategy are doomed to fail.

Effective and aligned leadership throughout every tier of an organisation provides the essential elements for transforming strategic vision into tangible success: clarity, alignment, and execution. If the leaders in your organisation were a truly united force, what would be different?

Imagine leadership teams that continually and seamlessly adapt to their environment whilst maintaining broader alignment and driving a powerful cultural transformation. Reshaping how teams collaborate, inspiring creativity and innovation, and creating a working environment in which high performance, inclusivity and well-being are the norm.

What might be possible for your business if every leader adopted positive work ways and aligned around a common framework?

If leaders truly united and aligned, just how powerful could the resulting ripple effect become, enhancing individual performance, team and organisational culture, and business outcomes?

Exploring Opportunities

Contemplate your organisation's leadership – how is it structured, and how well does it function as a whole? Is each tier of leadership effectively and consistently aligned with – and actively driving - your strategic vision of a thriving, connected, and high-performance culture?

Is your leadership proactively working in harmony as a united force, or is it fragmented and disjointed, lacking in coordination and collaboration, with disagreements that cause frustration and present unnecessary obstacles?

What difference could it make if leaders across all tiers consistently adopted and encouraged practices that foster Intellectual Mind states? Leadership is the face of organisational change. What opportunities might open up for your organisation if your leadership consistently created work environments where collaboration flowed naturally, challenges were met with creativity, and solutions emerged effortlessly?

If leaders consistently demonstrated positive ways of working, how might this influence trust, collaboration, and performance across your organisation and create a resilient and focused foundation for sustainable, positive change?

Questions to Explore

- How effective is your leadership in developing a thriving, high-performance culture?
- How could implementing positive work ways help to align your leadership and support them in driving transformational change across your organisation?
- What would be the simplest and most effective step that could be taken to start introducing positive work ways to your leadership teams?

Bridging Vision to Practical Action

Contemplate the practical steps your organisation might take to equip, engage, enthuse, and empower the leaders throughout your business on this journey. How might positive work ways concepts be introduced and shared with your leadership?

Could seemingly small actions, such as introducing solutions-focused questions in team meetings or encouraging reflective practices, be ways to familiarise leaders and get started? This isn't about imposing a new way of working on your leaders. It's about inviting them to explore what's possible and then supporting them in creating the conditions for success.

Could pilots and feedback inform broader initiatives that strengthen rollout across the organisation? What resources could be developed to guide and support leaders whilst they build confidence with the new knowledge and techniques?

Practical Steps

What does 'good' look like?

If every leader across your organisation adopted positive work ways, how would your organisation's culture change? What specific signs would signal success, for example, changes in communication, behaviour, process interfaces, personal interactions, outcomes, and culture?

What strengths can you build on?

What's already working well within your leadership team – what are their strengths?

What opportunities exist?

Where and how could leaders work together to explore and test some of these new approaches, and how might cross-functional collaboration help to enhance impact and effectiveness?

What's the first step?

What small step could be taken to introduce leaders to positive work ways?

Reflect and Act

How could your leadership team support an organisation-wide shift toward positive work ways?

- How would you introduce the concept of positive work ways?

- How could you roll out and embed positive work ways throughout different leadership groups and tiers?

Closing Thoughts

Positive work ways provide a framework that actively supports leadership in driving positive change and creating sustainable, long-term success through the development of a high-performance culture in which everyone can flourish.

4: Communication – Building a Culture of Connection

Introduction

Strategic vision sets an organisation's destination and roadmap, and goals define actions that leadership then drives to successful completion. Effective communication is central to it all and crucial to success.

Effective communication sends clear, aligned, and consistent messaging across all tiers, functions, and teams. It connects individual contributions to larger goals, sets expectations, provides feedback, motivates, inspires, supports, strengthens bonds, and builds trust.

Communication underpins everything – from determining compliance to engagement, motivation, well-being, and performance. What does communication look like in your organisation, and how effectively does it support the realisation of your strategic vision?

Are your vision and goals clearly and consistently communicated across all channels and to all stakeholders? Is existing communication actively engaging all employees and target audiences? Is it proactively contributing to the creation of a thriving and healthy work environment that encourages creativity, innovation, and high performance?

Is communication building and strengthening your organisation, or is it causing confusion, frustration, and misunderstanding? Is the corporate voice consistent and clear, with a supportive tone throughout the entire organisation? Do policies, procedures, and other forms of documentation interface seamlessly across different functions and teams?

How about interactions between leaders, teams, and individuals? Is there awareness and mindfulness of the influence their words may have on those around them? Imagine every interaction, from leadership updates to casual conversations, aligning with the principles of positive work ways. What would that look like?

Could more effective communication lead to greater alignment, as well as smoother workflows, interfaces, and interactions?

Exploring Opportunities

Communication goes far beyond the words we use – it's the tone, timing, and intent behind those words. Think about the different ways in which communication takes place across your organisation every day.

What's the prevailing tone in your leadership communications – does messaging mirror your strategic vision? Does it accurately reflect corporate voice? Is it motivating and engaging, and consistently repeated and aligned throughout the business? Could communicating in ways more closely aligned with positive work ways prove beneficial by raising engagement, strengthening resilience, and driving higher performance?

Written communications, such as policies and procedures, reflect your organisation's corporate voice. How they are framed is key—what message are they conveying in your organisation? Are they consistent, supportive, and clear in content, wording, and tone—or might they be causing unintentional confusion or defensiveness? Could even a simple reframing be enough to help raise engagement or improve compliance?

Every interaction, whether verbal or nonverbal, is instrumental in determining wider organisational culture. How might approaching communication through an alternative perspective of brain states help your business to utilise communication more proactively and strategically?

Questions to Explore

- Does your organisation's corporate tone have a positive or negative influence?
- How might the wording, tone, and framing across different forms of communication impact how people feel and perform?
- In what ways could positive work ways help to create a more positive corporate voice and tone for your organisation's culture?

Bridging Vision to Practical Action

Transforming communication across your business is a huge and daunting prospect. So, where might your organisation begin? How might you start shaping your communications to be more authentic, consistent, and engaging? Would you consider reframing some of your core policies to influence corporate voice and tone? Would you introduce meeting protocols to encourage more productive discussions? Would you embed positive work ways into leadership updates? How might these examples, in turn, set the tone for the wider business?

Practical Steps

What does effective communication look like for your business?
What would be different about the way people interacted if communication practices across the business were more engaging and aligned? What would you notice first, and how might this impact business outcomes?

What's already working?
Where do you already see examples of effective communication in your organisation? How might you build on these strengths?

Where are the gaps?
What aspects of communication could benefit most from improvement, and how might even small adjustments offer the potential to make a big difference?

What's one simple change you could make today?
Could experimentation with a policy reframe, introducing meeting protocols, or encouraging leaders to adopt more positive work ways in their interactions provide a starting point?

The accompanying exercises in Part 4 will help you start exploring these questions and more in further detail.

Reflect and Act

What role does communication play in shaping your organisation's culture and outcomes?

- How might reframing policies, messages, or meetings support greater alignment and engagement?

- What small steps could you take to start embedding positive work ways into your communication practices?

Closing Thoughts

Humans are social beings—they need positive interactions with others to flourish and perform at their best. An organisation built on a bedrock of positive communication, reinforced with positive leadership interactions that reflect clarity, trust, and alignment, creates a culture where people feel valued, engaged, motivated, and empowered.

5: Leadership and Workforce Development

Introduction

Leadership drives the execution of strategic vision and goals, and effective communication ensures alignment and consistency of messaging. To be successful, though, leaders need continuous development to grow and adapt, and their teams need to acquire the right skills and mindset to flourish and perform at their best.

Strategically aligned leadership and workforce development programmes facilitate an agile and adaptable organisation. Imagine your organisation's programmes doing more than teaching knowledge and skills.

What difference could they make if they were the vehicle for creating and driving strategic change across your entire business? Could streamlined programmes not only reduce training time but also amplify impact, enhance learning, and embed knowledge and skills more effectively?

What benefits could aligning programmes around a core concept with the potential to drive both high performance and well-being bring? Could positive work ways provide the thread to pull it all together for your business?

Exploring Possibilities

Contemplate the topics within your organisation's existing development programmes. Effective communication, high performance, behavioural safety, conflict resolution, difficult conversations, and well-being are likely on the list. All share common threads, so what benefit might alignment around a common framework bring?

Imagine leaders and teams consistently navigating challenges with the same tools, language, and mindset. How might this strengthen collaboration and improve performance across the business?

Could positive work ways transform your development programmes into a vehicle for strategic change?

Questions to Explore

- How strategically aligned are existing development programmes?
- Where and how could alignment be improved and streamlined to provide a more cohesive and strategic approach?
- In what ways could a core framework enhance the impact of training while reducing duplication and inefficiency?

Bridging the Vision to Practical Action

A complete overhaul of existing development programmes is a significant - and perhaps intimidating – undertaking. Identify a realistic, achievable starting point on which you can build over time.

Consider identifying any overlapping themes, followed by removing duplications and consolidating existing content. Or align messaging between programmes to develop a more streamlined, consistent, and impactful approach. Could positive work ways be incorporated to provide the framework around which to build?

Practical Steps

What does good look like?
What would highly effective strategic leadership and workforce development look like in your organisation?

Existing strengths
Where might it be possible to consolidate content or reduce duplication without losing impact? Where do existing programmes naturally align or overlap?

Explore opportunities
What benefits could exploring positive work ways bring to your leadership and workforce development programmes?

Next steps
What is one small change or first step that you could explore today? Could a pilot programme help better determine the value of wider integration?

Reflect and Act

How could you better align your leadership and workforce development programmes?

- What efficiencies might aligning and streamlining current programmes provide?
- What small steps could you take to start embedding positive work ways into development programmes?

Closing Thoughts

Effective leadership and workforce development programmes offer far more than resources for building knowledge and skills—they're also strategic drivers of cultural transformation.

Aligning programmes with your organisation's strategic vision and embedding positive work ways provides a strategic framework that supports collaboration, high performance, resilience, and growth.

6: Safety as a Brain State

Introduction

Conventional approaches to safety management tend to be largely compliance-driven, with a heavy reliance on rules, procedures, and enforcement to keep people safe. However, an increasing awareness of—and emphasis on—human factors over recent years has started to turn the tide.

Could exploring safety through the lens of brain states help to drive a more proactive, progressive, and strategic approach to safety throughout your organisation? How could creating environments that nurture behavioural and psychological safety - in every interaction, decision, and behaviour - help reduce reliance on rules alone to keep people safe?

In the UK, the Health and Safety Executive (HSE) emphasises the foundational role that a positive culture plays in effective behavioural safety initiatives. Could adopting positive work ways provide this foundation, embedding safety into daily practices? Could it enhance an existing programme or, for some organisations, remove the need for a separate programme entirely?

Imagine if improved safety and greater compliance were natural outcomes of an engaged, motivated, brain-friendly culture - what might that look like in your organisation?

Exploring Possibilities

How effective are your existing safety communications and procedures – are they easy to understand by their target audience? Are they framed in a positive tone, or might they inadvertently trigger negativity and defensiveness? Having read this book, could simply reframing some of these messages improve engagement, compliance, and outcomes?

Could positive work ways help to create a foundation where safe behaviours become second nature? Imagine the difference if safety became an organic outcome of how people think, communicate, and act across your organisation.

How might that influence behaviours, performance, well-being, culture, and business outcomes? How might a more proactive approach reduce or mitigate risk for your business?

Questions to Explore

- How effectively do your current safety practices engage the Intellectual Mind to create and support 'safe' brain states?
- How could implementing positive work ways help to align and integrate safety into core business activities?
- What would be the simplest and most effective step to start aligning your safety practices with positive work ways?

Bridging Vision to Practical Action

How could positive work ways support effective and impactful integration of safety across your organisation? Would a solutions-focused approach to incident investigations result in less friction and better outcomes?

How could the existing stress risk assessment process be used more effectively to drive proactive, leading data that improves visibility of trends across the business? Is it possible that even small actions, such as reframing safety signs and procedures, could positively influence perceptions and attitudes to safety?

Could the development and pilot of new approaches in individual teams or functions provide a base for a future, bespoke, organisation-wide behavioural safety programme?

Practical Steps

What does 'good' look like?
How would people behave, act, communicate, and interact differently if safety was seamlessly integrated throughout your organisation?

What's already there?
What influence on individual and team perspectives and behaviours might a simple reframing of existing safety messages and procedures have?

What opportunities exist?
How might building an awareness of the connection between brain states and safety guide incremental, positive change in safety culture?

What's the first step?

Where might you pilot a session on safety through brain states to gather feedback and build further momentum?

Reflect and Act

How might viewing safety through brain states help to change perspectives and attitudes across your business?

- Could reframing safety communications or adopting a solutions-focused approach to incident investigation help positively influence perception and outcomes?
- What is one small step that you could take to start integrating safety more effectively throughout your organisation?

Closing Thoughts

When safety is viewed through the lens of brain states, it comes to life as an intrinsic part of organisational culture. Cultivating work environments aligned with positive work ways leads to improved psychological and behavioural safety among individuals and teams.

7: Addressing Key Business Functions

Introduction

Imagine being part of an organisation in which every team and function truly collaborates, all working in harmony toward precisely defined goals that lead to a single, clearly articulated strategic vision.

Core processes operate efficiently, supported by optimally aligned systems that actively—and effortlessly—propel progress toward clear and realistic targets. Interfaces transition smoothly between teams and functions, assisted by seamlessly aligned shared policies and procedures, which define individual and collective roles and responsibilities and deliver clear and consistent direction, support, and guidance.

This isn't about overly rigid standardisation—it's about establishing a more collaborative, flexible and agile work environment that ensures progress toward an end goal isn't just possible – it's inevitable.

As well as providing useful approaches for forming precise, clearly articulated objectives, and improving communication and collaboration, how else might positive work ways support you?

Optimal alignment and integration of systems, perhaps? Smoother transitions between interfaces? Reduced duplication and fewer gaps? How might that improve performance, decision-making, culture, and business outcomes?

Exploring Possibilities

When you think about your organisation's key functions, how effectively do they contribute to delivering your vision and strategy? Are they working in harmony, or do gaps and inefficiencies exist that slow progress and create friction?

Could integrating positive work ways across core functions help to alleviate bottlenecks by smoothing interfaces and improving alignment? What opportunities might this provide for your business? Could it improve decision-making and enhance outcomes across the organisation?

Questions to Explore

- How effectively do business functions, core processes, and systems align and drive progress toward your organisation's strategic vision and goals?
- Where and how might positive work ways help strengthen collaboration and improve alignment?
- What is the smallest action with the greatest impact that you could take to get started and build further momentum?

Bridging Vision to Practical Action

Where and how could your organisation begin exploring ways in which to use positive work ways to improve alignment across different functions? What approach might work most effectively for your business?

Reviewing a single process, perhaps – or maybe homing in on some of the key interfaces between functions – exploring opportunities to reduce duplication, improve communication, and streamline workflow between teams.

Practical Steps

What does good look like?

How would your organisation operate if every function, team, system, process, policy, procedure, and interaction were seamlessly aligned with smooth interfaces and clear, consistent messaging? What would be different?

Where are the key interfaces?

Which interfaces have the most impact or could benefit most from greater collaboration or alignment?

What's already working?

Are there existing strengths across the organisation—sections of workflows or individual interfaces—that could serve as a foundation for further development?

Opportunities

How might you bring a greater diversity of experience and knowledge to encourage more creative thought?

What's the first step?

If you could improve just one small thing, what might that be? What small action would lead to the greatest impact?

The Part 4 workbook includes accompanying exercises for each of these chapters that provide more detailed guidance. These exercises use the templates provided toward the end of the book.

Reflect and Act

Which function would benefit greatest from strengthening collaboration, and how might positive work ways be used to achieve this?

- How could exploring ways to improve a couple of key interfaces also build future momentum?

- What small action could you take to improve alignment and strengthen collaboration?

Closing Thoughts

Positive work ways aren't about adding complexity—it's about simplifying and aligning processes to reduce friction, strengthen collaboration, and improve efficiency. By cascading this approach throughout your organisation, you build a workplace where every function actively and seamlessly contributes to a cohesive, flourishing, high-performance culture.

8: External Well-being Providers: Maximising Impact

Introduction

Occupational health services, employee assistance programmes, and other external well-being providers play essential roles in an organisation's day-to-day operations. Actively supporting line managers, employees, and HR teams and often involved in critical or highly sensitive moments, they directly influence decision-making, operational efficiency, and workplace culture.

With direct involvement in key areas, including absence management, physical and mental health assessments and support, health surveillance, return to work plans, workplace adjustments and regulatory compliance, these providers form an extension of your organisation.

This becomes even more complex when multiple providers are involved, each with their own models, language, and recommendations. Misalignment between providers—or between providers and the organisation—can lead to mixed messages, unnecessary delays, and frustration for both employees and managers.

Consider your existing service provision—how effective is it? If you asked each service user group - managers, employees, and HR teams - would it be meeting their expectations and needs? Are the KPIs presently in place successful in determining service impact and capturing current and future business needs?

Exploring Possibilities

Imagine streamlined processes and workflows that deliver targeted and effective support – underpinned by consistently aligned interfaces and messaging that actively drive positive work ways and reinforce your strategic vision.

Consider the impact eliminating bottlenecks and delays would have on reducing frustration and easing friction, improving productivity and business outcomes. Could small refinements to off-the-peg services help deliver more tailored and aligned programmes and solutions that proactively support and build resilience across your organisation?

Questions to Explore

- How aligned are existing providers with your strategic vision and goals?
- How well does the current provision meet service user and business expectations and needs?
- How might positive work ways help improve efficiency and effectiveness for your organisation?

Bridging Vision to Practical Action

What small changes might have the greatest potential to impact existing interfaces and service provision? If current offerings were mapped out against service user and business needs and goals, where would the greatest potential for improvement lie? Where and how could providers become more actively involved in organisational strategy, and what possibilities might emerge by greater alignment and collaboration?

Practical Steps

Review

How effectively does current provision reflect service user and business needs – what gaps or redundancy might be revealed by asking the different service user groups?

Alignment

How aligned are providers and services, both with your organisation and between different providers?

Consistency

How consistent is the messaging and approach across providers, and how does this compare with the internal messaging and approach?

Usage

Are all services being paid for being fully utilised, and if not, what are the reasons – are they under-promoted, or are they not required?

Collaboration

Could joint reviews between service users, providers, and other stakeholders help improve service design, delivery, and outcomes?

Reflect and Act

What does good occupational health and well-being support look like for your organisation?

- How might introducing positive work ways into these partnerships help optimise support for line managers, HR teams and employees?
- What small steps could provide the greatest impact on your business?

Closing Thoughts

External providers for occupational health, employee assistance programmes, and employee benefits play an essential role in supporting an organisation. Beyond providing services, they are an integral part of day-to-day operations, culture, and organisational success. Rethinking these services unlocks many opportunities.

9: General Supply Chain – Beyond Your Organisation

Introduction

Most organisations are heavily reliant on their supply chain. A robust and efficient supply chain that provides the right resources at the right time actively facilitates the achievement of targets and goals. Key suppliers are such an integral part of ensuring smooth operations and business continuity that organisations usually place great emphasis and resources on building strong and resilient supply partnerships.

But what if an organisation's supply chain holds potential beyond the provision of the right resources at the right time? Consider taking your supply chain beyond the more traditional measures of cost and efficiency. Imagine what it would be like leading an organisation that wasn't just successful - it also drove meaningful and impactful wider societal change.

Remember the ripple effect we discussed in Part One? Imagine the wider influence that your organisation might achieve by embedding positive work ways throughout your supply chain. As well as improving efficiency, strengthening resilience, and securing strong business outcomes, how far might the positive ripple extend, building and strengthening resilience on a scale far beyond the confines of your business?

Exploring Possibilities

How effective are shared interfaces? Are processes and systems seamlessly aligned and easy to access and navigate by the various target audiences? Are shared communications consistent with your corporate tone, driving a solutions-focused, proactive approach? Do suppliers actively support your organisational priorities and key initiatives across your business?

Could there be an opportunity to encourage collaboration and secure better alignment efforts between different suppliers? How could you use your existing systems and processes more effectively and actively encourage your supply chain to adopt more positive ways of working?

Social Value: A Ripple Effect Beyond Efficiency

Reflect on the potential that introducing positive work ways into your organisation opens up for wider positive societal impact. How much of a difference could small acts such as sharing some of your organisation's positive work ways training and support resources with suppliers and social value partners make? Think again about that ripple effect – how far might it be possible to extend it?

Questions to Explore

- How well aligned are your existing supply chain practices?
- In what ways might positive work ways strengthen and encourage even greater collaboration in existing supplier relationships?
- How easy would it be to share some or all of your positive work ways resources with your supply chain?

Bridging Vision to Practical Action

Introducing positive work ways across your supply chain doesn't have to be complex. Just a few small steps may be all it takes to instigate positive change. For example, aligning and smoothing interfaces, reframing the wording of contracts and negotiations, introducing solutions-focused language, or sharing knowledge by providing suppliers with access to positive work ways resources are all small steps that pave the way for positive change.

Practical Steps

Redefine supplier relationships

What would a truly effective supply base look like, and what additional benefits might the introduction of positive work ways bring – for your business, your suppliers, and beyond?

Revisit communications

How could communications be more consistent and aligned?

Rethink social impact

What opportunity exists to create meaningful and sustainable social value that supports your goals as well as those of suppliers and social value partners?

Celebrate and Share Success

How might recognising and sharing success stories inspire further alignment and collaboration within your supply chain?

Reflect and Act

How might viewing supply chain interactions through a different lens change your approach?

- How might optimising supplier relationships also lead to a wider societal impact and support long-term sustainable change?
- What small step could you take to start introducing positive work ways into your supply chain relationships?

Closing Thoughts

By integrating positive work ways into your supply chain, you open up the potential to create more than transactional relationships. You open up the possibility to develop partnerships that carry the ripple of positive change far beyond your organisation into the communities in which you operate and wider society.

What might your organisation achieve if every supplier, contractor, and partner embraced the positive work ways principles? Just how far could these ripple effects reach?

10: Measurement

Introduction

Every organisation depends on measurement to realise its strategic vision and goals. Access to relevant, reliable, and accurate data is fundamental to making well-informed, effective, and timely decisions. The right metrics and data provide a business with a clear and precise representation of what's happening across the company, from individual and team performance to organisational resilience and well-being.

What does effective measurement look like to your business? What difference could more refined metrics make—each with a definite purpose, collectively aligned and combined to provide a single, cohesive picture? Imagine replacing needless, costly, and confusing redundant data collection with a more unified approach. How might reducing needless data overload improve clarity, sharpen focus, and instil greater accountability throughout your organisation?

Moving Beyond Lagging Indicators

Lagging indicators—such as absence rates—focus on what's already gone wrong. While they undoubtedly have their place in an organisation's measurement framework, without the introduction of leading indicators to counterbalance, they risk trapping organisations in a reactive mindset.

When all attention is directed toward what is not wanted, we actually risk attracting more of it rather than less. Reframing lagging indicators into leading ones can be as simple as flipping them to reflect what we do want to happen or what we want more of.

Questions to Explore

- Reflect on your organisation's existing metrics—how balanced are they between leading and lagging?
- How might placing more focus on leading data help develop metrics that go beyond identifying problems and instead provide tools that drive more growth and opportunity?

- Could the development and integration of more dynamic and proactive metrics change your organisation for the better?

Bridging the Gap

Is the data currently being captured across your business telling you what you really need or want to know? Are you extracting the most valuable metrics, or are there more creative, innovative metrics waiting to be discovered? How could measurement be brought to life across your business?

How might onerous data capture or lengthy audits be broken down and integrated into business-as-usual activities? How could data capture be made quicker, more engaging, and more relevant?

Could minor changes be sufficient to develop more dynamic and engaging dialogues or replace unrelatable and uninspiring reports? How could measurement become a more natural and engaging part of daily operations across your business?

Tapping into Missed Opportunities

Consider how a different approach could simplify an existing measurement process or present findings in a more accessible, intuitive way. Here, I'll offer stress risk assessment as an example. Often viewed as an onerous, compliance-driven task, stress risk assessments have an all-too-often missed potential to furnish an organisation with a wealth of valuable data.

A little creativity, tailoring, and reframing are all that are required to create a quick and powerful tool that's capable of providing valuable insights and trends about leadership, inclusion, well-being, productivity, and culture.

Practical Steps

Strengths

What's already working well in your organisation's measurement practices, and how might building on these aid progress?

Reframe

Where could lagging indicators like absenteeism or turnover be quickly reframed into strengths-based metrics?

Collaborate

Could involving wider teams in the development of new metrics improve engagement and effectiveness?

Integrate

What processes or activities might accommodate creative and proactive measurement tools?

Pilot and Refine

How might pilots be used to try out new ideas before committing to large-scale change?

Reflect and Act

What does effective measurement look like for your business?

- How might reframing measurement help to engage and provide more dynamic metrics?
- What small step could you take to get started?

Closing Thoughts

A dynamic, proactive measurement strategy provides organisations with a more engaging and inspiring perspective. The right metrics, utilising well-developed questions, are transformational. Rather than pointing out what's already gone wrong, measurement needs to help an organisation uncover opportunities for future progress. A proactive measurement strategy, composed of carefully selected metrics, provides timely and meaningful data.

11: Support Resources: Bringing It All Together

Introduction

This book introduces the concept of positive work ways, adopting a solutions-focused approach to ask questions along the way that encourage exploration of how these ideas can be fully integrated into your organisation. Every question serves a purpose—helping you think critically, uncover possibilities, and create practical solutions that fit your unique workplace.

Throughout each part of the book, you've considered how these ideas can shape strategy, processes, functions, and leadership to gradually shift organisational culture. Now, the focus turns to creating resources that will support these changes in practice. The right tools can build confidence, increase awareness, reinforce learning, and help new ways of working become part of daily operations.

With a little creativity, you can develop tailored resources that will make positive work ways easier to apply throughout your organisation: whether through workplace guides, training materials, team exercises, or communication tools. This chapter provides practical steps to help you design simple, effective resources that embed these changes for the long term. Part 4 of the book also includes exercises you can use straight away to bring these ideas to life.

Creating a Culture of Positive Action

The ideas explored in this book—taken from the fields of solutions focus, positive psychology, and neuroscience—offer organisations the potential to create lasting change. However, without regular use and application, even the best approaches risk being forgotten or left behind. Regular and consistent reinforcement is needed to secure long-term, sustainable change.

Developing creative and practical solutions for your organisation that integrate these techniques and practices into daily operations will help build sustainable, positive habits that strengthen workplace culture and ensure they become second nature.

The exercises in this book can be applied in countless ways. Either on their own or in combination, they offer endless possibilities for the creation of tailored resources such as employee booklets, manager guides, workplace challenges, well-being initiatives, meeting activities, or team reflections. The key is finding the right fit for your organisation and making these ideas a natural part of how people work together.

Creative Applications for Interventions

Meeting Starters

Use the exercises in the workbook to gently set and encourage a positive tone. Or select a starter and some of the solutions-focused interventions to build more formal meeting protocols for use across the business.

Campaigns and Challenges

Lots of fun to be had on this one! Use techniques either individually or in combination to develop bespoke resources. Ideas to try:

- A month-long 'Challenge' where individuals and teams are challenged to practice a particular technique to explore its benefits and find ways to bring it into daily routines.
- A bespoke well-being calendar that transforms awareness initiatives into active drivers that support strategic vision and build resilience.
- Weave techniques into campaigns on any topic to highlight how inextricably these techniques and practices are tied to core business activities and performance.
- Run competitions asking for the most creative ideas on how activities can be integrated into working practices.
- Challenge leaders to run a whole meeting using only the solutions-focused questions and reframing negative templates at the end of the book.

Team Building Activities

Incorporate the exercises into team and corporate events, such as:

- Use leadership events to run role play with exercises such as difficult conversations, designed in a fun way to help your teams build confidence in a safe and relaxed environment.
- Host sessions for employees to brainstorm how they might best apply these techniques and practices in their roles.

Corporate Voice and Tone

Embed solutions-focused language into organisational communications and reframe problem-centred narrative into forward-thinking messaging that highlights strengths and possibilities.

Leadership Engagement

Encourage leaders to model solutions-focused inquiry in team discussions and decision-making.

Process Integration

Use solutions-focused techniques in strategy sessions, performance reviews, and even project kick-offs to align teams with organisational goals.

Breathing Exercises

Encourage the use of mindfulness or deep breathing techniques before meetings or in high-pressure environments.

Making It Accessible

To maximise engagement, consider creating physical and digital resources tailored to your organisation's needs:

Employee Booklets

Develop simple guides with examples of preferred interventions and explain how to apply them in daily work and personal life. The exercises in the workbook are designed to be plug-and-play, ready for you to go!

Training Reinforcement

Create bite-sized training modules that revisit key concepts and show how they align with ongoing projects and goals. Host a few webinars, sharing the load by getting senior leaders involved to raise the profile and impact.

Get workplace champions on board to run local initiatives and challenges using the different exercises. If your organisation uses toolbox talks or similar, then add it to the programme.

Recognition and Rewards

Celebrate individuals and teams who engage with and embody these principles. Use existing recognition programs to reinforce positive behaviours and encourage more engagement.

Digital Platforms

Use apps or intranets to share tips, challenges, and success stories.

Engagement Through Creativity

A strength of all the interventions covered in this book lies in their flexibility to be tailored to any audience or situation. With a little creativity, they can be adapted and/or combined to create a whole range of bespoke, powerful business resources tailored to your specific organisational needs. In addition to the many possibilities that we have explored so far, the Part 4 workbook provides even more ideas and guidance to inspire you and get you started.

The Strategic Advantage

Integrating these practices into your organisation goes beyond boosting morale and improving well-being. Individuals who engage with techniques and practices like the ones we've explored in this book tend to be healthier and more content. Healthier and content individuals, in turn, tend to be more collaborative, resilient, creative, innovative and productive.

Conclusion: Your Call to Action

This chapter is your final step - your call to action. You've explored ways these concepts can be integrated into all aspects of an organisation, from strategy to supply chain. Now, it's time to go further by bringing these ideas to life for your business, with creative, engaging initiatives that energise your teams and align them with your vision.

Part 3 Summary

Throughout Part 3, we have explored some of the many different ways that positive work ways can be integrated throughout an organisation to create impactful, sustainable change. Combined, the chapters in this book provide you with a roadmap for embedding more brain-friendly ways of working in your business.

Whether you decide to try a few low-key initiatives or commit to full-scale organisation-wide change, these techniques will provide a robust foundation for a more engaged, resilient, and high-performance culture.

Connecting the Dots: Key Themes

Positive work ways as the Core
This book revolves around the core concept that positive work ways aren't only beneficial for individual well-being - they hold truly transformative potential for entire organisations.

Integration Over Isolation
Each chapter highlighted the potential for integration into existing processes, whether through leadership and workforce development, safety, or external partnerships.

Solutions Focus as a Framework
Throughout, we've asked solutions-focused questions that ignite curiosity, encouraging readers to continually question, 'What does good look like?' to support exploration of the many potential possibilities for their organisation.

Simple and Practical
The practical steps in each chapter have served to highlight how small, considered changes continue to ripple out.

Reflection

As you consider the insights and strategies in Part 3, take a few moments to reflect:

- What elements of your existing organisation's strategic vision feel most aligned with positive work ways?
- How might starting to introduce and integrate these principles, in turn, create positive ripple effects across your business?
- What small, meaningful step could you take today to start embedding these techniques more deeply?

Bringing It All Together

This part of the book has been about exploring what's possible when organisations align their strategy, culture, and practices around positive work ways. But, most importantly, it's about recognising that every organisation's journey is unique.

The techniques and insights shared here are meant to guide rather than prescribe—they are intended to provide you with a flexible framework that can be adapted and tailored to your organisational context, goals, and aspirations.

Your organisation already has all it needs; the required tools, resources, and solutions are all there waiting - ready to create a culture of growth, performance, and resilience. A new journey starts here, and progress continues with every small action you take to introduce and reinforce these principles.

By applying these techniques, you're initiating a ripple effect of positive change that has the potential to extend far beyond the workplace, to encourage a healthier and more resilient society.

The future of your organisation starts now. Make it extraordinary.

Next Steps: Preparing for Implementation

Part 4 will take these concepts one step further again by offering ready-to-use resources and exercises designed to build confidence and help you and your teams start putting these ideas into action.

This next section provides everything you need to embed positive work ways into the core of your organisation, from practical tools to strategic frameworks.

Conclusion

'Every adventure requires a first step.'
— *Lewis Carroll*

What If?

What if organisations weren't just drivers of performance, but creators of ripples?

What if the way we work shaped not only culture, but also communities?

What if organisations held the key to stronger families, safer workplaces, and healthier societies?

What if that kind of change didn't need a grand initiative — just small, consistent shifts?

What if it started with one leader? One team? One person? One moment?

What if it started with you?

Because every ripple, every shift, every change…

starts with one simple question…

What's your Pharmacist doing?

Part 4: Workbook

Introduction

Whether you've read the previous sections or are jumping straight in here, this section provides a practical, hands-on guide to start implementing positive work ways - for yourself, your team, and your organisation. This workbook has been developed for active use by a broad audience. It starts with simple exercises that build familiarity and instil confidence, providing a solid foundation on which the rest of the exercises progressively build.

Whether you're a CEO focused on rethinking strategy, an HR leader looking for new ways to transform culture, part of a comms team working to raise engagement, a manager wanting to enhance team dynamics, or an individual interested in personal development - you'll find everything you need in this section to enable you to create impactful, tailored solutions.

These tools are intended to be flexible, accessible, and easy to implement, no matter how you use them. Every exercise is designed as a ready-to-go resource that can be quickly and easily adapted to any scenario, from personal reflection and team-building sessions to organisation-wide initiatives.

A brief introduction provides an overview and context to ensure each one is effective as a standalone resource, regardless of whether you have read the main book. If you've already read every chapter, you may notice a touch of repetition in places, but please rest assured that this is by design – and anyhow, a recap is no bad thing!

Using This Workbook

Start Where You Feel Inspired: Browse through the different workbook sections and exercises. You don't need to follow a set order - this is your journey, so let your curiosity lead the way and start with the exercises that resonate most.

Adapt as Needed: Each activity is flexible, and simple adjustments to the prompts will maximise the impact of how you want to use them. These tools are intended and designed to work for you, so tailor the worked examples, add personal touches, and collaborate with others to get the most out of them.

Reflect Often: Reflection is an integral part of the journey. Even seemingly small wins lead to positive change that continues to strengthen and build over time.

Recap: Brain States - Why These Techniques Matter

Positive work ways are based on a simple analogy of brain states – the Intellectual Mind vs. the Primitive Mind. Whereas the language of the Intellectual Mind is calm, rational, and solutions-focused, the language of the Primitive Mind is driven by survival responses such as anger, anxiety, and withdrawal.

Both brain states play essential roles in our survival, but balance is key – spending too much time in the Primitive Mind can negatively impact our well-being and make daily life more challenging.

This simple yet powerful analogy helps us recognise the influence our environment has on our own brain state and aids in understanding how our everyday interactions influence the brain states of those around us.

Viewing ourselves, others, and the world around us through the lens of Intellectual vs. Primitive Minds introduces an insightful and empowering perspective on personal well-being and the organisational landscape. It empowers us all to take greater control and actively influence our personal and collective well-being for the better.

When viewed through the lens of brain states, a poor culture in which firefighting and friction prevail reflects the language of the Primitive Mind, whilst a healthy and resilient culture reflects the language of the Intellectual Mind.

The different aspects of an organisation, such as communication, safety, inclusion, and performance, can also be understood through the lens of brain states. This makes it a compelling organisational framework and a simple yet effective vehicle for driving meaningful change throughout your business.

A brain-friendly organisational strategy simply encourages leaders and employees to spend more time in the Intellectual Mind. Solutions Focus and Positive Psychology provide ideal techniques to support this strategy because they are quick, simple, and evidence-based.

Applying these techniques individually and in combination across an organisation's different layers and functions provides a strategic and structured approach to introducing, embedding, and integrating more brain-friendly ways of working.

With regular and consistent application, the exercises in this workbook will help to create a ripple effect throughout your organisation. They will encourage people to think and act differently, transforming leadership and strengthening culture.

It's about unlocking untapped potential - strengthening connections, building resilience, and creating an environment where everyone thrives.

Workbook Contents

Section One: Individual, Team, and Organisational Exercises – Practical activities covering each technique from Part Two, helping you embed positive work ways at different levels.

Section Two: Strengthening Functional Alignment – Exercises for expanding positive work ways across teams to improve coordination and efficiency.

Section Three: Strengthening Functional Alignment – Tools for expanding positive work ways across teams to improve coordination and efficiency.

Section four: Strategic Organisational Integration – A structured approach to embedding positive work ways across the entire organisation, ensuring long-term impact.

Each section builds on the last, guiding you through a step-by-step process for creating real, lasting change.

Ready to Dive In?

Turn the page, choose an exercise you feel drawn to, and let your imagination take the lead. Whether you're reflecting on your personal growth, inspiring your team, or crafting organisational initiatives, this workbook is here to support you every step of the way. Let's begin!

Activity 1: Active Visualisation

Introduction

Imagine yourself stepping into a future where you are living your best life - confidently navigating any challenges that arise, supported by the people around you, and sailing toward success. Welcome to active visualisation - your brain's secret weapon for creating and rehearsing more positive outcomes, not only helping you plan and find more creative solutions but helping you get there, too.

But here's the key: active visualisation is more than just visualisation – yes, really! The true power lies in building rich, detailed pictures of success - how things look, feel, and work in practice. This detail helps embed the imagined outcomes into your brain, strengthening the neural pathways that guide action. The more vividly you imagine, the more internalised and powerful the outcomes become.

At first, this practice might feel a little unfamiliar - it's natural! But as with any new skill, it becomes easier and more natural with time. Your brain will adapt, and you'll find that each session flows more quickly and easily. Even a light touch will bring positive results, but dedicating a little extra time and detail will amplify the impact, turning 'what if?' into 'let's make it happen!'

Above all, like every intervention in this book, active visualisation should be a positive and fun experience. So, approach this exercise with curiosity, creativity, and an open mind – and enjoy!

Why Active Visualisation Matters

Your brain thrives on possibility. When you imagine success in vivid detail, it engages the Intellectual Mind, calming the stress response and allowing you to think with more clarity and creativity. By starting with your vision of success and then building the details around it, you are better placed to unfold – and mentally rehearse - the steps needed to achieve it.

Let's explore how to bring this tool to life for you, your team, and your organisation.

Individual Activity

Objective: Build a clear mental vision to explore and rehearse.

Set the scene: Find a quiet, comfortable space where you feel safe and can relax uninterrupted. Take a few deep breaths and close your eyes.

Step 1: Visualise Success

Imagine your goal or challenge as if it's already resolved. Engage as many of your senses as you can:

- What do you see, hear, and feel?
- Where are you, and what's happening around you?
- Who's involved? What are they doing and saying?
- What are you doing differently?
- What are you doing and saying differently?
- What's different in the way you are acting and thinking?
- What's different in how you respond to those around you?
- How good does it feel to have succeeded?
- How good does it feel to be calm, confident, and in control?
- Do you feel excitement? Relief? Happiness?

Spend a few moments exploring and basking in those wonderful positive feelings – imagining soaking them all up like a sponge.

Step 2: Identify an action

When ready, open your eyes and take a few moments to reorient yourself. Then, write down one or two small, specific steps you can take to start moving closer to your vision.

Step 3: Practice

The more you practice working with the same vision, the greater its impact will be. Find a few minutes over the next few days to repeat this exercise.

Step 4: Reflect

At the end of the week, take some time to reflect on your progress. How did it feel? What have you learned?

Team Activity

Objective: Unite a team around a clear, detailed vision of shared success.

Set the Scene:

Find a quiet, comfortable space where your team will feel safe and can relax uninterrupted. Start the session by providing an overview of Active Visualisation and its benefits, using the introduction and/or the relevant chapter in Part 2.

Do not rush this exercise. It is important to maintain a nice, relaxed, steady pace that leaves enough time between questions to allow participants time to explore, but not so slow that they are left wondering whether you are still there!

Top Tip:

First, practice the individual exercise on your own so that you are more familiar with the process. This will help you determine pace more easily and tailor the questions to ones you are comfortable with, and that fit your team.

Step 1: Visualise Success

When you're ready, take a nice deep breath, close your eyes, and bring your attention to your breathing.

I'd like you to start to imagine that we were the best team ever.

- What might that look like for you?
- What do you see…hear… feel?
- What's the first thing you notice that's different?
- How are people acting…speaking… and behaving?
- How are people working together?
- Notice what's different…
- And now bring your attention to you… What are you doing differently?
- How are you acting… what are you thinking?
- How are you responding to those around you?
- How does it feel to be part of a really successful team?

Spend a few moments exploring… and when you're ready, open your eyes.

Step 2: Facilitated Sharing
- Invite participants to share their experiences.
- Capture key themes and insights on a whiteboard or shared document.

Step 3: Build the Vision
- Pull the individual experiences together to create a narrative or visual representation of the team's shared vision.

- Get creative - use diagrams, drawings, storyboards, post-it notes, or bullet points.

Step 4: Take Action

- Identify one or two concrete steps the team can take toward the vision.
- Assign responsibilities to ensure follow-through.

Tip for Facilitators

Redirect any problem-focused comments by asking: 'If that challenge were resolved, what would success look like instead?'

Organisational Integration

Objective: Make active visualisation a regular tool for innovation and alignment.

In Meetings

Start meetings with a quick imagination exercise by asking participants questions like: 'What does success look like for this meeting? What will we have achieved by the end?'

Strategic Planning

Use Active visualisation at the beginning of planning sessions to envision long-term goals.

Team Huddles

Incorporate visioning exercises to keep alignment and motivation high.

Performance Reviews

Encourage employees to visualise their ideal performance and identify small steps to achieve it.

Organisational Campaigns

Launch initiatives that encourage employees to imagine the organisation's future success and how their role would contribute to that success.

Digital Adaptation

Collaborative Vision Boards

Use online tools and digital solutions to create shared visualisations.

Guided Visualisation Videos

Provide employees with recorded guides.

Breakout Discussions

For remote teams, host breakout rooms where small groups explore and share their visions.

Close-Out

Active Visualisation is far more than simply wishful thinking - it's a powerful tool for encouraging creative thought to explore possibilities and determine action. By adopting this practice, you enable yourself and those around you to see beyond challenges and focus on possibilities.

Activity 2: The Miracle Question

Introduction

Imagine waking up tomorrow morning to find that whilst you were sleeping, someone waved a magic wand, and the challenge you have been facing has completely vanished. What would you notice – how would you know it had vanished – what would be different?

The Miracle Question might initially sound a bit fluffy - but don't let its simplicity or fun disguise fool you. It provides a powerful, simple, and engaging way to define goals and inspire creative thought. Like the other exercises in this section, it is highly versatile. It can be used individually, with groups, or even across organisations where you want to generate creative new ideas.

Why the Miracle Question Matters

Directing focus to—and then actively imagining—our preferred future helps counter the brain's natural negativity bias. This allows our mind to circumvent any mental barriers that might be hindering our progress while exploring a world in which the challenge is resolved engages the Intellectual Mind.

Whether setting a personal goal, aligning and motivating a team, or conducting a strategic organisation-wide review, the Miracle Question inspires big-picture thinking while keeping progress grounded in small, achievable steps.

Individual Activity

Objective: Gain clarity on an ideal outcome and identify small, practical next steps.

Set the scene

Find somewhere quiet and comfortable where you won't be interrupted. Take a couple of deep breaths to help you relax and close your eyes to aid focus.

Step 1: Imagine the miracle

Imagine waking up tomorrow morning to find that while you were sleeping, someone waved a magic wand. The challenge you've been facing has been successfully overcome.

Step 2: Notice the changes
- What do you notice – what's different?
- What signs tell you that the challenge has gone?
- What's different about how your world looks and feels?
- What are you doing differently – and what's different about your interactions with others?

Step 3: Keep it small
- As you explore this new landscape and notice what's different, identify any small actions or changes that are contributing toward making the miracle possible.
- What's one seemingly small change that really stands out?
- What small change could you adopt to start bringing this new landscape closer to reality?

Step 4: Write it down
- Open your eyes, reorientate, and make a note of your key insights.
- Highlight one small step that would help you progress toward your vision.

Step 5: Act and reflect
Take that step and reflect on its impact.
- How did it feel?
- What did you learn?

Repeat the exercise to build momentum over time.

Team Activity

Objective: Align your team around a shared vision and identify practical next steps.

Set the Scene Find somewhere quiet and comfortable where you won't be interrupted.

Introduce the session, using content from Part 2 to provide an overview of The Miracle Question and its' benefits. Answer any questions and then ask participants to take a couple of deep breaths to help them relax and close their eyes to aid focus.

Step 1: Ask the Miracle Question
'Imagine waking up tomorrow morning to find that while you were sleeping, someone waved a magic wand, and the challenge we've been facing has been successfully overcome.'

Step 2: Individual Reflection

Prompt with questions:
- What's different - what tells you that the challenge has gone?
- What's different about how we work together?
- What are we doing well as a team?
- How does success feel?

Step 3: Keep it Small

Prompt with questions:
- What's one seemingly small change that really stands out?
- What small change could you adopt to start bringing this new landscape closer to reality?

Step 4: Team Reflection

- Invite participants to share their visions.
- Capture recurring themes and ideas on a whiteboard or shared document.

Step 5: Vision Building

- Using the shared insights, work together to develop a collective vision.
- Build as much detail as possible.

Step 6: Identify Next Steps

- Work together to pinpoint one or two small, achievable actions the team can take.
- Assign responsibilities to ensure follow-through.

Step 7: Act and Reflect

- Take the identified step and reflect collectively on its impact.
- How did it feel, and what did you learn?
- Repeat the exercise to keep progress moving.

Organisational Integration

Objective: Embed creative thinking into organisational strategy and innovation.

Strategic Planning

- Use the Miracle Question to kick off planning sessions:
- 'Imagine that a year from now, we will have resolved our biggest challenges.
- What's different about how we operate and succeed?'

Leadership Alignment

- Encourage leaders to reflect on organisational challenges.

- Apply the Miracle Question to define a bold, shared vision.

Workshops and campaigns

- Organise cross-functional workshops where teams collaboratively explore the Miracle Question.
- Share outcomes to improve alignment and encourage innovation across departments.

Digital Adaptation

Vision boards

Use online tools and digital solutions to combine collective insights from The Miracle Question and create shared vision boards.

Breakout sessions

Use breakout rooms in virtual meetings to divide larger teams into smaller groups. Ask each group to reflect on the Miracle Question together and then regroup to share visions.

Apps and surveys

Use online surveys and apps to collect individual reflections before discussing them in a group setting.

Close-Out

The Miracle Question creates a mindset shift by focusing on what success looks like and then identifying small steps that make it achievable. It is a versatile and fun way to encourage creative thinking.

Activity 3: What Does Good Look Like?

Introduction

When faced with challenges, our attention is often drawn wholly to what's wrong—which is great if we want to identify lots of problems, but it isn't very helpful in guiding us toward solutions that help us improve things.

This question helps achieve clarity and determine action in the here and now. Like all other solutions-focused questions, it is highly versatile—it can stop a negative conversation in its tracks and instead replace it with a more constructive dialogue.

Whether you are navigating a difficult conversation or exploring organisational culture, asking 'What Does Good Look Like?' encourages curiosity, uncovers possibilities, and aids more effective progress.

Why This Question Matters

Asking, 'What does good look like?' shifts your brain's focus from what's going wrong to what's possible, pushing the Primitive Mind out of play and getting the Intellectual Mind back at the helm.

It's time to explore another simple yet transformative solutions-focused question— 'What does good look like?' This deceptively simple yet powerful question equips you with a practical and flexible technique that can be useful in virtually any scenario.

Individual Activity

Objective: Clarify 'what good looks' like and identify steps toward achieving it.

Set the Scene

Think about an area of your work or life where you feel stuck or uncertain.

Step 1: Ask the Question
- Pause and ask yourself:
- 'What would good look like in this situation?'

Step 2: Build a Clear Picture
- Ask yourself questions that aid exploration and determination of what good would look like in this particular situation:
- What's different – how are you thinking, feeling, behaving, acting, and communicating differently?
- How are others responding to you - what's different in your interactions with those around you?
- Build a clear mental image of what this new landscape looks and feels like.

Step 3: Small Actions
Identify one or two steps you can take right now to start moving closer to that vision.

Step 4: Reflect and Act
- Take identified step and reflect on its impact.
- How did it feel?
- What did you learn?
- Repeat the exercise if needed.

Team Activity

Objective: Align your team with a collective vision of 'what good looks like' and determine the next steps to make progress toward achieving it.

Set the scene
Introduce the session, using content from Part 2 to provide an overview of the question and its' benefits.

Step 1: Ask the Question
Present the scenario or challenge and then pose the question to the team, framed in context to the challenge or scenario you wish to explore with them:
- 'What would good look like in this situation?'
- 'What would a good team look like here?'

Step 2: Individual reflection
Ask the team questions that aid exploration and determination of what good would look like in this particular situation:
- What's different – how are you thinking, feeling, behaving, acting, and communicating differently?
- What's different about our team – what are we doing differently?

- How does our team interact differently?

Step 3: Keep it small
- Prompt with questions:
- What's one seemingly small change that really stands out?
- What small change could you adopt to start bringing this new landscape closer to reality?

Step 4: Group discussion
- Facilitate a roundtable discussion where everyone shares their perspective.
- Encourage detail and focus on actions, not just outcomes.

Step 5: Build a shared vision
- Develop a clear vision of what a collective 'good' looks like.
- Capture shared themes and identify common goals, introducing as much detail as possible.

Step 6: Action steps
- Agree on one or two small, achievable actions the team can take to start aligning with the shared vision.
- Assign responsibilities to ensure follow-through.

Step 7: Act and reflect
Take the identified step and reflect collectively on its impact.
- How did it feel, and what did you learn?
- Repeat the exercise to keep progress moving.

Organisational Integration

Objective: Embed the question, 'What does good look like?' into organisational processes and meeting protocols to guide clarity, collaboration, and progress.

Strategic Planning
Encourage leadership teams to ask, 'What does good look like?' as a starting point for defining objectives.

Team meetings
Ask 'What does good look like' during team meetings to refocus discussions on progress and possibilities.

Employee feedback
Ask 'What does good look like' during one-to-ones or performance reviews to

create a forward-focused dialogue.

Cross-functional collaboration
When working with other departments, ask 'What does good look like?' to align on shared outcomes and avoid misunderstandings.

Organisational campaigns
Incorporate 'What does good look like?' into employee engagement initiatives to create a sense of shared purpose and alignment.

Digital Adaptation

Shared vision board
Use online tools and digital solutions to create a shared vision board for the team.

Reflection
Use in-meeting chats to pose the question, allowing team members to contribute at their own pace.

Break out rooms
Use breakout rooms during virtual meetings and ask participants to reflect on 'What does good look like' for a few minutes before reconvening to reflect and discuss as a group.

Close-Out

Asking, 'What does good look like?' may appear deceptively simple – but it's a question with profound potential to stop negative thinking in its wake. Forcing focus on the positives - directing attention from what's wrong to what's right, guides the way toward realistic, actionable steps and creative solutions that make progress both quicker and more effective.

Activity 4: Solutions-Focused Inquiry

Introduction

When challenges arise, it can be easy to get pulled in, placing all our focus and energy on what's gone wrong – and understandable, perhaps, given our brain's natural negativity bias. But what if, instead of problem hunting, we chose to go solution searching—what difference might that make?

Solutions-Focused Inquiry is a technique that does just that. It flips questions such as 'Why is this happening?' or 'What's the problem?' around and instead asks, 'What's already working?' or 'What's the next small step we can take?' and demonstrates the positive influence that seemingly minor shifts in communication can have on our interactions with others and on outcomes.

This subtle but powerful shift in questioning is sufficient to reframe our mindset from problem-centric to solutions-focused.

Why Solutions-Focused Inquiry Matters

When all our brains have to focus on is problems, or we are bombarded with too many questions asking us what went wrong, the Primitive Mind starts to creep in - and the Intellectual Mind starts to lose its control.

Framing questions in a way that encourages the exploration of possibilities and opportunities—not problems—helps bring the Intellectual Mind back into play so we can work more effectively.

Individual Activity

Objective: Use questions to reframe challenges and uncover practical next steps.

Step 1: Pause and Reflect
Think about a current challenge or goal you're facing.

Step 2: Ask Yourself
- What's already working in this situation?
- What small success have I had that I can build on?
- What's one small step I can take right now to make progress?

Step 3: Visualise Success

Imagine what it looks like when things improve.
- What's different?
- How will you know you're on the right track?

Step 4: Write It Down

Capture your answers and identify a straightforward action to take today.
- Focus on something achievable, no matter how small.

Step 5: Act and Reflect

Take that step and reflect on how it felt.
- What did you learn?
- How will you build on this progress tomorrow?

Team Activity

Objective: Use solutions-focused questions to search for solutions and build momentum.

Set the Scene

Introduce the session, using content from Part 2 to provide an overview of the technique and its' benefits. The templates section at the end of the book includes a solutions-focused question bank that provides more questions to get you started.

Rules

This exercise is about searching for opportunities by building on past successes and existing strengths and resources. It is simple, but like any new skill, it can take a little practice. If any participant responds with something they don't want, guide them back on track by asking them what they do want instead.

Step 1: Individual Reflection

Allow each participant member a few minutes to consider:
- 'What's one thing that's working well in this project or situation?'
- 'What's one small step we could take as a team to move forward?'

Step 2: Share and Discuss

Facilitate a roundtable discussion to share reflections. Encourage:
- A focus on specifics: Specific actions, strategies, and resources.
- Positive reinforcement: Highlight strengths, successes, and progress.

Step 3: Identify Priorities

Work as a group to identify one or two key steps. Ensure each step is specific, easy to achieve, and aligned with your shared vision.

Step 4: Follow Up

Agree on how you'll track progress. Review and repeat the above steps to continue progress.

Organisational Integration

Objective: Integrate and embed solutions-focused inquiry into organisational strategy and communications.

Leadership Advocacy

Introduce a protocol requiring leaders to model solutions-focused thinking in meetings and interactions:
- What's one strength we can leverage to tackle this challenge?
- What's already working, and how can we build on it?

Strategic Planning

Use solutions-focused questions to guide strategic planning, goal setting, and progress reviews:
- What's a small adjustment we can make to get closer to our desired outcome?
- What opportunities could we create by building further on what already works?

Team Check-Ins

Introduce solutions-focused questions into team meetings to serve as prompts, asking:
- What's a recent success we can celebrate?
- What's one small step we can take to build on that success?

Cultural Shifts

Use corporate communication to inspire and align employees by reinforcing solutions-focused language, highlighting progress, and celebrating wins.

Digital Adaptation

Brainstorming

Use online tools or apps to collect team reflections on questions like: 'What's already working, and how can we build on it?'

Interactive Polls

Use online tools during virtual meetings to gather real-time answers to questions like: 'What's one small step we can take this week?'

Individual Journaling Apps

Use apps for personal solutions-focused reflections.

Close-Out

Solutions-focused inquiry transforms the way we approach challenges, encouraging us to focus on what's going well and what's possible rather than getting hung up on what's wrong. This approach can improve the way we communicate - with ourselves and others.

Activity 5: Scaling

Introduction

When faced with big goals, we often plan and map out all the actions we think will lead to a successful outcome before even getting started. The result can be overwhelming spreadsheets and to-do lists. However, just like any journey, the landscape around us is continually changing—each step we take unveils new opportunities and closes previous ones down.

Scaling introduces a more responsive approach to personal, team, or organisational goals that provides both structure and flexibility. Maintaining a focus on progress while also keeping an eye on end goals - and pausing regularly to reassess the most optimal path forward - maximises any new opportunities or possibilities along the way.

Why Scaling Matters

Scaling helps reduce stress, calm the Primitive Mind, and bring the Intellectual Mind back into play. Whether you're working on your own, within a team, or leading change across an organisation, Scaling helps turn big, daunting challenges into manageable steps that build confidence.

Individual Activity

Objective: Use scaling to break down a big goal into small, manageable steps.

Set the scene

Reflect on a current goal.

Step 1: Define the scale

Define your goal by asking The Miracle Question or 'What does good look like?'

- Where do you want to be?
- What does success look like?

Step 2: Current position

Working with a scale of 1 to 10, where 10 represents the goal being met in full, where are you currently in relation to that vision?

- What puts you at that point?
- What got you to where you are?
- What's working well already?

Step 3: Next steps

Suppose you currently score a 3 on the scale - ask yourself:
- What's one small thing I can do to move from a 3 to a 4?
- What's the simplest action that would have the most significant impact?

Step 4: Act and reflect

Take the step, then reflect on what's changed:
- How far have you progressed up the scale?
- What new opportunities do you see now?
- What might the next step be?

This iterative process ensures you remain flexible and responsive whilst still keeping the long-term goal in sight.

Team Activity

Objective: Use scaling to align team efforts and build collective progress.

Step 1: Set the Scene

Introduce the session, using content from Part 2 to provide an overview of the technique and its' benefits.

Step 2: Define the Scale

Define your goal by asking The Miracle Question or 'What does good look like.'
- Where do you want to be?
- What does success look like?

Step 3: Current Position

Ask team members to rate progress individually on a scale of 1 to 10, with 10 being a successful outcome met in full.
- Aggregate the scores to find the team's average and explore the range:
- 'What's already working that's helped us get to this point?'
- Identify collective strengths to build on.

Step 4: Small steps

Brainstorm to identify small steps that would progress you up the scale:
- 'What's one small thing we can do to progress to the next step?'
- What's the simplest action that would have most significant impact?

Step 5: Act and reflect

Take the step, then reflect on what's changed.

- How far have you progressed up the scale?
- What new opportunities do you see now?
- What might the next step be?

Keep the focus on incremental improvement and shared accountability. Regularly revisit the scale in future meetings.

Organisational Integration

Objective: Use scaling to drive progress in organisational goals and processes.

Step 1: Define the Scale

During strategic planning meetings rate progress toward goals on a 1-to-10 scale, with 10 being a successful outcome met in full.

Step 2: Current Position

Leaders explore 'What's already working that got us here?' and 'What strengths can we build on?'

Step 3: Focus on the Next Step

Facilitate a solutions-focused discussion by asking, 'What's one small action we can take across the organisation to move one step closer to our goal?'

Step 4: Integrate Scaling into Processes

Scaling can be incorporated into reviews, strategy sessions, and team check-ins as a tool for tracking progress and momentum.

Digital Adaptation

Use a journaling app or digital notepad to track scale ratings, steps, and reflections.

Use pulse surveys or polls to gather input across departments and ensure widespread engagement.

Set reminders to revisit and reflect on progress regularly.

Close-Out

Scaling isn't about getting everything perfect—it's about making steady progress. By focusing on small, meaningful steps, you recognise your strengths, discover new opportunities, and adjust along the way.

Activity 6: Reframing Limiting Beliefs

Introduction

Limiting beliefs don't just influence how we interpret and perceive the world around us – they also impact how we respond to and navigate it. Formed throughout our lives from past experiences, decisions, and others' behaviour toward us, left unchecked, they can lead us to doubt our capability and prevent us from reaching our full potential.

But limiting beliefs do not only affect individuals—teams and even whole organisations can have limiting beliefs that negatively impact performance, culture, and business outcomes. The good news is that negative beliefs can be changed. By noticing them and taking the time to challenge and reframe them, it's possible to develop a more constructive perspective.

Why Reframing Negative Beliefs Matters

When a negative belief is reframed, new neural pathways develop that support the new way of thinking. These new pathways continue to strengthen with each repetition, building self-confidence, self-esteem, and resilience.

Individual Activity

Objective: Reframe an existing limiting belief.

Set the Scene

Find a quiet space without interruptions. Have a pen and paper on hand.

Observe

For example, 'This is too hard,' or 'I'm not good at this.'

Challenge

Is this belief based on facts or assumptions?
- What evidence exists that contradicts this belief – what are the exceptions?
- How could this situation be perceived differently?

Reframe
- Negative: 'I've never done this before, so I'll probably fail.'
- Reframed: 'I've never done this before, so this is a great opportunity to learn

something new.'

Anchor

- Identify one small step you can take to align with the new perspective.
- Repeated action helps to reinforce the reframed perspective - building confidence and resilience.
- Identify more small steps you can take to reinforce the new belief.

Tip: If reframing feels difficult at first, don't worry - it's all part of the process. You'll find that the more you practice, the easier it becomes.

Team Activity

Objective: Challenge and reframe limiting team beliefs hindering progress.

Set the scene

Introduce the session, using content from Part 2 to provide an overview of the technique and its' benefits.

- Schedule a dedicated session and create a safe, open space for discussion.
- Remind participants of the need for a constructive tone.
- The goal is to explore and reframe collectively.

Reflection

- Ask each participant to share a challenge the team is collectively facing.
- Agree on the challenge to work on collectively.
- Ask each participant to reflect on any limiting team beliefs that hinder progress.

Group sharing

- Invite team members to share their beliefs.
- Use sticky notes or a shared digital board.
- Review as a group, noting common themes.

Collective reframe

For each negative belief, gently and supportively challenge participants by asking:

- What evidence supports this?
- What evidence challenges it?
- How might we reframe this into something more supportive?
- Capture reframed beliefs on the board.

Act and reflect

- Agree on one or two small actions that participants can take to reinforce the reframed beliefs.
- Assign responsibilities to ensure follow-through.

Organisational Integration

Objective: Weave the process of challenging negative beliefs into organisational processes and communication.

Leadership

Encourage leaders to openly challenge their own limiting beliefs during meetings or strategy sessions.

Integration

- Include a 'belief challenge' step in project reviews or decision-making processes. Ask, 'What assumptions are we making? Are they limiting our thinking?'
- Adopt solutions-focused language that reinforces the reframe in internal communications.

Training and Development

Integrate this approach into leadership and workforce development programs.

Digital Adaptation

Shared Spaces

Use digital solutions and online tools to create a space where employees support and motivate each other by sharing examples of reframed beliefs.

Collaboration

Use online tools and apps to aid virtual brainstorming or collect anonymous contributions.

Close-Out

Challenging negative beliefs is about far more than simply changing your thoughts. Each time you reframe a limiting belief, you start building new, more supportive neural pathways in your brain that regular practice continues to strengthen.

Activity 7: Positive Self-Talk

Introduction

How often do you find yourself mid-conversation – with, well… yourself – batting back and forth in your head or even out loud? Repeatedly asking, 'Why did I do that?' or saying, 'I'll never get this right,' doesn't just zap our self-esteem - it can really get in our way and make daily life more challenging. But the great news is that you have all it takes - already within you - to flip the script.

Positive self-talk gets that inner voice working for you rather than against you. Stopping negativity in its' tracks gets you back into a more helpful and constructive dialogue. Like all new skills, it takes a little time to become a habit, but with regular practice, it will become second nature and turn your inner voice from your harshest critic into your biggest fan.

Why Positive Self-Talk Matters

How we talk to ourselves matters because it impacts how we think and perform. Negative self-talk can quickly drain our self-esteem and confidence, destroying our motivation. In contrast, more positive self-talk boosts our self-esteem and confidence, lowering stress, increasing motivation, and building resilience.

Individual Activity

Objective: Develop awareness of your inner narrative and reframe it into more constructive and positive self-talk.

Set the Scene

Take a moment to pause during your day. It's best to find a quiet space where you can relax without being disturbed. Reflect on the narrative playing in your mind.

Step 1: Review your Dialogue
- Reflect on your day or morning. #
- What tone has your self-talk taken?
- Have there been moments where you were critical of yourself or doubted your abilities?

Step 2: Reframe and Rewrite

For each negative or unhelpful thought, start to question its validity, taking the time needed to explore each question thoroughly before moving on. Ask yourself:
- Is this thought accurate, or is it my inner critic talking?
- What would a supportive colleague, friend, or coach say instead?
- Replace statements like, 'I'm so bad at this' with, 'I'm learning, and I'll get better with practice.'

Step 3: Speak It Out
- For additional reinforcement and to make this exercise more powerful, try repeating your positive self-talk out loud.
- It might feel silly, but hearing your own voice can strengthen the message and help it stick.

Step 4: Daily Check-In
- Commit to finding a few minutes each day to reflect on the tone of your self-talk, progressively reframing and reinforcing a more positive narrative.
- Over time, you'll notice a shift in how you approach challenges and setbacks.

Team Activity

Objective: Explore the collective narrative, positively reframing it to one that supports team success.

Set the Scene
Use the introduction in this workbook and/or the relevant chapter in Part 2 to set an encouraging and engaging tone for your team.

Step 1: Reflect as a Group
Ask team members to reflect on events over the past week or month, paying particular attention to team dynamics, interactions, and undercurrents.
- Has the team's collective narrative been positive and supportive - or has it leaned toward criticism or frustration?
- Were there times when it was more positive and times when negativity was more likely to drift in?

Step 2: Round the Table
Challenge everyone to share one positive aspect of the team's performance or dynamics. Get the discussion going by posing open questions that encourage reflection, such as:
- What are we doing well as a team?

- What's a recent success we can celebrate?

Step 3: Positive Start and Finish

Introduce a protocol of opening and closing meetings with a quick-fire round of positive affirmations. For example:
- At the start: 'What's one thing you're proud of accomplishing this week?'
- At the end: 'What's one thing we can look forward to next week?'

Step 4: Reinforce the Habit

Encourage the team to continually nurture a more positive collective self-talk by finding ways to inject more positivity into their daily interactions, emails, and conversations.

Organisational Integration

Objective: Develop and embed a positive narrative into organisational communication, core processes, and culture.

Leadership Modelling

Encourage leaders to adopt a positive narrative in their communications:

Celebrating Wins

- Explore opportunities for teams to celebrate wins more regularly - regardless of whether they are big or small.
- This could be through newsletters, town halls, webinars, or dedicated Teams channels.

Supportive Messaging

Provide support for managers and HR teams with tools that will help them incorporate more constructive, positive language in feedback and performance reviews.
- Develop formal protocols and crib sheets to provide support. (using the templates toward the end of this book).
- Encourage phrases like: 'You've shown great progress in...' or 'What strengths can we build on as we approach this goal?'

Collective Reflection

Use annual planning, strategic reviews, or retrospectives as opportunities to reflect and reframe setbacks as learning opportunities.

Digital Adaptation

Leverage the use of digital tools to encourage, optimise, and normalise positive self-talk:

Daily Prompts
Use online tools and digital solutions to send daily positive self-talk prompts. For example,

'What's one thing you've done well today?'

Journaling Apps
Search out apps that individuals can use to track and reframe negative self-beliefs.

Meeting Reminders
Add short affirmations or pose positive questions to calendar invites or virtual meeting agendas.

Close-Out

By practising positive self-talk daily, whether individually or collectively, we create a ripple effect, spreading optimism, strengthening resilience, and opening the door to more possibilities in our work and personal lives.

Activity 8: Affirmations

Introduction

When your inner critic starts to take over, how do you flip the script? This is where affirmations come in, and before you dismiss them as a little too 'out there,' consider this: every time you repeat an affirmation, you stop negativity in its tracks and instead start training your brain to focus on strengths.

Affirmations help transform that inner voice from your harshest critic into your greatest supporter. When effectively targeted and repeated consistently, affirmations can facilitate transformational change far beyond personal growth. Equally transformative for teams and organisations, affirmations can change mindsets, build resilience, and align values and goals.

Why Affirmations Matter

An inner critic fuels the Primitive Mind. Repeating affirmations helps to stop this cycle and get the Intellectual Mind back in play. In the process, it builds and reinforces neural pathways that gradually shift our mindset into one that's more confident, positive, and supportive.

Individual Activity

Objective: Develop and rehearse personal affirmations to drive positive change.

Set the Scene

Find a quiet space, take a couple of breaths to relax and bring your mind to the present.

Step 1: Develop
- Reflect on any doubts in your mind that may be hindering a current challenge or goal.
- Explore potential affirmations that may help reframe these doubts.
- Select 2 to 3 you feel most comfortable with. For example:
- 'I am capable of finding solutions to tough problems.'
- 'I am learning and growing every day.'

- 'I have the skills to lead with confidence.'

Step 2: Repeat
- Affirmations need to be repeated frequently and consistently to work at their best.
- Start by writing them down a few times each morning and evening.
- Repeat them in your head throughout the day, setting reminders for yourself if necessary.
- Once you feel comfortable to do so, start repeating them aloud.
- Finally, as your confidence continues to build, say your affirmations aloud each morning and evening whilst looking at yourself in a mirror.

Step 3: Reflect
Take a little time to reflect on your progress at the end of each week:
- How has this practice started to change how you feel?
- What positive shifts have you noticed in your mindset, thoughts, or actions?

Tip: Use language that feels natural to you. The more authentic and personalised the affirmation, the more impactful it will be.

Team Activity

Objective: Flip the team narrative.

Step 1: Set the Scene
Use the introduction in this book to provide an overview and set an encouraging and engaging tone for your team.

Step 2: Collaborative Affirmations
- Roundtable Sharing: Ask each team member to share one positive affirmation they'd like to adopt for themselves.
- Team Affirmation: Work together to create a shared affirmation that reflects the team's collective strength or vision.

Tip: Ensure team affirmations reflect shared values or recent successes to make them more meaningful.

Step 3: Repetition
- Display the team affirmation in a shared space.
- Encourage regular reflection.
- Make affirmations a part of team dialogue and meetings.
- Increase repetition during particularly demanding periods.

Step 4: Measure the Impact
- Try running this activity for a month.
- Ask team members to reflect on how it has influenced them individually and also as a team.
- Observe the positive ways in which the affirmation influences mindset, collaboration, and progress.
- Gather feedback to fine-tune or refresh the affirmation as needed.

Organisational Integration

Objective: Build affirmations into corporate strategy, culture, and communication to develop a shared sense of confidence and possibility.

Set the Scene
Use the content in this book to introduce and provide an overview of the concept of 'Corporate Affirmations.'

Develop
Collectively develop affirmations that articulate the organisation's shared aspirations, strengths, and values.

Strategy and Vision
- Use affirmations to actively support the organisation's strategy and vision.
- Ask leaders to integrate agreed affirmations into strategic plans.
- Use to guide how goals are set and communicated throughout the business.
- Frame organisational goals as affirmations to reinforce a growth mindset.

Embedding
- Embed corporate affirmations to reinforce messaging.
- Incorporate into core policies and procedures.
- Introduce into organisational communications and initiatives.

Collective Affirmations in Communication
- Adopt positive, affirmation-based language in announcements, campaigns, and updates.
- Weave affirmations throughout corporate communications to align and reinforce.

Creating a Shared Narrative
Create affirmations that resonate with employees across all levels and functions, making them part of the organisation's collective voice and reinforcing a shared narrative of positivity and possibility.

Digital Adaptation

Use digital tools to encourage and normalise the use of affirmations:

Daily Prompts
Use online communication tools to send daily positive affirmation prompts.

Affirmation Apps
Search out apps for individuals to create and prompt affirmations.

Shared spaces
Create shared digital spaces for teams to develop, share and reinforce individual and collective affirmations.

Meeting Reminders
Add short affirmations or positive questions to calendar invites or virtual meeting agendas.

Voice Notes
Encourage individuals to use voice recording apps to capture personal affirmations and play them back as needed.

Close-Out

Affirmations are invaluable for personal growth and provide a powerful way to shape an organisation's identity, culture, and voice. Whether used in teams or embedded into strategy, values, and communication, affirmations create a new and more positive collective narrative of confidence, resilience, and shared purpose.

Activity 9: Empathy

Introduction

Empathy is something that comes more naturally to some than others – it is our ability to see the perspectives of those around us and understand why they feel the way they do. It helps us trust and relate more easily to others, and when shown toward us, we feel heard and valued.

Even for those to whom it doesn't come naturally, empathy is a skill that most people can learn and develop with practice. Being able to step into someone else's shoes - and understand why they feel the way they do – is an important skill in practically every aspect of our daily life.

Whether we are innately more introverted or extroverted, humans are highly social by nature; to be truly healthy and thrive, we all need positive social connections in our lives, including at work. Healthy relationships need care and understanding to flourish, meaning empathy forms the bedrock for trust, stronger relationships, and collaboration.

Why Empathy Matters

Social relationships are fundamental to an organisation's success. The connections and interfaces between individuals, teams, departments, suppliers, and clients every day continually influence every aspect of how an organisation functions as a whole. Feeling heard and valued is a fundamental element of successful connections, making empathy essential for a resilient, engaged, and productive organisation.

Individual Activity

Objective: Develop empathy to build and strengthen connections with others.

Set the Scene

Reflect on a recent conversation in which someone shared a challenge they were facing or an emotion they were experiencing with you.

Reflect

What do you think they may have been feeling during that conversation? How heard and valued do you feel your response may have made them feel?

Plan Ahead

Identify an upcoming conversation that will provide you with an opportunity to practise empathy more intentionally – either at work or in your personal life. Consider these guiding questions:
- How can I create a safe space for this person to feel comfortable sharing openly?
- What might they need from me in this moment - validation, understanding, or support?

Empathy in Action

Throughout the conversation, maintain the following approach:
- Pause and be present: Clear your mind of distractions, ensure you will not be interrupted, and turn your phone off.
- Actively listen: Pay full attention and listen without interrupting, advising, judging, or second-guessing.
- Ask open-ended questions that invite them to share their perspective.
- Acknowledge their perspective and reflect back using paraphrasing to demonstrate you have really heard and understood them: 'it sounds like you're feeling...' or 'that must have been challenging.'

Reflect and Learn:

After the conversation, take some time to reflect:
- What did you learn about their perspective?
- How did they respond, and what might you do differently next time?

Team Activity

Objective: Promote a culture of empathy to strengthen team resilience.

Set the Scene

Use the introduction in this workbook and/or the relevant chapter in Part 2 to set an encouraging and engaging tone for your team.

Step 1: Empathy Map

As a team, select a recent challenge or project to focus on.
- On a digital whiteboard or flipchart, create an empathy map with the following sections:
- What might key stakeholders be thinking?
- How might they be feeling?

- What are they saying?
- What are they doing?

Use open-ended questions that encourage discussion, capturing insights as they arise in each of the map sections.

This is a really helpful way to encourage the team to step into others' shoes as well as to identify where and how collaboration and mutual support may be strengthened.

Step 2: Empathy in Action
Take time to reflect and explore as a team, asking:
- 'What actions can we take to address these feelings or needs?'
- 'How could we show more understanding in our daily interactions?'

Step 3: Ongoing Practice
Encourage the team to review the empathy map periodically and apply it in other areas to develop and maintain mutually healthy and robust relationships.

Organisational Integration

Objective: Promote empathy in leadership, culture, and communication.

Empathy in Leadership Development
Make empathy a cornerstone of leadership development programs, weaving it seamlessly throughout different programme modules. Provide opportunities to:
- Practice active listening in coaching scenarios.
- Practice holding empathetic conversations.
- Reflect on their own biases and perspectives.

Empathy-Based Communication
Develop communication guidelines that emphasise empathy. For example:
- Use inclusive language that acknowledges diverse perspectives.
- Frame messages with understanding and care, especially during times of change or challenge.

Empathy in Feedback Processes
Train managers to deliver feedback with empathy by using leadership meetings to practice role-play and providing crib sheets and quick reference guides to build confidence.

Measure and Reflect

- Regularly reflect on these findings to adapt and improve.
- Assess the impact of empathy initiatives using metrics such as employee engagement scores, retention rates, and qualitative feedback.

Digital Adaptation

Anonymous pulse surveys
Ask employees how supported and understood they feel, softening wording to encourage more open and honest responses.

Virtual workshops
Offer online empathy-building sessions for remote or hybrid teams.

Collaboration tools
Use digital platforms and apps for empathy mapping, quick tips, and team exercises.

Online resources
Develop e-learning modules or empathy guides that are accessible to all employees.

Close-Out

Great leadership and high-performing teams are impossible without empathy as a foundation. Promoting compassion throughout our personal and professional lives – be it in daily interactions with others, encouraging it within your teams, and finding ways to embed empathy into your organisation's culture develops an environment where trust, psychological safety, and collaboration flourish.

Activity 10: Authenticity

Introduction

Think about a leader you have known – someone you have worked for who really inspired you. What was it about them that stood out? Rather than simply saying the right words, were their actions consistently aligned with what they were saying, too? That's the core of authenticity – it's about knowing your values and staying true to them, showing up as your real self - every time, even when times get tough.

Most people can relate to situations where they have felt under pressure to adopt an identity that didn't align with their true self, especially perhaps in their working lives. Authenticity in the workplace isn't about oversharing and doing or saying as we please at any cost – it requires striking a balance between vulnerability and professionalism. It's about creating a work environment where people feel safe showing up as who they are, but without crossing professional boundaries.

Why Authenticity Matters

When we are truly authentic, our words, actions, and values are aligned in a way that builds trust and meaningful interpersonal relationships with others. Authentic leaders attract greater loyalty from their teams by creating environments where people feel more relaxed and psychologically safe. A culture of authenticity across a business not only enhances individual and team engagement, but it also enables organisations to navigate challenges with more integrity and resilience.

Individual Activity

Objective: Identify personal core values to guide future decisions and actions.

Set the Scene
- Find a quiet space where you won't be disturbed and take a few moments to settle your thoughts and calm your mind.
- Think about a recent situation where you felt truly aligned - or misaligned - with your values. Reflect on what that experience taught you about yourself.

Step 1: Identify Your Core Values

Reflect on moments when you felt proud, energised, or deeply satisfied.
- What values were at play during these times?
- Write down 3–5 values that resonate most with you.

If you need inspiration, online lists of values can be a helpful starting point.

Step 2: Plan for the Future
- Consider an upcoming decision, meeting, or event. Ask yourself:
- 'If I was acting in a way that aligned with my core values, what would that look like?'
- 'What would 'authentic me' say or do in this situation?'

Step 3: Imagine Success

Imagine yourself being truly authentic.
- What are you saying, doing, and feeling?
- What's different – notice the detail?
- How do your words and actions impact those around you?

Write down one or two practical steps you can take to personify this vision.

Step 4: Reflect and Grow
- After the event, find a few moments to reflect.
- Recognise where you acted authentically and any areas for growth.
- How might you refine your approach next time?

Team Activity

Objective: Explore and align shared core values.

Set the Scene

Use the introduction provided in this workbook and/or the relevant chapter in Part 2 to set an encouraging and engaging tone for your team.

Step 1: Individual Reflection

Ask each team member to reflect on and write down their top 3–5 personal values.

Step 2: Sharing and Understanding
- Facilitate a roundtable discussion where each person shares their values and why they're important to them.
- Encourage active listening and discourage debate - this is about understanding, not agreement.

Step 3: Collaborative Values Charter
- Collectively identify team themes or shared values.
- Collaborate to craft a simple 'Team Values Charter' reflecting what the team stands for and aspires to.

Step 4: Bring Values to Life
Use open questions to explore practical ways to integrate the charter into daily work. For example:
- 'How can we incorporate these values to guide decision-making?'
- 'How will we ensure collective accountability to these values?'

Step 5: Display and Reinforce
Share the charter in a visible space (e.g., a physical poster or digital workspace) and revisit it regularly as a team.

Organisational Integration

Objective: Develop a culture that demonstrates and promotes authenticity.

Authenticity in Leadership Development
- Encourage more authentic leaders by weaving authenticity throughout the core of leadership training programs.
- Include authenticity in every aspect of training, focusing on self-awareness, values-based decision-making, and authentic communication.
- Include role play so leaders become more comfortable in striking an appropriate balance between authenticity and professionalism.

Values-Driven Policies and Practices
Explore opportunities to improve and strengthen alignment between core policies and practices and the organisation's values. For example:
- Does the performance management process reflect fairness and transparency?
- Do diversity and inclusion initiatives align with the organisation's commitment to equity?

Cultural Rituals
Incorporate authenticity into cultural rituals. For instance:
- Start meetings with a 'values moment,' during which participants briefly share how a core value has influenced recent work.
- Celebrate employees who exemplify organisational values with recognition programs.

Measuring Cultural Authenticity

Gather regular feedback through pulse surveys, focus groups, or anonymous feedback channels to gauge employees' perceptions of how well authenticity is reflected in leadership and organisational practices.

Digital Adaptation

Use digital platforms to encourage and inspire more authentic interactions, such as:

Sharing

Create a virtual 'values spotlight' where employees can share stories of workplace authenticity in action.

Channels

Set up a dedicated channel for leaders and encourage them to share reflections on how they've navigated challenges with integrity.

Close-Out

Authenticity is far more than a leadership buzzword – it forms the bedrock for a flourishing and successful organisational culture. When people feel psychologically safe and able to work in alignment with their values, they feel more engaged and motivated - and this empowers them to perform at their best. Workplaces that embed authenticity throughout organisational culture create an environment where people feel valued, empowered, and ready to thrive.

Activity 11: Curiosity

Introduction

Curiosity goes beyond simply asking questions and searching for immediate answers—it's a mindset. It sparks and supports creative thinking and promotes the exploration of new possibilities. It enables us to see opportunities where others may only see problems.

In organisations, curiosity encourages individuals and teams to challenge assumptions, explore possibilities, and re-imagine new and more effective ways of working. Whether exploring personal challenges or developing organisational strategy, curiosity injects the energy, creativity, and focus to drive progress forward. It cultivates agility and sparks the innovation that enables organisations to maintain a competitive edge.

Why Curiosity Matters

Curiosity disrupts fixed thinking patterns, shifts us away from reactive thinking and engages the Intellectual Mind. Like any skill, curiosity becomes easier with practice, and it can be learned, so if it doesn't come naturally to you, don't worry - start small and allow the habit of asking more thought-provoking questions to become a natural part of your thinking.

Individual Activity

Objective: Use curiosity to explore a current challenge.

Set the Scene
Find a quiet space and take a few moments to relax and calm your mind.

Reflect
- Select a current challenge or situation you would like to explore.
- Summarise and write it down in one clear sentence.

Question
Write the question 'I wonder...' or 'What if...' at the top of a blank page.
- Explore at least three questions that would help to explore your challenge:
- 'I wonder what would happen if I approached this differently?'

- 'How might someone else see this differently?'
- 'What else might be influencing this?'

Contemplate
- Consider how asking these questions has influenced your perspective.
- Spend a few minutes reflecting on further questions and possible answers.
- Generate potential new solutions and next steps.

Act and reflect
- Choose the smallest step with the greatest impact.
- Implement and then reflect.
- Repeat the exercise to reinforce a more curious mindset.

Tip: Capture future questions and insights by writing them down as they arise.

Team Activity

Objective: Foster creativity and collaboration by encouraging curiosity within your team.

Set the Scene
Use the introduction provided in this workbook and/or the relevant chapter in Part 2 to set an encouraging and engaging tone for your team.

Step 1: Pose a Curiosity Prompt
Present a challenge or opportunity your team is presently facing. Use a question to kickstart the session, such as:
- 'What if we approached this challenge in a completely different way?'
- 'I wonder how we could solve this with half the resources we have now?'

Step 2: Individual Reflection
- Give the team 5–10 minutes for individual reflection.
- Ask them to note down a couple of questions they would like to explore.

Step 3: Collective Exploration
Encourage each team member to share one question they came up with.
- Discuss together and identify any common themes.
- Build further by combining insights and asking follow-up questions.

Step 4: Refine and Act
- Select one or two questions to explore further as a team.
- Define small, actionable steps based on the most promising ideas.

Tip: Use sticky notes or digital tools to capture and organise questions - a visual tool helps everyone see the breadth of ideas and find new connections.

Organisational Integration

Objective: Embed curiosity into organisational strategy and everyday communication.

Frame Curiosity as a Value
- Make curiosity a core part of leadership messaging.
- Encourage leaders to model curiosity by asking open-ended questions during meetings and reviews.

Ask Better Questions
Incorporate curiosity-driven prompts into strategic discussions, such as:
- 'What if we reimagined this process from the ground up?'
- 'I wonder how this would look if we collaborated across departments?'

Encourage Experimentation
- Create space for curiosity-driven pilot projects.
- Let teams explore 'what if' scenarios on a small scale before implementing changes.

Digital Adaptation

Interactive Brainstorming Tools
Use digital platforms to run virtual curiosity sessions, ask questions, and contribute ideas.

Prompts
Pose open-ended questions via email or shared platforms to generate curiosity and inspire new ideas and solutions.

Close-Out

When we adopt a curious mindset, we explore and connect new ideas more readily, transforming the way we think and solve problems. Embedding a little more curiosity into our personal habits, teams, and organisational culture unlocks a more creative way to navigate challenges and seize opportunities.

Activity 12: Gratitude

Introduction

You may think that gratitude sounds a little too 'fluffy' for a workplace intervention. Well, keep an open mind because gratitude has a surprising amount of research behind it, and it is truly powerful stuff. Gratitude is an emotion—one with transformative potential to improve mood, regulate emotions, strengthen relationships, and improve physical health.

If the word 'gratitude' doesn't feel right for you, your team, or your organisation, call it something else. Whether it's appreciation, thanks, or positives, the name doesn't matter—what counts is the reflection process, and the emotion stirred in us when we feel a sense of gratitude.

Why Gratitude Matters

Gratitude is a scientifically proven way to shift mindset, improve resilience, and enhance performance. Evoking feelings of thankfulness and appreciation for the positive things in our lives and the kindness and generosity of others engages the Intellectual Mind and, over time, rewires the brain so that we see positives and opportunities more quickly.

The great news is that it doesn't need endless hours of practice – it only takes a couple of minutes a few times a week to start making a significant difference. For organisations, gratitude creates a quick and accessible means to build a solid foundation for a more positive culture and support sustainable success.

Individual Activity

Objective: Implement a reflective gratitude practice to build personal resilience.

Set the Scene:
Find a quiet moment to reflect – somewhere without distractions. This could be in the morning, during a coffee break, or before bed.

Reflect
- Reflect on your day and focus on one or two things for which you feel gratitude.

- It doesn't need to be anything particularly significant or profound; it can be as simple as a supportive conversation, completing a task, or the sunshine outside.
- Emotions are personal - take some time to explore how you experience gratitude.
- The key is to ask: Why am I grateful for this? How does it make me feel?

Reflecting on the 'why' helps you connect emotionally and maximises the impact of the practice.

Write or Speak

- Write your reflections in a journal or notepad. If it feels comfortable, say them aloud.
- These extra steps strengthen positive emotions and reinforce the practice in your mind.

Be Consistent

- Find ways to incorporate gratitude practice into your everyday life, aiming for 3–5 times a week.
- It only takes a couple of minutes, but the impact can last all day – and beyond.

Track Your Shifts

At the end of the week, reflect on the positive ways in which gratitude practice has influenced your mood, mindset, or actions.

Team Activity

Objective: Develop a resilient and positive team environment.

Set the Scene

Use the introduction in this workbook and/or the relevant chapter in Part 2 to set an encouraging and engaging tone for your team.

Step 1: Team Gratitude Roundtable

Ask participants to reflect on something about the team they feel gratitude for.
- Ask them to direct their focus on the reasons **why** they're grateful.
- Allow time for reflection before inviting participants to share their reflections.

Step 2: Reflect and Discuss

Close by asking how participants felt about sharing and hearing these reflections.

- What positive changes did it have on their perspective of the day or week?
- How did reflecting on gratitude influence their energy?

Organisational Integration

Objective: Instil gratitude in organisational culture, strategy, and communication.

Embed Gratitude into Values and Policies

Review organisational values:

- Could they better reflect an attitude of gratitude and appreciation?

Make Gratitude Visible

Introduce organisation-wide initiatives, for example:

- Creating resources like a 'Wall of Gratitude' (digital or physical) allows employees to share thanks and recognition with their colleagues.
- Introduce gratitude protocols, such as starting or ending meetings with a quick round of gratitude.
- Incorporate gratitude themes into newsletters and leadership messages to encourage a more appreciative corporate voice.

Gratitude in Leadership Communication:

- Ask leaders to model gratitude more regularly and openly in their everyday work.
- Thank individuals and teams for their work, and recognising contributions in meetings, emails, or public forums.

Celebrate Wins with Reflection

During project debriefs or success celebrations, ask teams to reflect on:

- What went well, and why?
- Who contributed, and how can we show our appreciation?

Measure and Sustain

- Gather feedback on gratitude initiatives through pulse surveys or engagement metrics.
- Track shifts in employee sentiment, productivity, or collaboration to demonstrate the value of gratitude in action.

Digital Adaptation

Leverage digital tools to encourage and normalise gratitude:

Channels

Use online tools, intranets, and internal systems to create gratitude channels where employees can share daily or weekly reflections.

Prompts

Develop 'pop-up gratitude prompts,' such as a reminder on Fridays to share a positive moment from the week.

Recognition

Launch a gratitude recognition programme allowing employees to nominate peers for their contributions.

Apps

Use mood-tracking apps or journaling tools to help employees integrate personal gratitude practices into their daily routines.

Close-Out

Whether it's an individual moment of reflection, a team roundtable, or a company-wide initiative, gratitude can be transformative. Finding ways to bring reflective gratitude practice into organisations builds resilience, strengthens relationships, and improves physical and mental well-being, creating an organisational culture in which both people and business outcomes flourish.

Activity 13: Humour

Introduction

Humour provides a whole host of personal and workplace benefits. Think back over times when you have shared a genuine laugh with colleagues – how quickly and effortlessly has it boosted your mood, cut through tension, and helped conversations flow more easily?

Humour leads to happier work environments, improves job satisfaction, and gives people a greater sense of belonging. It also leads to much faster social bonding, key for successful networking and building effective relationships with those we need to work and collaborate effectively with every day.

Why Humour Matters

Humour is infectious—it creates a ripple effect, sending waves of positivity out into the environment around us. As well as helping to diffuse conflict, shared laughter strengthens bonds with those around us, reduces tension, and boosts morale.

Individual Activity

Objective: Introduce humour to lighten mood, reduce stress, and enhance creativity.

Recall

Reflect on moments when humour has lightened a stressful situation or helped you connect with someone.

Collect

- Collect things that make you laugh, such as funny clips, memes, or jokes.
- Compile them into a folder for easy access as a light-hearted prompt.

Develop

Look for opportunities to bring humour into your routine, such as:
- Sharing a light-hearted observation with a colleague.
- Starting your day with a funny podcast or video.

Reflect

- Reflect on the difference humour makes.
- Think about how humour influences your mood.
- How does it change interactions with others?
- In what ways does it help you feel more connected or creative?

Respect
Avoid any form of humour that could be misunderstood or offensive.

Team Activity

Objective: Use humour to strengthen the team and improve well-being.

Set the Scene
Use the content in this book to provide an overview. Set an encouraging and engaging tone for your team.

Share
Begin the meeting with a humorous icebreaker or story, and/or encourage team members to share a funny or uplifting moment from their week.

Brainstorm
Pose a light-hearted challenge such as creating a playful and motivating slogan for the team or developing light-hearted alternatives to common work jargon.

Reflect
Ask the team how humour has influenced their mood or collaboration.
- In what ways did it influence problem-solving and other team activities?
- How did it strengthen relationships?

Organisational Integration

Objective: Develop creative ways to introduce humour across the organisation.

Leadership Modelling
Encourage leaders to use humour to diffuse tension during high-pressure situations, strengthen team connections and improve team culture.

Incorporate Humour into Communications
Gently weave light-hearted touches into newsletters and internal campaigns to engage employees and make key messages more memorable.

Celebrate with Humour
Humour can be used in recognition programs by including creative awards and sharing light-hearted success stories.

Provide Training
Run accessible, short sessions and workshops on how to use humour effectively and appropriately in the workplace.

Measure the Impact
Use polls, surveys, and feedback sessions to gauge how humour is influencing workplace morale, engagement, and connection.

Digital Adaptation

Virtual Laughter
Dedicate a few minutes at the start of virtual meetings for humour by sharing light-hearted icebreakers.

Humour Channels
Create dedicated virtual channels for sharing appropriate jokes, memes, and uplifting stories.

Humorous Recognition
Use online tools and digital solutions to create and share humorous awards or captions for team achievements.

Light-hearted Prompts
Help teams through challenging times by sending encouraging, gentle prompts to team members to share something that made them smile.

Virtual Events
Host online virtual team-building events with fun activities to bring everyone together now and again.

Close-Out

Humour can strengthen relationships, build resilience, and create a happier and more productive work environment. When approached with forethought and consideration, appropriate, inclusive, well-placed humour can transform workplace dynamics and culture.

Activity 14: Breathing Practices

Introduction

Are you familiar with the saying 'count to ten'? Imagine for a moment that you're in the middle of a heated debate with a colleague; your heart races, your breathing becomes faster, and your stress levels rapidly rise. Someone intervenes, telling you both to 'take a few deep breaths.' But far more than being a myth, those simple words hold incredible power.

Breathing is far more than a reflex—it provides a quick and simple way to control our brain state. If we consciously slow and deepen our breathing during periods of stress, we tell our brain that everything is okay and it's safe to relax. Calming the Primitive Mind this way enables the Intellectual Mind to take back control, creating the space we need to bring clarity to the situation and make better decisions.

The Benefits of Breathing Practices

Becoming stressed activates our sympathetic nervous system, driving the stress response to prepare our body for fight or flight. As part of this process, our breathing gets quicker and becomes more shallow - and herein lies the reason that deep breathing is so reliably effective. Deeper, slower breathing deactivates the sympathetic nervous system, enabling the parasympathetic nervous system to take back over, calming the stress response and restoring emotional regulation and focus, leading to better decision-making.

Personal Activity

Objective: Use intentional breathing techniques to reduce stress and enhance focus.

Set the Scene: Find a quiet, comfortable space where you will not be disturbed.

Practice the 4-7-8 Technique
- Breathe in deeply through your nose for a count of 4.
- Hold your breath for a count of 7.
- Exhale slowly and completely through your mouth for a count of 8.

- Repeat this cycle 3-4 times.

Create a Breathing Awareness Challenge

For one day (or one week), pause and take just a couple of gentle, relaxed breaths:
- Before opening or responding to emails.
- Before speaking in meetings or during conversations.
- When any tense or stressful moments arise.

Reflect and Build a Habit

At the end of your day or week, take some time to reflect:
- What difference did pausing and bringing attention to your breath made in how you approached tasks and interactions.
- What impact did it make on how you felt, physically and emotionally?
- If you liked the results, keep going - regular practice will soon turn this into a habit that becomes second nature.

Team Activity

Objective: Foster a sense of calm and focus in team settings to reduce stress and improve collaboration.

Set the Scene

Use the introduction provided in this workbook and/or the relevant chapter in Part 2 to set an encouraging and engaging tone for your team.

Lead a Breathing Exercise

- Guide the team through a simple practice:
- Inhale through the nose for 4 counts.
- Hold the breath for 4 counts.
- Exhale through the mouth for 6 counts.
- Repeat this 3–4 times.

Reflect as a Group

- Ask the team to share how they feel after the exercise.
- Use this activity as a segue into meetings or brainstorming sessions.

Normalise Breathing Pauses

- Encourage team members to suggest a quick breathing break whenever tension or stress arises during discussions.
- Regular pauses build trust and resilience while fostering a positive team environment.

Organisational Integration

Objective: Embed breathing techniques into organisational culture.

Leadership Modelling

Encourage leaders to model breathing practices, demonstrating calm under pressure.

Training and Resources

- Offer workshops or resources on mindful breathing and its benefits.
- Instead of creating separate sessions, integrate brief guided breathing practices into existing training programs and courses.
- Include digital tools, such as guided breathing apps or short instructional videos, to give employees flexible, easy-to-access support between sessions.

Breathing Breaks

- Start meetings with a one-minute breathing exercise.
- Offer midday breathing sessions as part of wellness initiatives.

Digital Adaptation

Guided Tools and Resources

Share short videos or animations demonstrating breathing techniques on internal platforms or utilise popular apps with guided breathing exercises.

Prompts and Nudges

- Use software integrations to send reminders for breathing breaks.
- Create pop-up prompts in organisational systems that encourage employees to pause and take a few calming breaths.

Virtual Breathing Sessions

- Include brief guided breathing exercises in virtual meetings or webinars.
- Host optional midday breathing breaks online as part of wellness initiatives.

Track and Adapt

- Use engagement metrics or surveys to gauge participation and effectiveness of digital breathing initiatives.
- Gather feedback to refine and expand digital tools for greater impact.

Close-Out

Breathing practices provide simple, effective, and transformative ways to control our brain state, either as a quick fix in a heated moment or as a more regular practice.

Activity 15: Smiling

Introduction

While it may appear to be a simple social gesture, the impact of a smile can be transformational. Whether on the giving or receiving end, a smile can significantly affect our thoughts, emotions, and interactions with others.

Smiling plays an important role in our interactions and relationships with others. The human brain interprets an authentic smile as a signal that someone else is approachable and trustworthy. In addition to improving our mood and making us feel good, smiling helps to create stronger bonds with those around us, impacting both personal and professional relationships.

The Benefits of Smiling

Smiling tells your brain, 'Hey, everything's okay,' even when life gets stressful. And it's contagious, spreading positivity, calm, and a sense of connection in ways that words often can't do. By sending signals to calm down the Primitive Mind, smiling allows our Intellectual Mind back into play – but it has to be authentic.

Individual Activity

Objective: Smiling to reduce stress and improve mood.

Set the Scene
Take a moment to pause and take a couple of deep breaths to calm your mind.

Practice Smiling
Close your eyes and guide your thoughts toward something or someone who brings feelings of happiness, love, or gratitude. Slowly start to smile. It doesn't need to be overly forced - a gentle smile is fine.

Develop
Hold the smile for a few seconds and gradually encourage the smile to grow, noticing how your body and mind start to respond.

Practice
Set yourself a personal challenge for a day, week, or month.
- Smile briefly before opening or responding to emails.

Reflect

How does smiling influence your mood? How does it influence your interactions with those around you?

Team Activity

Objective: Creating a more positive and open atmosphere in team interactions.

Set the Scene

Start a team meeting or other team event by giving an overview and setting the tone using the introduction provided in this workbook and/or the relevant chapter in Part 2.

Smile Check-In

Ask participants to reflect on something that made them smile recently, either at work or in their personal life. Go around the room (or virtual space), inviting participants to share these moments with the rest of the team.

Encourage Smiling in Practice

Whenever the tension starts to rise when times get more challenging, encourage members to pause, take a deep breath, and smile before responding or continuing.

Reflection and Wrap-Up

Close the meeting by asking how incorporating smiles changed the energy of the discussion. Did it make collaboration easier or more enjoyable?'

Organisational Integration

Objective: Weave the power of smiling throughout the organisational culture to promote trust, strengthen relationships, and promote collaboration.

Smiling as a Leadership Tool

Encourage leaders to set the tone for open communication and trust by sprinkling smiles throughout their presentations, meetings, and one-to-one interactions.

Smiling Campaigns

Create a light-hearted campaign for your organisation, such as a 'Smile Week' to highlight the benefits of smiling, or 'Smile Spotlights,' where employees share stories of how a smile impacted their day.

Values-Driven Messaging

Frame smiling initiatives as part of a broader culture of positivity and connection. Combine them with other interventions to connect and align them with organisational values.

Regular Reflection

Incorporate 'smile moments' into team meetings or organisational check-ins, celebrating examples where smiles have made a difference in interactions or outcomes.

Digital Adaptation

Smile Prompts

Use internal platforms to send daily reminders encouraging employees to smile, such as 'Take a moment to smile and notice how it shifts your mindset.'

Share Stories

Create a dedicated virtual channel where employees can share moments that made them smile or instances where a smile brightened their day with colleagues.

Virtual Smile Challenges

Organise virtual 'smile challenges' to foster connection among remote teams. Encourage employees to share photos or stories of moments that made them smile.

Micro-Training Videos

Develop short, engaging video clips highlighting the science and benefits of smiling, making them accessible via the company intranet or wellness platforms.

Close-Out

The impact of a simple smile can be huge. As well as being a quick and powerful way to switch into a more positive brain state, smiling in the workplace helps to build rapport with others, strengthen our social bonds and improve collaboration. An authentic smile can even create a ripple effect, sending waves of positivity out to those around you.

Workbook Section 2

Section 2 contains quick and simple exercises for familiarisation and confidence-building before progressing onto more complex exercises in Sections 3 and 4.

1. **Understand the Goal**

    All the exercises included in this section are designed to help you introduce, implement, and embed positive work ways in your workplace. While this is the goal we work with for this book, these tools can be used in virtually any context.

2. **Scale Parameters**
    - A '10' represents a team consistently aligned with positive work ways.
    - A '1' represents a team experiencing frequent challenges, such as disengagement, conflict, or resistance to change.

3. **Tools to Get You Started**
    - This section introduces you to a range of versatile and adaptable tools. Blank templates are provided in the appendix.
    - These exercises are just ideas to get you started – experiment, mix and match, and get creative!
    - As your confidence grows, you'll soon start to develop your own personal approach and style.

4. **Set Your Intention**

    Write down what you hope to achieve from this workbook for yourself and your team.
    - Example: 'Improve communication and productivity in my team; positive team dialogue with increased emphasis on solutions rather than problems.'

5. **And Finally**
    - Skim over the exercises to get an overview before starting.
    - Check out the templates at the end of the workbook.

And above all else – have fun and enjoy the journey!

Exercise 1: Reflection

Purpose

Reflect on current team dynamics and identify how to start introducing positive work ways.

Key Points

- Starting with reflection identifies existing strengths to build on.
- Highlights areas where positive work ways will have greatest impact.
- Provides a baseline to monitor future progress.

Directions

Step 1: Understanding Current Dynamics

- Which aspects of team culture already support positive work ways?
  For example: 'Our team communicates openly, which helps create a transparent working atmosphere.'
- Where do you notice the most room for improvement?
  For example: 'We tend to fixate on problems rather than solutions when challenges arise.'

Step 2: Anticipating Challenges

- What might hinder the adoption of positive work ways?
  Example: 'Be more open to change, especially experimenting with different communication styles.'
- What small, constructive steps could you take to counter this?
  Example: 'I could role-model these behaviours in team meetings and ensure that it is an enjoyable and engaging process.'

Step 3: Defining Success

- What does the successful implementation of this first step look like for your team?
  For example: 'Team members feel comfortable sharing their views without concern of judgement or criticism.'
- How will you know if these changes are having a beneficial impact?

Example: 'Team working well together with fewer conflicts – using positive language patterns and adopting a more collaborative, solution-oriented approach to problem-solving.'

Reflection Prompts

- What aspects of the way the team works are most in alignment with positive work ways?
- What aspects of the way the team interacts are most in alignment with positive work ways?
- What's one aspect of positive work ways I feel most confident introducing into my team?
- What changes will let me know that my approach is making a positive difference?

Optional Activity

Use the Scaling for Success Template:

1. Define what '10' would look like for your team if they were fully aligned with positive work ways – consider how they would work and communicate.

2. Use the reflection prompts from the above exercise to help identify existing strengths and assess where the team currently sit on the scale.

3. Identify the smallest step that would help you move one point further up the scale toward alignment.

Exercise 2: If... Then Mental Preparation

Purpose

'If...then...' is a highly effective way to plan ahead by developing responses in advance. Here, we combine this technique with solutions-oriented language to disarm negativity in interactions with others and improve outcomes.

Key Points

- A solutions-oriented approach helps to maintain a positive focus.
- Advanced preparation builds confidence and leads to improved outcomes.

Directions

Step 1: Identify Scenarios

Identify 3 occasions when team dynamics have proved challenging, for example:

- A team member became frustrated or disengaged entirely from a conversation.
- Discussions became overly negative, resulting in resistance or friction between team members.
- Pessimism in one team member during a meeting rapidly spread to the entire team.

Step 2: Develop Responses

Refer to the Solutions-Focused Question and Reframed Response Banks.

- Develop responses that could have neutralised negativity on each occasion.
- Each response should be composed of 3 elements:
    - acknowledge
    - Validate
    - reframe/introduce possibility

Step 3: Rehearse

- Practice responses to familiarise yourself and build confidence.
- Rehearse or role-play with a friend or with a colleague to get a feel for how they work.

Step 4: Document

- Document responses and keep them on hand when you need them.
- These will form the basis of your toolkit as you progress.

Reflection Prompts

- How might this technique help with the effective navigation of common challenges you face?
- Which of your responses feels most natural in use, and how confident do you feel?

Next Steps

- Start using this technique more widely as your confidence builds.
- Over time, you will start to find this technique becoming more natural.

Develop your personalised version of the following template to keep on hand as a quick reference guide. This will provide support and help you stay on track more easily whenever you need it.

If This Happens...	Then I Will Respond By...
Someone responds negatively.	First, acknowledge concerns: 'What's one thing we can do to move forward?'
The group struggles to engage.	'I'd love to hear from everyone—what's one thing we can each do to make this work?'
A team member dismisses the exercise.	Validate their views: 'I understand this might feel unfamiliar. Let's focus on a couple of small steps that could make this more relevant for you.'

> **In-the-Moment Tips:**
>
> - **Pause Before Responding** and take a couple of breaths, allowing time to process your thoughts and emotions and regain your focus.
> - **Reframe Challenges** by using the responses you have developed to guide the conversation back toward looking for opportunities or solutions.
> - **Acknowledge and Validate** at the start of your response to demonstrate empathy and help diffuse tension.

Exercise 3: Personalised Crib Sheets

Purpose

The last exercise focused on preparing for interactions in which negativity was anticipated based on previous experience. Next we prepare to apply it more broadly and spontaneously by developing quick reference prompts for in-the-moment support.

Key Points

- Prompts use of solutions-focused language with others.
- Facilitates constructive and timely responses.
- Reassures whilst also promoting and demonstrating the value of positive language patterns to others.

Crib Sheets Overview

Solutions-Focused Crib Sheet

- Guides conversations toward opportunities and successful outcomes.
- Brings focus to what's working, potential opportunities, and practical next steps.

Reframed Response Crib Sheet

- Reframes negativity quickly, calmly, and constructively.
- Acknowledges, validates, and then reframes negative dialogue.

Directions

Step 1: Identify Scenarios

- Reflect on recent interactions that have proved challenging in your daily routine.
- These will help 'test' your crib sheets as you develop them

Step 2: Set Tailored Questions and Responses

- Refer to the Solutions-Focused Question Bank and Reframed Response Bank.
- Select questions and responses that feel most natural to you.

- Aim to develop 3-5 generic questions and 3-5 generic responses.
- Test them and tailor to suit by experimenting with your example scenarios.

Step 3: Complete Templates
- Fill in the template with your tailored questions and responses.
- Add examples or notes if useful.
- These will form the basis of your toolkit as you progress.

Step 4: Rehearse Responses
- Run through each question and response mentally and say them aloud to help memorise them and until they feel natural.
- Test them out with a friend or with a colleague to get a feel for how they work.
- Gradually start to introduce the questions and responses into interactions with others.
- As confidence grows, you'll find they feel more natural, and you'll eventually use them without any thought!

Reflection
- Which solutions-focused questions feel most relevant to your daily interactions?
- How confident do you feel in using your selected responses to reframe negativity as it arises throughout your day?
- What adjustments might you make to tailor these questions and responses to suit your personal style?

Next Steps
- Practice using your crib sheets in low-pressure day-to-day interactions or team discussions.
- Update your crib sheets regularly based on what works and what doesn't.
- Encourage team members and colleagues to create their own crib sheets.

Develop personalised versions of the following templates and keep them on hand to provide a quick reference guide to support you and help you keep things on track more easily when you need it.

Solutions-Focused Crib Sheet Example

Question	Notes/Examples
What's already working well?	'Our communication has been smoother than usual recently.'
What's the smallest step we can take?	'Prioritising the top three tasks for this week.'
How will we know we've succeeded?	'Stakeholders provide positive feedback, or we meet key milestones.'

Reframed Response Crib Sheet Example

Negative Response	Positive Reframe	Next Steps
'We don't have enough time.'	'What can we achieve with the time we have?'	Focus on the top three priorities.
'This won't work.'	'What's one aspect we could adapt to make it work?'	Identify one small-scale trial opportunity.

Exercise 4: Active Visualisation – 'Imagining Success'

Purpose

Active visualisation is a useful way to prepare and rehearse events in advance. Exploring and preparing for successful outcomes before they occur helps to prime our brain.

Key Points

- Creates a safe space in which to explore and rehearse a future scenario.
- Rehearses solutions-focused conversations.
- Practising in a low-pressure environment builds confidence.

Directions

Set the Scene

- Think about an upcoming scenario in which to use the solutions-focused questions and responses previously developed.
- Push yourself just a little, but not too far, out of your comfort zone.
- Aim to build on previous exercises and expand your use of solutions-focused language.

Prepare

- Mentally prepare by reflecting on a couple of questions prior to commencing.
- What's the goal of the meeting?
- What would a successful outcome look like?
- What challenges might require reframing?

Rehearse

- Find somewhere quiet where you can relax without being disturbed.
- Take a few deep breaths to help relax.
- Close your eyes and rehearse the scenario as if it were actually taking place.
- Use solutions-focused questions and responses.
- Practice handling negativity that may arise.
- Practice engaging quieter participants.

Build Detail

Picture yourself feeling calm and confident, building as much detail as possible.

- Imagine using solutions-focused language in a natural and relaxed manner.
- Calm, confident, and unphased by any negativity arising.
- Picture yourself effortlessly reframing any negativity as it arises and keeping the conversation solutions-oriented.

Reflect and Refine

- Reflect on the questions and responses that felt most natural and worked best, and refine as needed.
- You can't overdo this one, so practice away—just be sure to keep it positive and solutions-oriented!

Reflection

- How did you feel during – and after - the visualisation exercise?
- How well did your questions and responses align with the starting goals?
- Would further repetition help you feel even more prepared and confident?

Next Steps

- Use this technique regularly prior to important meetings or discussions.
- The more you practice and use this technique, the easier and more powerful it becomes.

Optional Activity: Role-Play with a Colleague

1. Pair up with a colleague to rehearse responses using role-play.
2. Take turns playing different roles to experience both sides of the conversation.
3. As you become more comfortable, try challenging each other a little more - to develop skills further and build confidence.
4. Exchange open and honest feedback with each other so you can refine your approach.

Reflection

1. What elements of this exercise proved most helpful?
2. What specific adjustments will you make to your phrasing or tone?
3. How might this exercise influence your confidence during real interactions?

Exercise 5: Solutions-Focused Team Conversations

Purpose

This builds on the previous exercises, encouraging wider adoption by introducing solutions-focused language into a team environment.

Key Points

- Introduce teams to solutions-focused language.
- Develop a common team solutions-focused language.

Steps to Take

Run as one longer workshop or split over a couple of shorter sessions – one exercise per session.

Preparation

- Use content from this book and your personal experience with the exercises to provide an overview of solutions-focused language with the team.
- Provide copies of the Solutions-Focused Question Bank and Reframed Response Bank and blank crib sheets.

Set a Positive Tone

- This exercise presents a great opportunity for the team to have some constructive fun together – so frame it that way!
- This is new and unfamiliar, so some participants may find these exercises a little uncomfortable at first – that is OK.
- Encourage a light-hearted, relaxed, and experimental approach to help reduce resistance or negativity.
- If any negativity arises, simply apply what you have learned so far, simply acknowledge, validate, and then reframe. It is an opportunity for you to practice!

Facilitate Session

Either run one longer workshop with breaks between or split over two sessions, encouraging practice between sessions to maintain momentum.

- Start with exercise 2: 'If... then'
- Guide team through the steps, allowing time for discussion and completion of templates.
- Once templates are completed, discuss collectively.
- Split into pairs and allow time for practice and refinement.

Discuss as a group and then take a break or end session one here.
- Complete exercise 3: 'Personalised Crib Sheets' guiding through the steps.
- Once everyone has created their own crib sheets, discuss them as a group.
- Split the team up into pairs and provide scenarios to use for role-play practice.
- Reconvene and discuss as a group.

Group Activity

Select a current or recent challenge the team has faced as scenario for the group to work with.
- Facilitate a group discussion with the following rule: solutions-focused language must be used.
- Every time someone drifts toward negative language, use it as a group opportunity to reframe.
- Aim for 30 minutes of continuous solutions-focused language across the entire team.

Summarise
- At the end of the session, discuss as a group and ask team members to share their experiences of using solutions-focused language.
- Work as a team to find solutions to any negative feedback together. For example, if someone says a particular question or scenario didn't work, ask what could have worked instead.
- Agree on the next steps—for example, extending the challenge to the next team meeting, participants agreeing to practice between themselves, etc.

Reflection Prompts
- How engaged were the team during these exercises?
- How did using solutions-focused language change conversations?
- What positive feedback did the team provide about their experiences?
- How could you build on these exercises to encourage regular use of solutions-focused language?

Next Steps

Practice Makes Perfect

- Repeat this approach in future team meetings to build consistency and confidence.
- Be sure to reflect after each future session or team meeting.

Scale and Adapt

- Gradually incorporate more questions and techniques as you and your team become comfortable.
- Once the team are comfortable with the solutions-focused language, run a session using Active Visualisation with them.
- Use the exercises throughout this workbook to have fun and encourage the team to explore different tools and techniques.
- Approaching this way will help to build team skills as well as a resilient team culture.

Example:

Original Statement	Reframed Statement	Positive Outcome
'We don't have enough time.'	'What can we achieve with the time we have?'	Focus shifts to effective prioritisation of tasks on hand.
'This task is too complex.'	'What smaller steps could we take?'	Reduces overwhelm and sharpens focus.
'This process always fails.'	'What's one part of this process that works?'	Takes focus off failure and on to success.

Exercise 6: Solutions-Focused Goal-Setting

Purpose

This exercise introduces the Universal Template as a versatile, solutions-focused approach, to setting individual or team goals.

Key Points

The questions can be amended to suit context but must remain solutions-focused.

Preparation

Review the template to familiarise and select a goal you would like to work with.

Steps to Take

Introduce session

Provide an overview of the purpose of the session and share template.

Follow Template

- Guide team through each step, using the questions provided as a guide and tailoring them as required.
- Ask sufficient questions to explore each step fully before moving on.

Reflection

At the end of the exercise, reflect with the team.
- What difference did approaching goal setting this way make?
- How did it influence team perspectives?
- What's one other area where you could adopt this technique?
- How could this technique help embed positive work ways across the team?

Next Steps

- Practice using the Solutions Focus Universal Template on another topic.
- Explore exercises later in the workbook for more detailed guidance.

Revisit this exercise regularly to refine goals and evaluate progress.

Exercise 7: Introduction to Scaling

Purpose

This exercise uses the Scaling Template to introduce Scaling to define success, assess current positioning, plan next steps, and track future progress. This exercise can also be combined with the previous one.

Key Points

Scaling promotes small, realistic steps toward a common goal.

Preparation

- **Determine the Goal**: Select a new or existing team goal for this exercise.
- **Data**: Gather any relevant available data, observations, or team feedback.

Steps to Take

Define success, applying a scale of 1-10.

'10' represents the goal met in full, and 1 represents the goal not met at all.
- Core Question: What does a '10' look like?
- Example: 'If we were at a 10 in communication, what would that look, sound, or feel like in our team?'

Assess Current Position
- Core Question: Where are we now on a scale of 1 to 10?
- Example: 'What's already working well, and what's helping us stay at this level?'

Identify Opportunities
- Core Question: What would take us one step closer to a 10?
- Example: 'What challenges are we facing, and how could we turn them into opportunities?'

Determine the Next Step
- Core Question: What's the smallest step we can take to move closer to a 10?
- Example: 'What simple action could we take right now to make progress?'

In-the-Moment Prompts

- **If responses vary**: 'What common ground can we build on to align our vision of success?'
- **If energy dips**: 'What's one small thing we can do today to move forward?'

Reflection

How did defining '10' help to align a collective vision of success with the team?
- How does using Scaling help the team to understand our current position?
- How might Scaling help focus our future efforts and motivate the team to keep going?
- What impact could Scaling have on helping the team meet successful outcomes?

Next Steps

- Use scaling results with other stakeholders to improve alignment.
- Use scaling in meetings to define strategies and measure progress.
- Find creative ways to utilise Scaling across your team and with colleagues.

Exercise 8: Team Challenge

Purpose

The techniques in this book provide fantastic resources for team challenges, this exercise provides a way to encourage collective exploration.

Key Points

Introduces an element of fun and embeds positive work ways into everyday work activities.

Templates

Refer to the relevant chapter and corresponding exercise from the main book or workbook section.

Steps to Take

Preparation

Introduce the idea of a challenge to the team, discuss and gather thoughts and review the techniques either individually or collectively as preferred.

Select technique

Ask the team to select the technique they're most interested in exploring together.

Set Scene

Start with a team review and discussion of the selected technique and its benefits.

Define Challenge

Encourage creativity to find as many ways as possible to weave into working day.

Set Duration

- Agree to use the selected technique consistently over a defined period (e.g., one week or one month).
- Agree on how techniques will be adopted – for example as individuals, across team discussions, meetings, or routine tasks.

Implement and Track

Use the chosen technique consistently for the agreed timeframe, encouraging the team to note their experiences, successes, and challenges.

Review and Reflect

At end of challenge, discuss the influence on individual well-being and team dynamics.

In-the-Moment Prompts

- **If enthusiasm dips**: 'What's one small change that we could make to keep this challenge engaging?'
- **If challenges arise**: 'How can we adapt this technique to suit our situation better?'

Reflection

How did practising this technique affect the dynamics and morale within the team?

- What did the team find most impactful or surprising?
- How could this technique be refined or expanded for future use?

Next Steps

- Show appreciation for the team's participation and acknowledge successes, no matter how small.
- Consider exploring another technique in the future to build on your progress.
- Use insights from this challenge to guide the next exercise.

Workbook Section 3

Taking Positive Work Ways to the Next Level

The exercises in this section of the workbook are designed to embed positive work ways into everyday practices. Whether you work in HR, Operations, Communications, or any other business function, these will help get you started.

Building on the Foundations

If you've completed earlier sections, you've already familiarised yourself with the main techniques and templates. If you haven't yet completed the exercises in the previous section, don't worry—you can still use this section as a standalone guide and refer back as and when you need.

What You Will Learn in This Section

1. **Advanced Application:** Explore how to use the same simple tools and techniques to explore and address more complex scenarios.

2. **Alignment:** Explore how positive work ways can align and smooth interfaces between teams, departments, and functions.

3. **Collaboration:** Explore how positive work ways can encourage and facilitate greater collaboration and engagement across an organisation.

Approach and Structure

The exercises in this section are designed to be both practical and supportive, providing the details necessary to guide you through each one:

1. **Difficult Conversations:** This module explores how to use a solutions-focused approach to navigate even the most complex discussions with ease and confidence.

2. **Policy and Procedure Review:** This module demonstrates how to apply the Universal Template to review and optimise policies and procedures into vehicles that actively encourage positive work ways.

3. **Goal Setting with Scaling:** This module uses scaling exercises to show

how to align functional goals with organisational values.

4. **Engagement & Collaboration Across Teams:** This module explores how adopting positive work ways can encourage greater cohesion and collaboration across departments and functions.

5. **Developing a Framework for Integration:** This module explores how adopting positive work ways can encourage greater cohesion and collaboration across functions.

Application 1: Difficult Conversations

Purpose

This module provides a step-by-step guide on using a solutions-focused approach to navigate difficult discussions with greater ease, confidence, and effectiveness.

Navigating Difficult Conversations

Difficult conversations are a part of every workplace, particularly when covering sensitive areas such as performance management, conflict resolution, and organisational change. While they can feel uncomfortable, they present great opportunities for growth that are often missed. Adopting a solutions-focused approach helps maintain a constructive dialogue between parties and leads to quicker and more successful outcomes - for everyone involved.

Why It Matters

Tense situations can often feel high stakes for either one or all parties involved. When intense emotions start running high, the risk of misunderstandings and resistance greatly increases - and if left unchecked, things can quickly escalate. Being able to manage any interaction with ease is a fundamental leadership skill – one that is essential for supporting healthy workplace relationships, regardless of any challenges posed.

Difficult Conversations Toolkit

The exercises at the start of the workbook section provided a gentle introduction to solutions-focused language, setting a firm foundation on which to now build. If you haven't already done so, it would be worth completing those first—it will be time well spent and will develop your skill and confidence more quickly.

Tools You'll Need

Revisit the following, using responses and reframes from earlier exercises:
- Crib Sheets
- Solutions-Focused Question Bank
- Reframed Response Bank

Revisit Crib Sheets

Reflect on the crib sheets that you developed. If you have not previously undertaken the exercises in question, take a quick look before continuing.

Review Suitability

Are the questions and responses that you selected appropriate, or would they benefit from a little tweaking?

Identify Gaps

Are there specific challenges you have in mind that may require additional questions or responses?

Rules for Staying Solutions-Focused

Here are a few principles to guide your approach – keep these in mind throughout the exercise:

1. **Get Comfortable with Silence**

   Silence often means the other person is thinking deeply, so resist the urge to interrupt or intervene.
   - If necessary, repeat or rephrase the same question, or allow them more time to think by going to grab a coffee or rescheduling.

2. **Avoid Giving Suggestions**

   Your role is to facilitate their thought process by asking questions that help them work through potential solutions for themselves.
   - This helps keep their Intellectual Mind engaged, enabling them to think constructively and develop solutions more quickly.
   - This is a core element of the process, so avoid the temptation to 'help' by suggesting what you think they should do.
   - As they think through and develop solutions, they are also mentally rehearsing them, increasing the likelihood of them being implemented.
   - If they ask, 'What do you think I should do?' refrain from advice and instead try reflecting back: 'What do you think would work best for you?'

3. **Stick with One Question**

   Instead of jumping between questions, stick with the same core question, rephrasing it slightly if needed.
   - This avoids overwhelm and helps to keep the Intellectual Mind engaged.

Step 1: Planning for Success

Preparation is everything. Taking time to prepare will help you feel more confident and ensure the conversation remains constructive and focused.

1. Reframe the Objective

Frame the purpose of the conversation on the desired solution or outcome, e.g.

- Instead of 'Addressing missed deadlines,'
  Reframe as 'Exploring how to support consistent and timely delivery of work.'
- Instead of 'Resolving team conflict,'
  Reframe as 'Improving team communication and collaboration.'

2. Reframe Key Points

Place focus on solutions when listing key points to discuss.

- Instead of 'You are repeatedly missing deadlines.'
  Reframe as 'What changes may help you to meet deadlines more consistently?'
- Instead of 'The team isn't working well together,'
  Reframe as 'What strengths can we build on to improve collaboration?'

3. Prepare Questions

Use the **Solutions-Focused Question Bank** to craft your questions and update your crib sheet in advance, for example

- What would a good outcome look like for you?
- What would be different for you if you achieved that outcome?
- What's one small step you could take toward that outcome?

4. Anticipate Emotional Reactions

Consider how the other person might feel (e.g., defensive, frustrated) and plan how you'll validate their emotions, for example

- I can see this feels overwhelming. Let's explore what a positive outcome might look like for you.

Step 2: Rehearsal

Building confidence through practice ensures you're ready to navigate the conversation effectively.

Role-Playing for Confidence

1. **Scenario**

   Select a real or hypothetical situation, such as addressing underperformance or managing conflict.

2. **Add Rules**

   The 'leader' cannot give suggestions.

   Stick to the reframing crib sheet and solutions-focused questions.

   Get comfortable with silence – build this into the role play!

   Experiment with different ways to frame the same question.

3. **Reflect**

   What worked well?

   What felt uncomfortable?

   How did sticking to the rules highlight the flexibility of these tools?

Step 3: Having the Conversation

Bring everything together during the conversation:

1. **Start with Empathy**

   Acknowledge the other person's feelings, for example:

   - I hear you, and I can see how challenging this has been for you
   - I can't imagine how difficult this must be for you.

2. **Provide a Positive Boost**

   Highlight their resilience, effort, or courage, for example:

   It takes a lot of strength to share this with me today.

3. **Redirect to Solutions**

   Use reframing and solutions-focused questions to move toward action:

   - If things improved, what would that look like for you?
   - What's one small step we could take to improve this?

Step 4: Reflecting and Learning

After the conversation, reflect:

1. **What worked well?**

   Example: Validating their emotions helped build rapport and instil trust quickly.

2. **What was challenging?**

   Example: I felt uncomfortable sitting in silence at first.

3. **What will you try next time?**

   Example: Rehearse more ways to reframe potential negative comments.

4. **How will you refine your toolkit?**

   Example: Add more reframes for addressing resistance to policy changes.

In-the-Moment Prompts

When the conversation feels challenging, keep these reminders on hand:
1. Allow silence to work—resist the urge to fill it.
2. Stay with one question and then rephrase it if needed.
3. Keep redirecting to small, actionable steps.

Next Steps

1. Review and revise personalised crib sheets.
2. Practice a role-play or carry out an active visualisation exercise for an upcoming conversation.
3. Reflect after each future discussion to build and reinforce skills.

Final Thoughts

Difficult conversations don't have to feel overwhelming. By staying solutions-focused, validating emotions, and overcoming the discomfort of silence, you'll quickly develop a skillset that transforms challenges into opportunities. Remember, every conversation is a chance to practise, refine, and build your skills.

Application 2: Shaping Corporate Voice

Purpose

This exercise guides you through the review and/or development of policies and procedures that support positive work ways and actively encourage a positive, supportive, and inclusive organisational voice.

Changing the Tone

Policies and procedures do far more than set rules—they reflect corporate voice and determine how your business communicates with employees, clients, and other stakeholders. Every word, tone, and phrase matters. The previous workbook section focused on how to start introducing positive work ways at the individual and team levels. Now, we broaden the scope and explore how to take these same principles to influence the policies and procedures that underpin organisational culture.

Reinforcing the Connection and Flow

Individuals to Functions

Adopting positive work ways at departmental and functional levels consolidates individual efforts, influences wider dynamics, and initiates a ripple effect across the wider business.

Policies as Catalysts

Reframing supporting processes actively drives, supports, and reinforces these positive changes.

Looking Ahead

Organisation-level integration occurs when policies and procedures become part of a broader strategy that supports long-term, systemic change.

Tools You Will Need

- Universal Template
- Solutions-Focused Question Bank
- Reframed Response Template

Exercise: Reviewing Policies and Procedures

Preparation

Select a Policy or Procedure

Select a document with a significant impact on your department or function (e.g., absence management or incident investigation).

Gather Input

Prior to commencing, collate as much information as you can. Include stakeholder feedback and needs, internal metrics (e.g., engagement surveys, occupational health data, absence data, stress risk assessments, focus groups, audit findings, and exit interviews), and any relevant external data (e.g., national data, professional body findings, guidance, trends, compliance requirements).

Universal Template

Title Policy / Procedure name

Date

Review Team Members

Step 1: Define Your Vision

(This step establishes a clear, forward-focused vision for success.)

Core Question: What does good look like?

If this policy/procedure aligned with positive work ways and fully met stakeholder needs, how would that look?

Additional Questions
- If things were working optimally, what would be happening?
- What would success look like?
- How would we know we were making progress?
- What positive impact would this have on individuals, teams, or the organisation?

Things to Consider
- Overarching strategic goals and values.
- Stakeholder needs.
- Internal and external interfaces.
- Industry priorities and professional standards.
- External and internal data.

Your Questions:

[Insert here]

Your Vision

[Insert here]

Metrics

- What will be the key signs of progress?
- With 10 being the vision realised in full, where do we currently sit on a scale of 1–10?

Step 2: Existing Strengths

(This step identifies strengths that could be used to build on further.)

Core Question: What's already working well?

What aspects of the policy/procedure already support positive work ways?

Additional Questions

- What's already working well in this policy/procedure?
- Have we seen success in other areas of the business that may be useful?
- What existing strengths, skills, or resources could help?
- Who else might have useful insights or experience?

Things to Consider

- Existing communication channels.
- Employee network groups and workplace champions.

Your Questions

[Insert here]

Your Strengths

[Insert here]

Metrics

- What existing data or observations show we have a foundation to build on?
- How can we track what's already working well as we move forward?

Step 3: Explore Opportunities

(This step helps generate ideas and practical options for moving forward.)

Core Question: Where and how could this policy or procedure align greater with positive work ways?

Additional Questions
- What if we approached this from a completely different perspective?
- What is one change we haven't tried yet that could move us forward?
- If there were no constraints, what ideas would we explore?
- Who may be able to provide fresh ideas?

Things to Consider
- Simplify, streamline, or combine with similar policies or procedures.
- Enhance flexibility to reflect different business needs.
- Encourage greater collaboration or innovation.
- Communicate content more effectively to all target audiences.
- Introducing language that engages the Intellectual Mind.
- Removing language that causes defensiveness or resistance.
- Introduce solutions-focused approaches or techniques.
- Raise engagement by creating a practical, supportive resource.

Your Questions

[Insert here]

Your Opportunities

[Insert here]

Metrics
- How will we determine the feasibility of these opportunities?
- How will we measure future success?

Step 4: Take Action

(This step ensures practical and achievable action.)

Core Question: What's the smallest, most effective action that could be taken to start aligning this policy/procedure with positive work ways?

Additional Questions
- What is the smallest action with the greatest impact that we can take?
- What support, resources, or tools do we need to implement this effectively?
- How can we integrate this action to improve efficiency?
- What will we do if we hit an obstacle?
- How can we integrate this action to improve efficiency?
- How and where can we run a pilot

Your Questions

[Insert here]

Your Steps

[Insert here]

Metrics

- What early indicators of success will we look for?
- How will we measure engagement, efficiency, or other relevant improvements?

Step 5: Reflect and Review

Core Question: What progress has been made, and what insights can guide the next steps?

Additional Questions

- On a scale of 1–10, where are you now compared to your starting position?
- What's improved since we started?
- What's working well that we should continue doing?
- What have we learned that could help with the next steps?
- What's the next small adjustment we can make to keep moving forward?

Consider

- How does stakeholder feedback inform the next steps?
- Are there any perceived barriers or challenges that require reframing before moving forward?

Your Questions

[Insert here]

Your Reflections

[Insert here]

Final Measurement & Progress

- On a scale of 1–10, where are we now compared to where we started?
- How does current progress compare to our original baseline?
- What feedback or data supports the impact of our changes?
- What new opportunities have emerged that we hadn't considered before?

Application 3: Goal Setting with Scaling

Purpose

Introduce scaling as a structured process for setting departmental and functional goals that align with positive work ways and broader organisational goals and objectives.

Why It Matters

Developing departmental and functional goals that actively support positive work ways and align with overarching organisational goals and objectives drives high performance and successful goal fulfilment. Scaling provides a simple and flexible tool that facilitates iterative improvement toward that future goal.

Preparation

Revisit Crib Sheets

Review your previously selected solutions-focused questions and reframes and refine them if necessary.

Review Scaling Template

Refer to the template provided at the end of the book.

Gather Relevant Data

In preparation, gather any available, relevant data beforehand, including stakeholder feedback, performance metrics, and any other internal or external data that may prove useful.

Rules for Staying Solutions-Focused

Keep these principles in mind throughout this exercise:

Size Matters

Scaling is about identifying small, feasible steps that drive steady progress. It is an iterative process: identifying and then taking the smallest steps that will secure the greatest results, and then reviewing their impact before repeating the process

Balanced Input

A diverse range of perspectives throughout the process will provide most impactful solutions and reflect all stakeholder needs.

Stay Curious

Use open-ended questions at every step to uncover as many opportunities and insights as possible along the way.

The Scaling for Success Framework

Follow these steps to align goals and drive progress:

Step 1: Define the Scale

Key Question: With 10 representing the goal being successfully met in full, and adding as much detail and definition as possible, what does '10' look like?

Example Response

Definition of 10:

- Teams across the function consistently align with positive work ways:
- Collaboration is strong, interfaces are smooth, and communication is positive.
- Any issues arising are resolved quickly adopting a solutions-focused approach.
- Meetings are engaging and productive, and a high-performance culture prevails.
- Stakeholders' report increased satisfaction with outcomes.

Step 2: Assess Current Position

Key Question: Where are we now on a scale of 1–10?

Example Response

Current Position: 5

- Teams occasionally share updates but lack regular, structured collaboration.
- Stakeholders' express frustration with missed opportunities to align priorities.

Step 3: Explore Opportunities

Key Question: What's helped us to reach this level, and how can we move forward?

Example Response

Opportunities:

- Use existing tools (e.g., shared digital platforms) to facilitate updates.
- Use pilots to show the potential impact on business outcomes.

Barriers (reframe to create opportunities):

- Conflicting schedules limit meeting availability.
- Many teams work in silos and are resistant to working more collaboratively.

Step 4: Identify Next Steps

Key Question: What's the smallest feasible step that would facilitate progression up the scale by one or two points?

Example Response
- Schedule monthly cross-team meetings with a protocol for attendance.
- Build collaboration slowly – bring two or three core teams together first before expanding participation gradually over time.
- Use voting as a means to secure the best fit for meetings and schedule in advance.
- Assign leaders and deputies to provide flexibility around other diary commitments.
- Create a common dashboard to track progress and promote visibility.
- Run short cross-team sessions on the concepts of positive work ways, emphasising the importance of collaborative working and how individual actions contribute to overall success.

Step 5: Reflect and Review

Key Questions: What progress have we made, and how can we build on it? What further opportunities could we explore to continue progressing up the scale?

Example Response

Progress:
- Stakeholder satisfaction increased by 10% in quarterly feedback surveys.
- Cross-team meeting attendance improved by 30%.

Insights:
- Small wins are boosting employee engagement.
- Teams are requesting more structured tools for collaboration.

Reflection Prompts

- What did using the template reveal?
- How might you apply this approach to other areas?
- What additional resources or adjustments could enhance future scaling activities?

Next Steps

- Try applying Scaling to a different goal or priority.
- Share your results and reflections with colleagues to encourage further cross-functional collaboration and learning.
- Reflect on how scaling exercises help improve alignment and progress by clearly defining a shared vision and adopting a small-step approach.

Application 4: Engagement & Collaboration Across Teams

Purpose

This module explores how adopting positive work ways can encourage greater cohesion and collaboration across departments and functions - setting the stage for broader organisational alignment.

Why It Matters

Organisations are composed of diverse individuals and teams continually working toward common goals—collaboration is, therefore, fundamental to organisational success. Adopting positive ways of working clearly defines success, enhances communication, improves alignment and collaboration between individuals and teams, and provides support along the way.

Tools You'll Need

- **Solutions-Focused Question Bank**: To encourage reflective discussions and explore opportunities.
- **Reframing Bank**: To constructively reframe any challenges that arise.
- Scaling Template: To track progress and identify iterative steps.
- **Part 2 Techniques**: For ideas and inspiration that can be tailored to context.

Universal Template

Title: Improving collaboration, engagement, and alignment.

Date

Review Team Members

Step 1: Define Your Vision

(This step establishes a clear, forward-focused vision for success.)

Core Question: What does good look like?
How would the department or function look if it were optimally aligned with positive work ways?

Additional Questions

- How would individuals and teams be communicating and interacting?
- How would different processes and interfaces operate?
- What's the working environment and culture like?
- What would 'good' look and feel like?
- What positive impact would this have on individuals, teams, or the organisation?

Things to Consider
- Overarching strategic goals and values.
- Stakeholder needs.
- Internal and external interfaces.
- Industry priorities and professional standards.
- External and internal data.

Encourage input that reflects the organisation's diversity to build a clear, shared vision of what good looks like for everyone.

Your Questions
[Insert here]

Your Vision
[Insert here]

Metrics
- What will be the key signs of progress?
- With 10 being the vision realised in full, where do we currently sit on a scale of 1–10?

Step 2: Existing Strengths

(This step identifies strengths that could be used to build on further.)

Core Question: What's already working well?
What are the current engagement levels across the various teams within the department or function?

Additional Questions
- What's already working well in terms of collaboration or shared goals?
- How do individuals and teams perceive their connection and input to functional culture and success?
- Have we seen success in other areas of the business that may be useful?

- What existing strengths, skills, or resources could help?
- Who else might have useful insights or experience?

Things to Consider
- Existing communication channels.
- Employee network groups and workplace champions.

Your Questions

[Insert here]

Your Strengths

[Insert here]

Metrics
- What existing data or observations show we have a foundation to build on?
- How can we track what's already working well as we move forward?

Step 3: Explore Opportunities

(This step helps generate ideas and practical options for moving forward.)

Core Question: Where and how could this function align greater with positive work ways?

Additional Questions
- Where could communication be enhanced and how?
- Where could siloes benefit from greater openness and collaboration?
- Where could techniques such as gratitude, optimism or empathy be used to promote a more positive and supportive working environment?
- Could introducing scaling more widely help to keep everyone aligned on shared progress across teams?

Things to Consider
- Simplify, streamline, or combine different processes.
- Communicate content differently to the various target audiences.
- Introduce techniques to engage the Intellectual Mind.
- Create practical and tailored support resources.

Your Questions

[Insert here]

Your Opportunities

[Insert here]

Metrics
- How will we determine the feasibility of these opportunities?
- How will we measure future success?

Step 4: Take Action
(This step ensures practical and achievable action.)

Core Question: What's the smallest, most effective action that could be taken to start aligning this department/function with positive work ways?

Additional Questions
- What is the smallest action with the greatest impact that we can take?
- What support, resources, or tools do we need to implement this effectively?
- What's one thing we can commit to today that will build momentum?
- How can we integrate this action to improve efficiency?
- How and where can we run a pilot?
- What will we do if we hit an obstacle?

Things to Consider
- Review the opportunities generated in the previous step.
- Which opportunities would prove simplest and quickest to implement?
- Which opportunities have the potential for the greatest impact?
- Use scaling to sort through and rank the opportunities to determine the most suitable ones.
- Identify the smallest and quickest opportunities that will result in the greatest impact.
- Encourage exploration and invite feedback before deciding on action.

Your Questions
[Insert here]

Your Steps
[Insert here]

Metrics
- What early indicators of success will we look for?
- How will we measure engagement, efficiency, or other relevant improvements?

Step 5: Reflect and Review

Key Question: What progress has been made, and what insights can guide the next steps?

Additional Questions
- On a scale of 1–10, where are you now compared to your starting position?
- What's improved since we started?
- What's working well that we should continue doing?
- What have we learned that could help with the next steps?
- What's the next small adjustment we can make to keep moving forward?

Consider
- How does stakeholder feedback inform the next steps?
- Are there any perceived barriers or challenges that require reframing before moving forward?
- Use scaling creatively to measure progress and refine initiatives within and between different teams.
- Refine existing metrics in use across the business to highlight the progress of specific actions.
- Obtain feedback from individuals and teams.
- Create a shared platform to document successes.

Your Questions

[Insert here]

Your Reflections

[Insert here]

Final Measurement & Progress
- On a scale of 1–10, where are we now compared to where we started?
- How does current progress compare to our original baseline?
- What feedback or data supports the impact of our changes?
- What new opportunities have emerged that we hadn't considered before?

Reflection Prompts
1. What strengths or opportunities have emerged from this exercise?
2. What positive changes have you noticed in communication and collaboration?
3. What additional support or tools could enhance progress?

Next Steps

1. Continue experimenting, using feedback to refine and expand actions.
2. Encourage teams to reflect on what works well and has the greatest positive impact.
3. Reflect on how successes could be scaled to extend beyond the department or function.

Application 5: Developing a Framework for Integration

Purpose

This module explores how adopting positive work ways can encourage greater cohesion and collaboration across departments and functions - setting the stage for broader organisational alignment.

Why It Matters

Organisations are composed of diverse individuals and teams continually working toward common goals—collaboration is, therefore, fundamental to organisational success. Adopting positive ways of working clearly defines success, enhances communication, improves alignment and collaboration between individuals and teams, and provides support along the way.

Tools You'll Need

- Solutions-Focused Question Bank
- Reframing Bank
- Scaling Template
- Part 2: Techniques

Universal Template

Title: Integrate positive work ways into functional systems and processes.
Date
Review Team Members

Step 1: Define Your Vision

(This step establishes a clear, forward-focused vision for success.)

Core Question: What does good look like?
How would things look and operate differently if positive work ways were consistently implemented, integrated, and embedded throughout every level of the department or function?

Additional Questions

- How could integrating positive work ways improve alignment with wider organisational goals?
- In what ways would integrating positive work ways into core processes and systems improve interfaces, workflows, performance, and efficiencies?
- How might interweaving positive work ways throughout the layers of the department or function positively impact working environments and employee well-being?
- What specific business outcomes could be enhanced and how?
- How might embedding positive work ways at the core of this department or function positively impact other areas of the business?

Things to Consider

- Overarching strategic goals and values.
- Stakeholder needs.
- Internal and external interfaces.
- Industry priorities and professional standards.
- External and internal data.

Your Questions

[Insert here]

Your Vision

[Insert here]

Metrics

- What will be the key signs of progress?
- With 10 being the vision realised in full, where do we currently sit on a scale of 1–10?

Step 2: Identify Current Strengths

(This step identifies strengths that could be used to build on further.)

Core Question: What's already working well?

What's already working well in this function that can support integration?

Additional Questions

- Where are positive ways of working already happening?
- What feedback or metrics highlight areas of success?
- Have we seen success in other areas of the business that may be useful?

- What existing strengths, skills, or resources could help?
- Who else might have useful insights or experience?

Things to Consider
- Existing communication channels.
- Employee network groups and workplace champions.

Your Questions
[Insert here]

Your Strengths
[Insert here]

Metrics
- What existing data or observations show we have a foundation to build on?
- How can we track what's already working well as we move forward?

Step 3: Explore Opportunities

(This step helps generate ideas and practical options for moving forward.)

Core Question: Where and how could this function align greater with positive work ways?

Where could integrating positive work ways be simplest and most impactful?

Additional Questions
- Which processes or systems would offer the greatest benefit from aligning with positive work ways?
- Which systems or processes would most easily support – or have the highest impact from – positive work ways?
- What techniques (e.g. solutions-focused language, gratitude, reframing, optimism) would be the best fit?
- What pilots with positive work ways could be expanded into other teams, or could be transferred to processes or systems?
- Which processes or systems would align most easily with positive work ways?

Things to Consider
- Simplify, streamline, or combine different processes.
- Communicate content differently to the various target audiences.
- Introducing techniques to engage the Intellectual Mind.
- Create practical and tailored support resources.

Your Questions
[Insert here]

Your Opportunities
[Insert here]

Metrics
- How will we determine the feasibility of these opportunities?
- How will we measure future success?

Step 4: Take Action

(This step ensures practical and achievable action.)

Core Question: What are the smallest actions with the greatest impact that could be taken to start integrating positive work ways?

Additional Questions
- What's one small, high-impact, change that could be introduced straight away?
- What support, resources, or tools do we need to implement this effectively?
- What's one thing we can commit to today that will build momentum?
- How can we integrate this action to improve efficiency?
- How might bigger actions be tested or piloted on individual teams before scaling up?
- What will we do if we hit an obstacle?

Things to Consider
- Review the opportunities generated in the previous step.
- Which opportunities would prove simplest and quickest to implement?
- Which opportunities have the potential for the greatest impact?
- Use scaling to sort through and rank the opportunities to determine the most suitable ones.
- Identify the smallest and quickest opportunities providing greatest impact.
- Encourage exploration and invite feedback before deciding on action.

Your Questions
[Insert here]

Your Steps
[Insert here]

Metrics

- What early indicators of success will we look for?
- How will we measure engagement, efficiency, or other relevant improvements?

Step 5: Reflect and Review

Core Question: What progress has been made, and what insights can guide the next steps?

What impact has the action had – how far up the scale have we progressed?

Additional Questions

- On a scale of 1–10, where are you now compared to your starting position?
- What's improved since we started?
- What's working well that we should continue doing?
- What have we learned that could help with the next steps?
- What's the next small adjustment we can make to keep moving forward?

Consider

- How does stakeholder feedback inform the next steps?
- Are there any perceived barriers or challenges that require reframing before moving forward?
- Use scaling creatively to measure progress and refine initiatives within and between different teams.
- Refine existing metrics in use across the business to highlight the progress of specific actions.
- Obtain feedback from individuals and teams.
- Create a shared platform to document successes.

Your Questions

[Insert here]

Your Reflections

[Insert here]

Final Measurement & Progress

- On a scale of 1–10, where are we now compared to where we started?
- What feedback or data supports the impact of our changes?

Reflection Prompts

- What strengths or opportunities have emerged from this exercise?
- What positive changes have you noticed in communication and collaboration?
- What additional support or tools could enhance progress?

Next Steps

- Continue experimenting, using feedback to refine and expand actions.
- Encourage teams to reflect on what works well and has the greatest positive impact.
- Reflect on how successes could be scaled to extend beyond the department or function.

Workbook Reflection: Progress and Insights

Use the following prompts to reflect on your progress within this section of the workbook.

What Have You Learned?
- How have the tools and exercises in this section helped build your skills and confidence in adopting positive work ways?
- What stands out most – what specific aspects have you noticed?

Where Do Opportunities Exist?
- Do any areas still feel challenging or unclear?
- If so, what steps might you take to find solutions and improve understanding?

What's One Next Step?
- What small, practical step could you take to build on your progress?

Which Tools or Exercises Resonated Most?
- Which modules particularly resonated or proved especially effective?
- What insights could you take from these into a wider organisational context?

What Would You Share?
- What aspects would you highlight if you were to present your learnings to other leaders or areas of the business?

What Is Your Legacy?
- What longer-term, lasting positive impact could the changes you have already initiated have on you, your teams, and beyond?

Practical Tip: Set the Stage for Organisational Change

Take a moment to consider what organisation-wide integration with positive work ways could look like. Use the reflection prompts below to get started:

- If your function were to model positive work ways for the entire

organisation, what might that look like?
- How might you share your successes and ideas with senior leaders?
- What opportunities exist for cross-functional collaboration that could pave the way for broader organisational shifts?

Final Encouragement

As you complete this section, take a moment to feel good about the positive progress you've made in contributing to a healthier and more productive organisation. Change doesn't happen overnight, but every small, consistent step creates a ripple effect.

Introduction to Organisational Integration

Welcome to the Final Workbook Section

So far, the exercises in this workbook have explored how positive work ways can be applied to individuals, teams, and business functions. This final section brings everything together, guiding you as you explore the ways you can start integrating these principles across your entire organisation.

Building on Previous Exercises

The techniques and exercises we've covered so far remain essential, but now the focus shifts to scaling them.

The exercises within this workbook section are designed to help change the way your business operates, helping you:

- Apply these principles at an organisational level.
- Align efforts with business strategy and values.
- Achieve greater consistency across your business.
- Secure a sustainable culture shift.
- Nurture an engaged, productive, and resilient workforce.

Before You Start

- Take a moment to reflect on where your organisation is now:
- How much progress have you made?
- What does success look like for your organisation?
- What steps will bridge the gap between today and your long-term vision?

What's Next?

Each module in this section provides practical exercises covering how to align positive work ways with:

1. Aligning Organisational Strategy and Vision.

2. Strategic Goal Setting.

3. Engaging Leaders with positive work ways.

4. Strategic communication to drive positive ways of working.

5. Incorporation into Leadership and Workforce Development.

6. Aligning Safety with positive work ways.

7. Functional alignment between different parts of the business.

8. External Well-being Providers and positive work ways.

9. Rethinking Measurement.

10. Support Resources – Bringing it all Together.

Wherever you choose to start, these exercises combine all the different elements from the book, helping you create a workplace where positive work ways become the norm. Let's begin.

Module 1: Aligning Strategic Vision

Purpose

This module provides a clear, actionable framework for integrating positive work ways into your organisation's existing strategy and vision.

Why it Matters

By following this step-by-step exercise, senior leaders will explore what successful integration looks like, identify key considerations, and outline an actionable approach tailored to their business context.

Tools You'll Need

- Universal Template
- Solutions-Focused Question Bank
- Reframing Bank
- Scaling Template

Follow the template steps using the guide questions provided to get you started. Replace or add further questions in order to thoroughly explore each core question in turn before proceeding.

Keep additional questions solutions-focused, using the Solutions-Focused Question Bank as a guide around which to frame your own tailored questions. If helpful, use the reframe bank to help reframe any negative goals and the scaling template to determine progress as you go.

Universal Template

Title: Aligning Organisational Strategic Vision.

Date

Review Team Members

Step 1: Define Your Vision

Core Question: What does good look like?
If positive work ways were fully embedded in our strategy, what would success look like?

Questions to Explore
- If we had already fully integrated positive work ways, what would be different?
- What would have improved from where we are now, and how do we know?
- What positive changes are visible in leadership, decision-making, and collaboration?
- How are employees, teams, and stakeholders engaging with this approach?
- What impact is there on business outcomes, culture, and performance?
- What would we see, hear, or feel if this vision were fully realised?

Strategic Considerations
- How does this vision align with our long-term business priorities?
- What would make this vision practical and strategically valuable?

Your Questions

[Insert here]

Your Vision

[Insert here]

Metrics
- On a scale of 1–10, how clearly defined is our vision?
- What specific indicators will show we are moving towards this vision?

Step 2: Existing Strengths

Core Question: What's already working well?
What strengths do we already have that can support this vision?

Questions to Explore
- What elements of our business already align with positive work ways?
- What existing behaviours, values, or processes align with this strategy?
- Where in the organisation already aligns with this vision?
- What structures or frameworks already support positive work ways?
- What past successes can we build on to accelerate this shift?

Strategic Considerations
- How can we build on these strengths?
- Which strengths provide a solid foundation?
- Which may need further development?

Your Questions

[Insert here]

Your Strengths

[Insert here]

Metrics
- On a scale of 1–10, how well do our current strengths support this vision?
- What existing data or success stories indicate we are on the right track?

Step 3: Explore Opportunities

Core Question: Where does integrating positive work ways offer the greatest strategic value?

Objective: To identify high-impact opportunities where integrating positive work ways into the strategy will strengthen business priorities and drive measurable value.

Questions to Explore
- Where could positive work ways make the biggest positive difference across the organisation?
- What areas of the business would benefit most from improved alignment with this vision?
- If we strengthened our approach in one key area, what would be the biggest gain?
- What untapped opportunities exist to reinforce this vision within our strategy?
- Where could small shifts have a significant impact on business outcomes, engagement, or performance?

Strategic Considerations
- Which business functions or strategic initiatives would gain the most from this integration?
- How can we ensure opportunities align with both short-term wins and long-term sustainability?
- What emerging trends or external factors make this the right time to explore these opportunities?

Your Questions

[Insert here]

Your Opportunities

[Insert here]

Metrics

- How will we determine whether these opportunities are viable?
- On a scale of 1–10, how well do these opportunities align with existing priorities?

Step 4: Take Action

Core Question: What are the first practical steps we can take to align our strategy with positive work ways?

Objective: To translate strategic opportunities into concrete, measurable actions that begin embedding positive work ways within the organisation's strategy.

Questions to Explore

- What is the simplest, most immediate action we can take to begin integrating this vision?
- Who needs to be involved in taking the first steps, and how can we engage them effectively?
- What existing initiatives or processes could we adjust slightly to bring this vision to life?
- What's one small change we can implement now that will create a visible impact?
- What strengths from Step 2 can we apply immediately to support early success?

Strategic Considerations

- How do we ensure actions are practical, achievable, and aligned with our strategic priorities?
- What early wins will help build confidence and momentum?
- How do we embed accountability, so actions lead to lasting change rather than temporary initiatives?

Your Questions

[Insert here]

Your Steps

[Insert here]

Metrics

- What short-term behaviours or results will indicate we are making progress?
- How will we track and measure engagement in these initial steps?
- On a scale of 1–10, how effectively are these actions aligning with our broader strategic goals?

Step 5: Reflect, Review, Repeat

Core Question: What progress have we made, and what insights will guide our next steps?

Objective: To assess progress, identify learnings, and ensure continuous alignment with the strategic vision for positive work ways.

Questions to Explore

- What positive changes have we noticed since taking action?
- What's working well that we should continue or scale up?
- What unexpected benefits or opportunities have emerged?
- What have we learned that could make our next steps even more effective?
- If we took one more small step forward, what would it be?
- How can we ensure this remains a continuous strategic focus rather than a one-time initiative?

Strategic Considerations

- How do we ensure leadership and teams stay engaged in this vision over time?
- What structures or review processes will keep this strategy aligned with business goals?
- How will we integrate feedback loops to refine and improve our approach?

Your Questions

[Insert here]

Your Reflections

[Insert here]

Final Measurement & Progress

- On a scale of 1–10, where are we now compared to our starting point?
- What measurable improvements (e.g., engagement, efficiency, collaboration) indicate progress?
- What key indicators will tell us whether we're on track for long-term success?

Reflection Prompts

- What insights have emerged about the alignment between your current strategy and the principles of positive work ways?
- How has this process clarified what success looks like for your organisation?
- What is the first tangible step you will take toward integrating these practices into your strategy?

Next Steps

- Draft a high-level roadmap that outlines your approach to integrating positive work ways into your strategy.
- Prepare to refine this roadmap in the next module, which focuses on Strategic Goal Setting.
- Engage your leadership team to review and align on your vision and initial steps.

Module 2: Strategic Goal Setting

Purpose

This module provides two structured exercises to ensure strategic goals are clear, solutions-focused, and aligned with positive work ways. The first exercise reframes existing goals to shift focus from problems to opportunities, and the second guides the development and cascading of goals to ensure they drive meaningful action at every level.

Why It Matters

Goals shape organisational focus and impact. Without the right goals, progress is unclear, and alignment is lost.

Tools You'll Need

- Universal Template
- Solutions-Focused Question Bank
- Reframing Bank
- Scaling Template

Follow the template steps using the guide questions provided to get you started. Replace or add further questions in order to thoroughly explore each core question in turn before proceeding.

Keep additional questions solutions-focused, using the Solutions-Focused Question Bank as a guide around which to frame your own tailored questions. If helpful, use the reframe bank to help reframe any negative goals and the scaling template to determine progress as you go.

Exercise 1: Reframing Strategic Goals (Quick Exercise)

Purpose

All goals have a positive intention, but they can often be negatively framed. Reframing a negatively framed goal involves identifying the positive intention and then flipping the perspective.

Process

1. Write the goal down in its current form.
2. Does the goal focus on a problem - does it focus on reducing an unwanted behaviour, action, or outcome?
3. Flip the perspective - so place the focus on what behaviours, actions or outcomes are wanted.
4. How can the goal be flipped to emphasise strengths, progress, and desired outcomes rather than fixing issues?
5. End of process - it really is that simple!

Example

Original Goal	Reframed Goal
Reduce employee turnover by 15%.	Build a workplace culture that supports growth and engagement, improving retention by 15%.
Increase operational efficiency by 20%.	Foster cross-team collaboration and innovation to achieve a 20% improvement in operational efficiency.
Improve customer satisfaction by 10%.	Enhance team alignment and communication to achieve a 10% improvement in customer satisfaction.

Exercise 2: Developing & Cascading Strategic Goals

Purpose

Develop strategic goals that align with positive work ways, ensuring that they are well structured, measurable, and cascaded effectively across all levels of the organisation.

Universal Template

Title: Develop and cascade strategic goals.

Step 1: Define Strategic Goals

Core Question: What goals will best support our strategic vision for positive work ways?

Objective: To guide leaders in identifying the right strategic goals that align with the organisational vision and drive meaningful impact.

Questions to Explore
- What key goals will move us closest to achieving our strategic vision?
- What measurable outcomes will indicate success in embedding positive work ways?
- What would we see, hear, and experience if these goals were fully realised?
- How can we structure these goals to maximise impact and long-term value?
- How do we ensure these goals are practical, actionable, and aligned with our vision?

Strategic Considerations
- Are these goals ambitious but achievable?
- How do these goals contribute to the long-term success of the organisation?

Your Questions
[Insert here]

Your Strategic Goals
[Insert here]

Metrics
- How well do these goals align with our vision? (Scale of 1–10)
- How will we measure whether these goals are driving the intended impact?

Step 2: Identify Strengths That Support These Goals

Core Question: What strengths already exist that will help us achieve these goals?

Objective: To ensure that strategic goals build on what's already working, making them easier to achieve and sustain.

Questions to Explore
- What existing processes or systems already align with these goals?
- Where have we seen success in similar areas, and how can we build on that?
- What strengths within our teams or culture will help drive progress?
- What resources or capabilities do we already have that can accelerate implementation?
- How can we make the most of what's already working to embed these goals faster and more effectively?

Strategic Considerations
- How do our existing strengths give us a competitive advantage in achieving these goals?

- Where can we scale up what's already working rather than reinventing processes?

Your Questions

[Insert here]

Your Strengths

[Insert here]

Metrics

- What existing data confirms we have a strong foundation to build on?
- How well do current strengths align with these goals? (Scale of 1–10)

Step 3: Explore Opportunities for Alignment & Impact

Core Question: How can we refine and optimise these goals to maximise their impact?

Objective: To explore ways to enhance strategic goals so they create maximum value across the business.

Questions to Explore

- Where will achieving these goals create the greatest value across the organisation?
- What opportunities could aligning these goals more closely with our vision unlock?
- What small adjustments could significantly accelerate progress?
- How can we refine these goals to enhance engagement and impact?
- What practical steps will make these goals easier to embed and sustain?

Strategic Considerations

- How do these goals connect across different business areas, ensuring a whole-organisation impact?
- How do we ensure these goals remain flexible, adaptable, and scalable?

Your Questions

[Insert here]

Your Opportunities

[Insert here]

Metrics

- What measurable indicators will confirm these opportunities are viable?

- How well do these opportunities align with business priorities? (Scale of 1–10)

Step 4: Take Action & Finalise the Goals

Core Question: How do we ensure these goals are clear, actionable, and ready to be cascaded?

Objective: To refine, simplify, and structure strategic goals so they are measurable and drive real-world impact.

Questions to Explore
- How can we structure each goal, so it is clear, measurable, and actionable?
- What is the first concrete step we will take to begin achieving each goal?
- Who will take ownership, and how will accountability be built in?
- What key milestones will indicate we are on track?
- How can we make these goals easy to communicate, understand, and embed at all levels?

Strategic Considerations
- Are these goals simple enough to be easily understood across all levels?
- How do we ensure that they remain adaptable while staying focused on impact?

Your Questions

[Insert here]

Your Finalised Goals & Action Plan

[Insert here]

Metrics
- How well do these finalised goals align with the strategic vision? (Scale of 1–10)
- How will success be measured at different levels of the organisation?

Step 5: Cascading Goals Across the Business

Core Question: How do we ensure these goals are understood, adopted, and embedded at every level?

Objective: To create a structured plan for translating high-level strategic goals into department, team, and individual objectives.

Questions to Explore
- How can we communicate these goals clearly and meaningfully across the organisation?
- What's the best way to adapt these goals for different teams while maintaining alignment?
- How do we ensure leaders actively model, reinforce, and embed these goals?
- What simple structures or processes will help track progress and maintain focus?
- How do we ensure goal-setting remains a continuous, evolving process rather than a one-time exercise?

Strategic Considerations
- What's the best cascading approach (e.g., phased, piloted, organisation-wide)?
- How do we ensure leaders and teams take ownership of these goals rather than seeing them as top-down directives?
- What support, training, or resources will make goal alignment seamless?

Your Questions
[Insert here]

Your Cascading Plan
[Insert here]

Metrics
- How consistently are goals being cascaded across different levels?
- How well do teams and leaders understand how their goals align with the overall vision?

Step 6: Reviewing, Measuring & Sustaining Progress

Core Question: How do we track success and ensure continuous alignment?

Objective: To establish a structured process for monitoring, refining, and sustaining goals over time.

Questions to Explore
- What measurable progress have we made so far, and how can we build on it?

- What early successes can we strengthen and scale?
- What adjustments will help refine and improve goal alignment?
- How can we ensure these goals stay relevant, flexible, and impactful over time?
- What tracking and review processes will keep us on course for sustained success?

Strategic Considerations

- What review mechanisms will ensure that goals are regularly refined and not static?
- How do we embed continuous feedback and adaptability into strategic goal-setting?

Your Questions

[Insert here]

Your Steps

[Insert here]

Metrics

- What KPIs confirm that goals are embedded in daily operations and decision-making?
- How do engagement and business outcomes reflect progress?

Module 3: Engaging Leaders with Positive Work Ways

Purpose

This module provides a structured approach for communicating the vision for positive work ways throughout leadership teams in a way that will ensure understanding, support, and commitment.

Why It Matters

Leaders set the tone for how change is received and adopted. If they are unclear, resistant, or disengaged, the message will not reach employees meaningfully. Taking the time to engage leaders first ensures that positive work ways are introduced with consistency, confidence, and genuine commitment across the business.

Tools You'll Need

- Universal Template
- Solutions-Focused Question Bank
- Reframing Bank
- Scaling Template

Follow the template steps using the guide questions provided to get you started. Replace or add further questions in order to thoroughly explore each core question in turn before proceeding.

Keep additional questions solutions-focused, using the Solutions-Focused Question Bank as a guide around which to frame your own tailored questions. If helpful, use the reframe bank to help reframe any negative goals and the scaling template to determine progress as you go.

Universal Template

Title: Communicate positive work ways vision and engage leadership.
Date
Review Team Members

Step 1: Define Your Vision

Core Question: What does good look like?

If all leaders understood, supported, and aligned with positive work ways, what would success look like?

Questions to Explore

- What would I see, hear, and experience when talking to leaders if they were fully on board?
- What discussions would be happening at senior, mid-level, and frontline leadership levels that show this is understood and valued?
- If leaders were fully engaged in this, how would they describe positive work ways in their own words?
- What would tell me that leaders not only understand the message but are committed to driving it forward?

Strategic Considerations

- What do leaders need to believe about this for them to support it fully?
- What level of understanding will leaders need before they feel comfortable advocating for it?
- How will I recognise when leadership alignment has been achieved?

Your Questions

[Insert here]

Your Vision

[Insert here]

Metrics

- On a scale of 1–10, where are we currently?
- What measurable indicators will confirm leaders are effectively engaging with and communicating positive work ways?

Step 2: Identify Existing Strengths

Core Question: What's already working well?
What existing communication channels, leadership behaviours, or cultural factors will support this?

Questions to Explore
- Where do leaders already communicate effectively across the business, and how can I use that?
- Which past leadership messages or changes gained strong buy-in, and what made them successful?
- What structures—meetings, leadership forums, or networks—already exist that could help deliver this?
- Who are the most trusted and influential leaders that others naturally listen to?
- What examples of existing behaviours or company values align with positive work ways that I can highlight?

Strategic Considerations
- How can I introduce this using existing leadership structures rather than creating new ones?
- Who are the key leaders who need to support this first to set the tone?
- What proven engagement strategies can I use to reinforce this message?

Your Questions

[Insert here]

Your Strengths

[Insert here]

Metrics
- On a scale of 1–10, where are we currently?
- What existing data confirms leaders are engaging with similar initiatives?

Step 3: Explore Opportunities

Core Question: Where is the greatest potential for positive impact?

How do I introduce this in a way that maximises buy-in and avoids resistance?

Questions to Explore
- Where do leaders naturally look for guidance, and how can I make sure positive work ways are part of those conversations?
- How can I adapt this message to resonate with senior executives, mid-level leaders, and frontline managers?
- What opportunities exist to connect this to leadership priorities, so it feels

relevant rather than 'another initiative'?
- How can I position this so that it feels useful and necessary rather than an extra task?
- What are the easiest ways for leaders to see early results, so they become advocates rather than sceptics?

Strategic Considerations
- How do I ensure that leaders receive the right message at the right time in the right way?
- What methods will help leaders feel involved rather than simply informed?
- What can I put in place to make this easier for leaders to absorb, apply, and communicate?

Your Questions

[Insert here]

Your Opportunities

[Insert here]

Metrics
- How will we determine whether our leadership engagement strategies are effective?
- What leading indicators will show early signs of leadership buy-in and ownership?

On a scale of 1–10, how well do our current communication approaches align with leadership needs?

Step 4: Take Action

Core Question: What small steps will create meaningful progress?

What actions will help leaders understand, commit to, and reinforce this message?

Questions to Explore
- What is the simplest and most effective way to introduce this message?
- How can I ensure leaders have time to process and respond to this message rather than just receive it?
- What structured approach will ensure this message reaches all leadership levels without overwhelming them?

- How do I create opportunities for leaders to ask questions and shape their role in this?
- What will I put in place to ensure early conversations turn into long-term commitment?

Strategic Considerations
- What key steps will ensure alignment before moving forward?
- How can I support leaders in feeling confident discussing this before expecting them to endorse it?
- What early signals will show that this message is being received well and not just acknowledged?

Your Questions

[Insert here]

Your Steps

[Insert here]

Metrics
- What leadership behaviours will indicate that communication is effective?
- On a scale of 1–10, how well are these actions supporting leadership engagement?

Step 5: Reflect, Review, Repeat

Core Question: What progress have we made, and what insights will guide our next steps?

How do I measure and sustain leadership alignment and buy-in?

Questions to Explore
- What feedback from leaders tells me they understand and support this?
- Where have I seen strong alignment, and what helped make that happen?
- What concerns or resistance have surfaced, and how can I address them constructively?
- What adjustments can I make to improve understanding and engagement?
- How do I keep this message alive in leadership discussions, so it doesn't fade over time?

Strategic Considerations
- How do I ensure that this continues to be reinforced at all leadership levels?

- What mechanisms will keep leaders involved and accountable for embedding this?
- How do I track leadership commitment beyond the initial rollout?

Your Questions

[Insert here]

Your Reflections

[Insert here]

Final Measurement & Progress

- On a scale of 1–10, how effectively are leaders engaging with and communicating positive work ways?
- What measurable improvements (e.g., clarity, consistency, leadership confidence) indicate progress?

What key indicators will confirm sustained leadership commitment?

Final Notes & Follow-Up Actions

- Maintain ongoing leadership alignment through structured engagement and feedback loops.
- Refine and adapt communication tools based on leader feedback and observed challenges.
- Establish a system for tracking leadership confidence and effectiveness in messaging.

Module 4: Strategic Communications with Positive Work Ways

Purpose

This module helps define what good communication looks like so that positive work ways is understood and used across the organisation.

Why It Matters

Without a clear vision, communication can be inconsistent or ineffective, making it harder for people to apply positive work ways in their daily work.

Tools You'll Need

- Universal Template
- Solutions-Focused Question Bank
- Reframing Bank
- Scaling Template

Follow the template steps using the guide questions provided to get you started. Replace or add further questions in order to thoroughly explore each core question in turn before proceeding.

Keep additional questions solutions-focused, using the Solutions-Focused Question Bank as a guide around which to frame your own tailored questions. If helpful, use the reframe bank to help reframe any negative goals and the scaling template to determine progress as you go.

Universal Template

Title: Communicate the positive work ways vision and engage leadership.
Date
Review Team Members

Step 1: Define the Communication Vision

Core Question: What does good look like?
If communication fully supported positive work ways, what would success look like?

Questions to Explore

- How would Positive work ways be communicated in a way that feels clear and consistent?
- What role would core policies, procedures, and other written frameworks play?
- What would people need to see and hear to know that positive work ways are an organisational priority?
- How should messaging be structured to keep it practical and useful at all levels?
- What would confirm that communication is influencing behaviour, not just sharing information?

Strategic Considerations

- How do we ensure consistency across different communication channels and formats?
- What formats are most effective for reinforcing positive work ways in written, verbal, and digital communication?
- How will we track whether communication is driving real action?

Your Questions

[Insert here]

Your Vision

[Insert here]

Metrics

- On a scale of 1–10, where are we against our vision?

Step 2: Identify Existing Strengths in Communication

Core Question: What's already working well?

Which communication channels across the organisation could be utilised?

Questions to Explore

- Do any existing core policies or procedures already align, either wholly or partially, with positive work ways?
- Could previous messaging strategies that proved successful be useful?
- What communication channels (formal and informal) already exist that we can use to introduce positive work ways?

- Where does communication already align with positive work ways, and how can we expand on this?
- How do different parts of the organisation currently receive and process information, and what does this tell us about the best ways to introduce this?

Strategic Considerations
- How can we build on existing communication strengths rather than starting from scratch?
- Which leaders, teams, or functions have already set a strong example in reinforcing positive behaviours?
- Where does communication naturally work well, and how can that be replicated?

Your Questions

[Insert here]

Your Strengths

[Insert here]

Metrics
- What percentage of leadership messages (meetings, newsletters, policy updates) already align with positive work ways?
- What is the current engagement rate with existing internal communications?

Step 3: Explore Opportunities

Core Question: Where is the greatest potential for positive impact?

Where could communication have the greatest impact in embedding positive work ways across the organisation?

Questions to Explore
- How could positive work ways be communicated in a practical and useful way?
- Where are the most frequently used communication interfaces, and how might positive work ways be integrated into those spaces?
- What approaches would help leaders and teams feel personally responsible for embedding positive work ways in their work?
- How might written and spoken communication consistently reinforce the principles of positive work ways?

- What needs to be in place for communication to reinforce the behaviours and mindsets that positive work ways promote?

Strategic Considerations
- How can communication ensure that positive work ways are understood as a core way of working rather than just an initiative?
- How can we adapt communication over time to strengthen positive work ways as a lasting part of organisational culture?
- How will we integrate messaging into existing communication routines rather than treating it as an add-on?

Your Questions
[Insert here]

Your Opportunities
[Insert here]

Metrics
- On a scale of 1-10, how well do the identified communication opportunities align with and support positive work ways?
- To what extent have different communication channels, formats, and audiences been considered when identifying ways to embed positive work ways?

Step 4: Take Action

Core Question: What small steps would provide the greatest impact?

What small, practical steps would lead to greater alignment and effectively communicate positive work ways across the organisation?

Questions to Explore
- What step might be most impactful in starting to align communication with positive work ways?
- Who would need to be responsible for delivering these messages, and how?
- What steps might it be beneficial to update or introduce first?
- What structured approach will we use to reinforce and sustain these messages over time?
- How will we track whether the actions are understood, used, and implemented?

Strategic Considerations
- What is the quickest, most practical way to align policies and leadership messaging?
- How can communication be structured to reinforce action rather than just awareness?
- What regular touchpoints will keep this visible without overwhelming employees?

Your Questions
[Insert here]

Your Steps
[Insert here]

Metrics
- **Practical Implementation**: Percentage of leadership teams that have identified concrete actions for embedding positive work ways within their scope.
- **Resource Utilisation**: Uptake of leadership toolkits, frameworks, or training sessions provided for preparation.
- **Early Progress Indicators**: Instances where leaders have already started embedding positive work ways in their behaviours or decision-making before the formal rollout begins.

Step 5: Reflect, Review, Repeat

Core Question: What progress have we made, and what should we adjust?

How do we measure, refine, and sustain the communication strategy to ensure positive work ways stays embedded over time?

Questions to Explore
- What signs tell us that our communication efforts are making a real impact?
- What evidence informs us that our action is proving effective?
- What feedback could be useful in determining any changes or future steps?
- What adjustments need to be made to improve reach, relevance, or impact?
- How will we ensure communication remains a long-term, embedded part of how we work rather than a short-term initiative?

Strategic Considerations
- What processes will help to maintain consistency and alignment in

communication across the organisation?
- What steps will be most impactful in making positive work ways an integral part of our strategic communications?
- What tracking methods will ensure we continue improving communication without creating unnecessary complexity?

Your Questions

[Insert here]

Your Reflections

[Insert here]

Metrics
- On a scale of 1-10, where are we?
- What are the engagement rates with the amended communications?

Final Reflection and Next Steps

- What's one immediate step that would progress us toward our desired outcome?
- What next steps will we take to maintain the momentum in aligning communication with positive work ways?

Module 5: Incorporation of Positive Work Ways into L&D Programmes

Purpose

This module explores how leadership and workforce development programmes can be utilised to integrate and embed positive work ways throughout an organisation.

Why It Matters

Positive work ways rely on an analogy of brain states. Aligning development programme frameworks and training content with positive work ways provides the foundational awareness needed, strengthens performance and resilience, and supports long-term organisational change.

Tools You'll Need

- Universal Template
- Solutions-Focused Question Bank
- Reframing Bank
- Scaling Template

Follow the template steps using the guide questions provided to get you started. Replace or add further questions in order to thoroughly explore each core question in turn before proceeding.

Keep additional questions solutions-focused, using the Solutions-Focused Question Bank as a guide around which to frame your own tailored questions. If helpful, use the reframe bank to help reframe any negative goals and the scaling template to determine progress as you go.

Universal Template

Step 1: Define the Vision

Core Question: What does good look like?

If everyone were equipped with the appropriate mindset, skills, and tools to incorporate positive work ways, what would that look like?

Questions to Explore
- What would be different about the working environment?
- How would people be working and communicating differently?
- How would everyday activities such as decision-making and problem-solving improve?
- How would teams be interacting, collaborating, and navigating challenges differently?
- If development programmes centred around positive work ways, what other benefits might that lead to?
- How might the integration of positive work ways into daily work activities influence employee well-being, motivation, and resilience?

Strategic Considerations
- How does this vision align with existing leadership and workforce development strategies?
- What long-term benefits could this approach create for organisational performance, engagement, and adaptability?
- Could leadership and workforce development based on positive work ways also help reduce programme complexity and training overload?

Your Questions

[Insert here]

Your Vision

[Insert here]

Metrics
- On a scale of 1–10, how well do existing programmes align with strategic priorities?
- Percentage of training aligned with positive work ways principles.

Step 2: Identify Existing Strengths

Core Question: What's already working well?

Where are programmes already in strategic alignment?

Questions to Explore
- Where does existing content have a natural alignment with positive work ways?

- What aspects of current programmes already support either high performance or resilience?
- Where and how does present training actively reduce friction, inefficiencies, or duplication?
- Are there any areas in which existing training structures already encourage positive ways of working?
- Where do existing training and support resources already promote a proactive approach?

Strategic Considerations
- Where could we build on any strengths in existing programmes rather than start from scratch?
- Which existing training models best support long-term learning and engagement?
- Where have past development programmes successfully changed workplace culture?

Your Questions

[Insert here]

Your Strengths

[Insert here]

Metrics
- Overlap of duplication in existing content.
- Engagement and effectiveness scores from previous programmes.

Step 3: Explore Opportunities

Core Question: Where is the greatest potential for positive impact?

How could positive work ways be integrated into leadership and workforce development to create meaningful and lasting change?

Questions to Explore
- **Standalone Module**: What benefits might a dedicated training module on positive work ways provide, and how could it complement existing programmes?
- **Embedded Learning**: Where do existing courses naturally align with positive work ways, and how might they be successfully integrated?

- **Full Programme Realignment**: What would be the impact of designing leadership and workforce development entirely around positive work ways as a core framework?
- What factors will determine whether a standalone, embedded, or fully realigned approach works best in your organisation?
- How could different learning formats strengthen effectiveness?
- What role could senior leaders play in reinforcing and embedding positive work ways throughout development programmes?
- Where could training be streamlined or consolidated to reduce duplication while maintaining impact?
- What tailored support resources (e.g., quick-reference guides, practical toolkits) would help sustain learning beyond formal training?

Strategic Considerations
- Which approach would fit best with organisational priorities, capacity, and long-term goals?
- How might positive work ways be incorporated into training frameworks in a way that ensures learning is practical, relevant, and easy to apply?
- How might a sequential or phased approach ensure effective incorporation without creating overwhelm?

Your Questions

[Insert here]

Your Opportunities

[Insert here]

Metrics
- Percentage of development programmes incorporating positive work ways.
- Early feedback from trial or pilot sessions on engagement and effectiveness.

Step 4: Take Action

Core Question: What small steps will have the greatest impact?

Which actions will bring positive work ways into leadership and workforce development effectively and sustainably?

Questions to Explore
- Which approach (standalone, embedded, or full realignment) are we

implementing?
- What are the first steps we will take to initiate progress?
- Who needs to be involved, when, and how?
- What action will we take to instil consistency across different courses and audiences?
- What support resources (e.g., guides, toolkits) will be helpful?
- Who will develop training content and accompanying support resources?
- Where could pilot programmes help assess and refine before scaling?
- Who will communicate these actions to key stakeholders to ensure alignment and buy-in?
- What timelines and milestones will ensure steady progress without disrupting existing programmes?

Strategic Considerations
- How will these actions be implemented in a way that avoids any disruption?
- Are these actions the most appropriate ones for our organisation?
- Is the required resource secured, available ready to go?

Your Questions

[Insert here]

Your Steps

[Insert here]

Metrics
- Percentage of actions initiated within defined timeframes.
- Number of courses updated, created, or revised to incorporate positive work ways.
- Participant engagement and feedback from pilot sessions.

Step 5: Reflect, Review, Repeat

Core Question: What progress has been made, and what requires further refinement?

How will the impact of positive work ways in leadership and workforce development programmes be assessed, adapted, and sustained?

Questions to Explore
- How have we progressed?

- What has feedback informed regarding learning effectiveness, engagement, and real-world application?
- What additional refinements could improve how positive work ways are embedded into daily operations?
- How well do the learning formats, tools, and resources support long-term behaviour change?
- What next steps will ensure continued integration and improvement?

Strategic Considerations

- What mechanisms will ensure ongoing feedback and continuous refinement of L&D programmes?
- What steps will provide leadership reinforcement and on-the-job application?
- How will progress be measured and reported to secure continued leadership buy-in?

Your Questions

[Insert here]

Your Reflections

[Insert here]

Metrics

Percentage of employees/leaders applying positive work ways in their roles.

Module 6: Aligning Safety Strategy with Positive Work Ways

Purpose

This module provides a structured framework for integrating positive work ways into existing safety strategies to develop a more proactive approach.

Why It Matters

Safety isn't just about policies and compliance—it's about behaviours, conversations, and accountability at all levels. By applying positive work ways, organisations can shift safety from a tick-box exercise to an engaged, collaborative process where people feel safe speaking up, taking ownership, and contributing to continuous improvement.

Tools You'll Need

- Universal Template
- Solutions-Focused Question Bank
- Reframing Bank
- Scaling Template

Follow the template steps using the guide questions provided to get you started. Replace or add further questions in order to thoroughly explore each core question in turn before proceeding.

Keep additional questions solutions-focused, using the Solutions-Focused Question Bank as a guide around which to frame your own tailored questions. If helpful, use the reframe bank to help reframe any negative goals and the scaling template to determine progress as you go.

Universal Template

Title: Strengthening safety through positive work ways
Date
Review Team Members

Step 1: Define the Vision

Core Question: What does good look like?

If positive work ways were fully integrated into the safety strategy, what would success look like?

Questions to Explore

- What would a strong, proactive safety culture look like at every level of the organisation?
- How would policies, procedures, and reporting systems reinforce positive safety behaviours?
- What leadership behaviours would demonstrate a strategic commitment to positive work ways in safety?
- How would communication and training ensure that safety is consistently prioritised and understood?
- What visible signs would confirm that the safety strategy enhances both operations and employee well-being?

Strategic Considerations

- How does this vision align with long-term business goals and regulatory priorities?
- How can integrating positive work ways into the safety strategy strengthen organisational performance?
- What mechanisms would ensure that safety remains an ongoing strategic priority rather than a compliance exercise?

Your Questions

[Insert here]

Your Vision

[Insert here]

Metric

On a scale of 1–10, where are we now?

Step 2: Identify Current Strengths

Core Question: What's already working well?

What existing strengths could be utilised and built on?

Questions to Explore

- Are there any areas where safety already feels proactive?

- Which policies and procedures already align either wholly or partially with positive work ways?
- Where do leaders successfully promote ownership and accountability for safety?
- What communication or training methods reinforce positive safety behaviours?
- Where have teams embedded safety practices that align with positive work ways?

Strategic Considerations
- How can existing strengths be expanded to reinforce positive work ways in safety?
- What successful safety initiatives could be scaled across the organisation?
- Which organisational behaviours support psychological safety and open safety discussions?

Your Questions

[Insert here]

Your Strengths

[Insert here]

Metric

Percentage of employees who feel comfortable reporting safety concerns.

Step 3: Explore Opportunities

Core Question: Where is the greatest potential for impact?

Where could positive work ways strengthen the safety strategy and culture?

Questions to Explore
- What new approaches could make the safety strategy more brain-friendly and solutions-focused?
- How could policies and procedures be refined to encourage proactive rather than reactive safety behaviours?
- Where could communication methods better reinforce engagement with safety practices?
- What small shifts in leadership approach could further embed positive work ways into safety?
- How might adopting a solutions-focused approach influence future outcomes?

Strategic Considerations
- How might safety strategy be utilised to embed positive work ways without adding complexity?
- What systems could be amended to reinforce proactive safety mindsets?
- Where could integrating positive work ways have the greatest long-term impact on safety culture?

Your Questions
[Insert here]

Your Opportunities
[Insert here]

Metric
On a scale of 1–10, how well does current safety communication encourage engagement?

Step 4: Take Action
Core Question: What small steps will create the greatest progress?
What steps will embed positive work ways into the safety strategy?

Questions to Explore
- What are the first actions we will take?
- Who is responsible for making it happen?
- What targets will be required to track progress effectively?
- How can it be ensured that this will be communicated clearly to those who need to act?
- What resources or support do we need to move forward without delay?

Strategic Considerations
- What safeguards will ensure these actions are sustained long-term?
- How will leadership reinforce and model these actions throughout the organisation?
- What process will we use to assess whether these actions are driving real change?

Your Questions
[Insert here]

Your Steps
[Insert here]

Metric

Percentage of employees actively involved in new safety initiatives.

Step 5: Reflect, Review, Repeat

Core Question: What progress have we made, and what should we adjust? How do we ensure the long-term integration of positive work ways into safety?

Questions to Explore

- What behavioural changes show that safety culture is improving?
- How can feedback be utilised to help determine next steps?
- Where is the integration of positive work ways proving most impactful?
- What further refinements would help build further momentum?
- What steps can we take to improve alignment with positive work ways further?

Strategic Considerations

- What tracking methods will help keep engagement high?
- How can leadership continue reinforcing these behaviours?
- How do we ensure this remains a long-term shift rather than a temporary effort?

Your Questions

[Insert here]

Your Reflections

[Insert here]

Metrics

On a scale of 1–10, how embedded are positive work ways in safety practices?

Final Reflection and Next Steps

- What's the next step to maintain progress?
- What are the next actions to sustain and build on this progress?

Module 7: Functional Alignment

Purpose

This module explores how positive work ways can be integrated into functional processes and interfaces.

Why It Matters

Disconnected teams slow progress and create inefficiencies. Strengthening alignment ensures smoother collaboration, clearer communication, and better business outcomes.

Tools You'll Need

- Universal Template
- Solutions-Focused Question Bank
- Reframing Bank
- Scaling Template

Follow the template steps using the guide questions provided to get you started. Replace or add further questions in order to thoroughly explore each core question in turn before proceeding.

Keep additional questions solutions-focused, using the Solutions-Focused Question Bank as a guide around which to frame your own tailored questions. If helpful, use the reframe bank to help reframe any negative goals and the scaling template to determine progress as you go.

Universal Template

Title

Date

Team Members

Step 1: Define the Vision

Core Question: What does good look like?
What would your organisation look like if every function, system, and process were aligned and working seamlessly together?

Questions to Explore
- How would the organisation operate if all functions, processes, policies, and systems were effectively aligned?
- What impact would clearer, more consistent messaging across functions have on workflow, decision-making, and outcomes?
- How might positive work ways help smooth interfaces and reduce inefficiencies?
- What would teams and leaders notice if every function supported the organisation's strategic vision?
- How would alignment impact culture, performance, and operational success?

Strategic Considerations
- How does this vision fit within existing organisational priorities?
- What signs would indicate that alignment is improving?
- How can this vision be embedded sustainably rather than as a short-term initiative?

Your Questions

[Insert here]

Your Vision

[Insert here]

Metrics

On a scale of 1–10, where are we presently?

Step 2: Identify Existing Strengths

Core Question: What's already working well?
Where do existing systems, processes, or frameworks already support alignment across functions?

Questions to Explore
- Where are functional teams already aligned and working efficiently toward shared goals?
- What existing policies or frameworks provide clarity and consistency across departments?
- Where do processes naturally create smooth handovers and reduce bottlenecks?

- What communication methods help maintain alignment and minimise misunderstandings?
- How have past improvements in coordination led to better outcomes, and what can we learn from them?

Strategic Considerations
- How can existing alignment be maintained as the organisation evolves?
- Where might small adjustments to existing structures enhance efficiency without major change?
- Where could greater alignment between teams be achieved without increasing the present workload?

Your Questions

[Insert here]

Your Strengths

[Insert here]

Metrics
What percentage of processes already support cross-functional alignment?

Step 3: Explore Opportunities

Core Question: Where is the greatest potential for positive impact?
Where and how could positive work ways improve alignment and streamline interfaces between functions?

Questions to Explore
- What areas of the business could benefit most from increased alignment?
- How could interfaces between functions be more efficient?
- How might taking a different approach to decision-making help outcomes?
- Where could individual processes or workflows be combined or streamlined?
- How could clarification of roles and expectations between teams help ease workflows?

Strategic Considerations
- What future possibilities might stronger function alignment create for the organisation?
- How could refining key touchpoints between functions create better long-term outcomes?

- How might these improvements contribute to a more adaptable and efficient organisation?

Your Questions

[Insert here]

Your Opportunities

[Insert here]

Metrics
- How well do cross-functional teams work together on shared priorities?
- How often do misaligned processes create delays or confusion?

Step 4: Take Action

Core Question: What small steps will have the greatest impact?

Which actions will lead to improved functional alignment and efficiency?

Questions to Explore
- Which actions from Step 3 offer the greatest potential for progress, and how will we prioritise them?
- What small steps will make it easier to embed positive work ways?
- What small steps will support greater alignment and smoother interfaces?
- Who needs to be involved, and how will responsibilities be determined?
- What steps will ensure these actions are followed through effectively?

Strategic Considerations
- How might the integration of these actions into existing processes improve their effectiveness?
- What resources, tools, or training might make implementation easier?
- How could we optimise alignment between key decision-makers and stakeholders?

Your Questions

[Insert here]

Your Steps

[Insert here]

Metrics

Number of actions successfully implemented.

Step 5: Reflect, Review, Repeat

Core Question: What progress has been made, and what requires amendment? How could ongoing effectiveness be monitored to ensure continued impact?

Questions to Explore

- What progress has implementing the actions achieved?
- How have these changes influenced operational efficiencies?
- What early signs indicate that the actions taken are having the anticipated outcomes?
- What amendments could improve the effectiveness of these actions?
- Where will further integration of positive work ways help evolving business needs?

Strategic Considerations

- How will we ensure regular review and adaptation of our approach?
- What structures or processes will maintain accountability and prevent drift?
- How can we recognise and sustain progress without introducing unnecessary complexity?

Your Questions

[Insert here]

Your Reflections

[Insert here]

Metrics

How many function interfaces have been improved and streamlined?

Final Reflection and Next Steps

Reflection Prompts

- How will continued improvement be maintained?
- How could we build further momentum?
- How could this contribute to broader organisational change?

Next Steps

- Finalise the integration plan and confirm key stakeholders and roles.
- Begin piloting cross-functional initiatives, focusing on high-impact areas first.
- Schedule reviews to monitor progress, gather feedback, and refine.

Module 8: Leveraging External Well-being Providers

Purpose

This module explores how to align external well-being providers with their internal culture, ensuring their services actively support workplace goals rather than operating in isolation.

Why It Matters

When well-being providers align with organisational priorities, they reinforce positive working practices, improve support consistency, and strengthen employee and business outcomes.

Tools You'll Need

- Universal Template
- Solutions-Focused Question Bank
- Reframing Bank

Follow the template steps using the guide questions provided to get you started. Replace or add further questions in order to thoroughly explore each core question in turn before proceeding.

Keep additional questions solutions-focused, using the Solutions-Focused Question Bank as a guide around which to frame your own tailored questions. If helpful, use the reframe bank to help reframe any negative goals and the scaling template to determine progress as you go.

Universal Template

Title: Aligning External Well-being Providers with positive work ways.
Date
Review Team Members

Step 1: Define the Vision

Core Question: What does good look like?

If external providers were effectively aligned with positive work ways, what would success look like?

Questions to Explore
- What would be different about how external providers communicated, advised, and supported employees and leaders if they aligned with positive work ways?
- If external providers and internal teams were collaborating well, what would that look like in practice?
- If alignment was working at its best, what would employees, managers, and senior leaders notice about how external providers support them?
- How would interactions between providers and the organisation create smoother, more proactive ways of working?
- If external providers were fully integrated into the business strategy, what long-term benefits would that create for people, processes, and performance?

Strategic Considerations
- How will it be ensured that external providers enhance internal approaches without any omission or duplication?
- How might existing relationships or agreements could support this shift?
- How will we measure whether external providers are meaningfully contributing to positive work ways?

Your Questions
[Insert here]

Your Vision
[Insert here]

Metrics
Where are we now on a scale of 1–10?

Step 2: Identify Existing Strengths

Core Question: What's already working well?
Where is alignment already strong, and how can this be built on this?

Questions to Explore
- Where are providers already reinforcing positive work ways in their services, language, or recommendations?
- What processes, reporting structures, or referral pathways are smooth and

efficient?
- How effectively do providers presently support employees?
- Where have we seen strong, effective partnerships between internal teams and providers, and what made them successful?
- What strengths could be scaled or replicated across multiple providers?

Strategic Considerations
- How do we ensure that we utilise these strengths rather than reinventing existing processes?
- Which providers already demonstrate the strongest alignment, and what can we learn from them?

Your Questions

[Insert here]

Your Strengths

[Insert here]

Metrics
- How many provider services are already partially or wholly in alignment with positive work ways?
- Which provider processes or partnerships have the best feedback?

Step 3: Explore Opportunities

Core Question: Where is the greatest potential for positive impact?
What changes would make external provider relationships and internal processes more effective?

Questions to Explore
- How could external providers better support positive work ways in their services and interactions?
- Where could provider processes be amended to improve efficiency and ease of use for employees and leaders?
- What would make it easier for internal teams and providers to work together more effectively?
- How could external providers help improve long-term outcomes rather than just responding to issues?
- What practical steps could strengthen consistency between provider

approaches and internal ways of working?

Strategic Considerations
- How might minor changes lead to the most significant outcomes?
- How could we ensure provider services support rather than hinder our organisation?
- What gaps exist in the current approach, and how can they be addressed without unnecessary changes?

Your Questions
[Insert here]

Your Opportunities
[Insert here]

Metrics
- How many provider services directly align with positive work ways?
- How often are provider recommendations aligned with internal approaches?
- How many identified process gaps or inefficiencies have been addressed?

Step 4: Take Action

Core Question: What small step will have the greatest impact?

What actions will align external providers more closely with positive work ways and organisational needs?

Questions to Explore
- What is the first specific change we will introduce to strengthen how providers align with positive work ways?
- What is the first action we will take?
- Who is responsible for making it happen?
- What targets will be required to track progress effectively?
- How can it be ensured that this will be communicated clearly to those who need to act?
- How can feedback be utilised to determine next steps?

Strategic Considerations
- How do we ensure providers implement changes efficiently?
- What safeguards will ensure the long-term sustainability of actions?

Your Questions

[Insert here]

Your Steps

[Insert here]

Metrics
- How many agreed changes have been actioned?
- How quickly are providers adapting to these changes?

Step 5: Reflect, Review, Repeat

Core Question: What progress have we made, and what requires amendment? How will we track progress and build on what's working?

Questions to Explore
- How effectively are the changes improving alignment with both positive work ways and organisational needs?
- What feedback from employees and leaders suggests that provider support is working effectively?
- What further steps will be required to ensure alignment continues to improve over time?
- Where is the alignment of positive work ways proving most impactful?

Strategic Considerations
- How often should provider alignment be reviewed, and what existing process could be utilised to keep it on track?
- What additional support or adjustments might providers need to align with positive work ways fully?
- How will we ensure that providers evolve alongside organisational changes rather than falling behind?

Your Questions

[Insert here]

Your Reflections

[Insert here]

Metric
How many provider services and interfaces adopt a solutions-focused approach?

Module 9: Rethinking Measurement

Purpose

This module guides organisations in creating meaningful ways to track progress, ensuring measurement drives action rather than just reporting on past performance.

Why It Matters

Effective measurement highlights what's working, identifies areas for growth, and ensures positive work ways remain a core part of organisational success.

Tools You'll Need

- Universal Template
- Solutions-Focused Question Bank
- Reframing Bank
- Scaling Template

Follow the template steps using the guide questions provided to get you started. Replace or add further questions in order to thoroughly explore each core question in turn before proceeding.

Keep additional questions solutions-focused, using the Solutions-Focused Question Bank as a guide around which to frame your own tailored questions. If helpful, use the reframe bank to help reframe any negative goals and the scaling template to determine progress as you go.

Universal Template

Title
Date
Review Team Members

Step 1: Define the Vision

Core Question: What does good look like?
What would it look like if measurement fully supported positive work ways?

Questions to Explore

- Imagine every metric in your organisation had a meaningful role—what difference would that make?
- How could measurement provide a single, cohesive picture instead of fragmented data?
- What would measurement look like if it actively engaged teams rather than just reporting numbers?
- How could a stronger focus on leading indicators create more opportunities for growth?
- How might a more engaging approach to measurement encourage greater action at all levels?

Strategic Considerations

- How does measurement currently influence decisions across the organisation?
- What's the simplest way to make measurement useful and practical at every level?
- How do we ensure measurement supports learning rather than just tracking performance?

Your Questions

[Insert here]

Your Vision

[Insert here]

Metrics

- How well do current measurement systems align with organisational goals?
- On a scale of 1–10, how clearly does measurement support progress rather than just compliance?

Step 2: Identify Existing Strengths

Core Question: What's already working well?
Where do existing metrics already support positive work ways?

Questions to Explore

- What measurement practices already provide useful insights, and how could building on these strengthen progress?
- Where is data already collected but not being utilised optimally?

- How might data from existing processes—such as performance reviews, leadership updates, or team meetings— form a basis for more powerful metrics?
- How could existing measurement and data capture become more practical and useful?
- Where has measurement provided helpful insights or guided decisions in the past?

Strategic Considerations
- How could existing tools and data be optimised rather than introducing new systems?
- What existing measurement practices naturally support solutions-focused thinking?
- How could we adjust lagging indicators to highlight progress and strengths?

Your Questions

[Insert here]

Your Strengths

[Insert here]

Metrics
- How many existing measurement tools already support a forward-focused, solutions-driven approach?
- How frequently are existing insights used to inform action rather than just reporting?

Step 3: Explore Opportunities

Core Question: Where is the greatest potential for positive impact?

How could we make measurement more engaging, dynamic, and proactive?

Questions to Explore
- Could existing data be turned into something more relevant and useful with a simple reframe?
- Where could simplifying how data is presented make insights clearer and easier to apply?
- How might different formats, such as visuals or real-time dashboards, improve understanding and engagement?

- What small adjustments could make measurement more interactive and encourage participation?
- How could we simply and practically measure the impact of positive work ways across the organisation?
- What alternative or creative ways could we gather insights beyond surveys and reports?
- How could qualitative data, such as personal stories or reflections, bring measurement to life?

Strategic Considerations
- What safeguards are needed to ensure measurement drives positive action rather than becoming a box-ticking exercise?
- How can we align measurement with existing organisational priorities without creating additional complexity?
- What opportunities exist to integrate measurement into everyday work rather than treating it as a separate task?
- How can we ensure measurement captures both quantitative trends and qualitative insights for a fuller picture?
- What would make measurement more engaging and relevant so that employees see value in participating?

Your Questions

[Insert here]

Your Opportunities

[Insert here]

Metrics
- How well do current measurement efforts capture real insights rather than just numbers?
- How many opportunities exist to simplify or enhance measurement without adding complexity?

Step 4: Take Action

Core Question: What small steps will help move this forward?
What practical steps will improve measurement and make it more effective?

Questions to Explore
- What's one small change we can make to measurement today?

- How can we refine how data is shared and discussed to ensure it drives action?
- What adjustments will make measurement more engaging and relevant across the organisation?
- Where can we test a more dynamic or creative measurement approach?
- How will we track whether changes are improving decision-making and encouraging learning?

Strategic Considerations
- What's the simplest, most practical improvement that could create meaningful change?
- How can we ensure changes to measurement support strategic goals?
- What systems will help track and refine progress over time?

Your Questions

[Insert here]

Your Steps

[Insert here]

Metrics
- How many new measurement approaches have been tested?
- How well do updated measurement processes support real-time learning and action?

Step 5: Reflect, Review, Repeat

Core Question: What progress have we made, and what's next?

How do we ensure measurement remains relevant and continues to evolve?

Questions to Explore
- What progress have we seen in making measurement more insightful and useful?
- Where have measurement changes led to real improvements in decision-making?
- What feedback suggests we need to adjust or refine our approach?
- What opportunities have emerged that we hadn't considered before?
- What's the next small improvement we can make to ensure measurement stays valuable?

Strategic Considerations

- How do we ensure measurements continue to adapt over time?
- What regular check-ins or feedback loops will help sustain momentum?
- How do we make sure measurement remains a tool for learning rather than just tracking?

Your Questions

[Insert here]

Your Reflections

[Insert here]

Metrics

- How often are measurement insights used to inform real changes?
- How frequently is measurement reviewed and updated based on insights?

Final Reflection and Next Steps

Reflection Prompts

- What's one insight from this session that changes how we think about measurement?
- What's one immediate action we'll take to improve measurement?
- How will we track our progress in refining measurement itself?

Next Steps

- Choose 2–3 priority areas to improve measurement.
- Test small changes before making major adjustments.
- Set a review date to assess impact and refine further.

Module 10: Support Resources – Bringing It All Together

Purpose

This module brings it all together to explore the development of tailored resources that reinforce positive work ways throughout your organisation.

Why It Matters

Without practical tools and reinforcement, learning fades. Well-designed resources make it easier for employees to apply positive work ways, sustaining change over time.

Tools You'll Need

- Universal Template
- Solutions-Focused Question Bank
- Reframing Bank
- Scaling Template

Follow the template steps using the guide questions provided to get you started. Replace or add further questions in order to thoroughly explore each core question in turn before proceeding.

Keep additional questions solutions-focused, using the Solutions-Focused Question Bank as a guide around which to frame your own tailored questions. If helpful, use the reframe bank to help reframe any negative goals and the scaling template to determine progress as you go.

Universal Template

Title

Date

Review Team Members

Step 1: Define the Purpose

Core Question: What does good look like?

What would it look like if every leader and team had access to tailored resources that actively encouraged positive work ways?

Questions to Explore
- How would resources facilitate the adoption and integration of positive work ways across different parts of the organisation?
- How would these resources influence ways of working, decision-making, and interactions across teams?
- What visible changes would we see in decision-making, team interactions, and workplace behaviours if these resources were actively used?
- If the right resources were in place, how would they be used, accessed, and embedded in everyday work?
- How would it feel to work in an organisation where every resource reinforced positive work ways as the norm?
- What would employees and leaders be saying, doing, and noticing if these resources were shaping a more confident, engaged, and consistent workplace?

Strategic Considerations
- In what ways would core business strategies reinforce this vision?
- What lasting cultural shifts would we expect to see if these resources were fully embedded?
- If these resources were in place, how would they be driving business outcomes and operational success?

Your Questions
[Insert here]

Your Vision
[Insert here]

Metrics
On a scale of 1–10, how well do present support resources reinforce positive work ways?

Step 2: Identify Existing Strengths

Core Question: What's already working well?
Where do existing resources already aid the integration and reinforcement of positive work ways?

Questions to Explore
- Which existing workplace resources (e.g., training materials, policies, internal toolkits) already support positive work ways, even if indirectly?
- Where are teams already utilising self-generated tools or informal methods to embed positive work ways in their daily work?
- How do current communication channels (e.g., team meetings, intranet, newsletters) support the reinforcement of positive work ways?
- What learning and development programmes or workplace initiatives already align with positive work ways?
- Where has positive work ways already had a noticeable impact, even if it hasn't been fully embedded?

Strategic Considerations
- How might incorporation into existing resources avoid duplication?
- Which existing practices could be formalised or scaled to provide greater impact and consistency?
- What past lessons from previous training or cultural initiatives can inform how we strengthen these support resources?

Your Questions
[Insert here]

Your Strengths
[Insert here]

Metrics
Number of existing resources that align with positive work ways.

Step 3: Explore Opportunities

Core Question: Where is the greatest potential for positive impact?
What types of support resources would encourage the adoption of positive work ways throughout the organisation?

Questions to Explore
- What types of support materials would best support the integration of positive work ways?
- How might adopting a more creative approach lead to more user-friendly, relevant, and impactful resources?

- How could different positive work ways techniques be combined to maximise engagement and impact?
- What fun, engaging, or unexpected ways might employees want to experience these concepts rather than just read about them?
- How could we design resources that encourage curiosity, experimentation, and peer-led learning?
- How might technology be utilised to create innovative and creative resources to support positive work ways?
- How could positive work ways be embedded into team rituals or cultural moments to ensure they become second nature?

Strategic Considerations
- How can resource creation balance creativity with practicality, ensuring solutions are engaging but also easy to use?
- Which approaches would allow for both organisation-wide consistency and flexibility for different teams or functions?
- How can it be ensured that resources are adaptable, so they remain relevant as needs evolve?
- How can these resources be designed to be intuitive, accessible, and easy for employees to use without formal training?
- How might positive work ways techniques be utilised to replace or strengthen existing initiatives and campaigns?

Your Questions
[Insert here]

Your Strengths
[Insert here]

Metrics
- Number of new resource formats identified for development.
- Pilot engagement levels for newly introduced materials.

Step 4: Take Action

Core Question: What small steps will have the greatest impact?
Which resources should be prioritised and developed first?

Questions to Explore
- Which support resources will we prioritise first?

- What is the first step that will be taken to initiate progress?
- What teams need to be involved, when, and how?
- Which individuals will be responsible for each step?
- What process will be utilised to ensure all resources are aligned, engaging, practical, and fit for purpose?
- Who will be responsible for testing and rolling out the completed resources?
- Where will pilot programmes be run to assess and refine before scaling?
- Who will communicate agreed actions to key stakeholders to ensure alignment and buy-in?
- What timelines and milestones will ensure steady progress without disrupting existing programmes?

Strategic Considerations
- How will these actions be implemented in a way that avoids any disruption?
- Are these actions the most appropriate ones for our organisation?
- Is the required resource secured, available, and ready to go?

Your Questions
[Insert here]

Your Steps
[Insert here]

Metrics
- Percentage of identified resources created and implemented.
- Usage rates of new materials in workplace initiatives.
- Percentage of identified resources created and piloted.

Step 5: Reflect, Review, Repeat

Core Question: What progress have we made, and what should we adjust?
How will we assess, refine, and sustain the use of support resources?

Questions to Explore
- How effectively are resources supporting the adoption and integration of positive work ways across the organisation?
- What feedback indicates strengths or gaps in resource development?
- How well are different teams engaging with and using available resources?
- What amendments could improve accessibility, usability, or impact?

- How will we ensure continuous updates and improvements?
- What long-term measures will ensure positive work ways resources remain an integral part of organisational culture?

Strategic Considerations
- How can resources evolve alongside organisational priorities and needs?
- What will be put in place to ensure ongoing review, feedback, and iteration?
- How will we determine the long-term impact on workplace behaviours, engagement, and performance?
- How can we ensure resources remain adaptable and relevant as business needs evolve?

Your Questions

[Insert here]

Your Steps

[Insert here]

Metrics
- User satisfaction ratings of developed resources.
- Percentage of employees actively engaging with resources.
- Effectiveness ratings from follow-up assessments or feedback loops..

Final Summary

You've now completed the final phase of this workbook—**organisational integration**. In this phase, we brought together the concepts, strategies, and practical tools you explored at the individual, team, and functional levels to embed positive ways of working across your organisation.

Throughout this phase, you've:

Aligned positive ways of working with organisational strategy and vision.

Optimised strategic goals to reinforce solutions-focused thinking and engagement.

Created a methodical means to cascade these principles across leadership, teams, and business functions.

Developed targeted plans for integrating positive ways of working into external partnerships, including suppliers and well-being providers.

Designed measurement frameworks that drive curiosity, momentum, and positive change.

Explored creative communication and resource strategies to sustain engagement beyond initial implementation.

Your Next Steps

This workbook is not the end of the journey—it's the foundation for **continuous learning, adaptation, and refinement**. To **keep the momentum going**, consider:

Reviewing your progress: What has worked well so far? Where are the biggest opportunities for refinement?

Engaging stakeholders: Who else needs to be involved in sustaining these changes?

Embedding positive ways of working into long-term planning: How can this approach remain a core part of your organisational culture, leadership development, and strategic goals?

Measuring and celebrating success: What early indicators of progress can you track? How can you communicate wins to reinforce engagement?

Final Thought

Positive ways of working are not a project—they are a strategic enabler of engagement, productivity, and long-term organisational success. Every conversation, decision, and interaction are an opportunity to reinforce a culture where solutions-focused thinking, collaboration, and resilience thrive.

What might your organisation achieve if every employee, leader, and partner fully embraced these principles?

This is your opportunity to turn positive ways of working into a sustainable competitive advantage. What's the first step you will take today?

Templates Section

Universal Template

(For use across all topics in the workbook, adaptable for different organisational contexts.)

Title: [Exercise Name]

Date: [Insert Date]

Team Members Involved: [Names]

Step 1: Defining the Vision

(This step helps establish a clear, forward-focused vision for success in this area.)

Core Question: What does good look like?

- What would success look like if this were working at its best?
- How would this positively impact day-to-day operations?
- What would employees, leaders, and teams be doing differently?
- How would this change improve communication, decision-making, and collaboration?
- If this approach were fully embedded, what long-term benefits would we expect to see?
- What challenges or inefficiencies would this solve?
- How would this shape workplace culture and team dynamics?
- How would external stakeholders, clients, or customers experience this change?

Add Your Questions

[Your Response]

Your Responses

[Your Response]

Step 2: Existing Strengths

(This step helps you explore where you are now and what's already working.)

Core Question: What's already working well?

- Where do we already see elements of this approach in action?

- What existing processes, structures, or resources could support this change?
- Which teams or individuals are already demonstrating best practices?
- What successful past initiatives could provide insights for this effort?
- How have similar changes been introduced effectively in the past?
- What strengths within the organisation can be leveraged to drive this forward?
- How do our values, goals, or strategies already align with this vision?
- Where have we seen engagement, enthusiasm, or momentum for similar ideas?

Add Your Questions

[Your Response]

Your Responses

[Your Response]

Step 3: Exploring Opportunities

(This step helps generate ideas and practical options for moving forward.)

Core Question: Where is the greatest potential for positive impact?

- Where could this approach be introduced with the most immediate effect?
- What small changes could lead to significant improvements?
- How could this be adapted to fit different teams, roles, or business areas?
- What creative or unconventional approaches could enhance its impact?
- How might technology or new tools support this effort?
- What existing systems or processes could be simplified, improved, or repurposed?
- How could different perspectives or expertise help strengthen this initiative?
- Where might quick wins help build momentum and engagement?

Add Your Questions

[Your Response]

Your Responses

[Your Response]

Step 4: Next Steps

(This step ensures concrete, practical next steps.)

Core Question: What small steps will have the greatest impact?

- What are the most practical first steps we can take?
- Who needs to be involved in implementing these actions?
- What barriers might slow progress, and how can we address them?
- How can we ensure consistency and clarity in the rollout?
- Where would a small pilot test provide useful insights before scaling up?
- What support, tools, or resources are needed to make this sustainable?
- How can we introduce these actions without disrupting existing operations?
- How will we communicate these steps effectively across the organisation?

Add Your Questions

[Your Response]

Your Responses:

[Your Response]

Step 5: Reflect and Review

Core Question: What progress has been made, and what amendments are required?

- What impact have these actions had so far?
- What feedback have we gathered from employees, leaders, or stakeholders?
- What adjustments could improve effectiveness or engagement?
- Where have we seen the most success, and what made it work?
- What lessons have we learned that will inform future improvements?
- How will we track progress over time to ensure lasting change?
- What additional support or reinforcement is needed?
- How will we sustain this progress and prevent it from fading over time?

Add Your Questions

[Your Response]

Your Responses

[Your Response]

Solutions-Focused Question Bank

A universal guide to fostering more positive, constructive conversations—at work, home, and beyond.

A structured set of guiding questions to shift communication patterns away from problems, criticism, and negativity toward curiosity, strengths, and solutions.

How to Use This Question Bank

This isn't just a problem-solving tool—it's about changing the way people think, interact, and communicate in every setting. **The aim is to:**

- **Encourage** conversations that build energy and momentum.
- **Develop** a habit of noticing what's working and how to build on it.
- **Embed** solutions-focused thinking as the default, not just a technique for 'stuck' moments.
- **Replace** problem-heavy discussions with constructive, energising dialogue.

Where can you use these questions? → Everywhere!

- In leadership discussions
- In team meetings
- In performance conversations
- In personal relationships
- In everyday workplace interactions
- In goal-setting and coaching

The more you use these questions, the more natural they become—until solutions-focused communication becomes your default.

Core Solutions-Focused Question Categories

1. Setting the Direction (Shaping a Shared Focus from the Start)

- What's the best possible outcome we could aim for here?
- What would tell us we're making real progress?
- If this were already sorted, what would be different?

- If we could fast-forward to a successful result, what would we see happening?
- How will we know we've got this right?

Your Questions:

[insert here]

2. Unlocking Strengths & Resources (Finding What's Already Working)

- What's already working well that we could build on?
- What strengths or skills do we already have that could help here?
- When have we handled something similar successfully? What worked then?
- Who else might already have some great ideas or experience we can use?
- What's happening when things feel easy or effective for us?

Your Questions:

[insert here]

3. Reframing Challenges (Turning Obstacles into Opportunities)

- If we assumed this challenge had a hidden opportunity, what might it be?
- What's one useful thing we can take from this situation?
- What's one part of this that's easier than we originally thought?
- What would happen if we looked at this from a different angle?
- If someone else had this problem and solved it brilliantly, what do you think they did?

Your Questions:

[insert here]

4. Defining a Clear Vision of Success (Making the Future Real & Motivating)

- If we could design the perfect outcome, what would it look like?
- What would be happening if this was already going exactly as we wanted?
- What will be different when we've made progress?
- How will we know we've reached a great result?
- If we walked into a meeting six months from now and saw this working brilliantly, what would we see?

Your Questions:

[insert here]

5. Generating Momentum (Getting into Action Quickly & Effectively)

- What's the smallest step we could take right now to move forward?
- If we had to take action in the next 10 minutes, what would we do?
- What's one small change that could create a ripple effect?
- What's the easiest first step we can take?
- If we were already halfway to the result we want, what's something we'd have done differently?

Your Questions:

[insert here]

6. Strengthening Collaboration (Building Constructive & Engaging Relationships)

- How can we support each other to make this work well?
- What's something we appreciate about the way we work together?
- How can we help each other stay on track?
- What's one thing we're already doing well as a team?
- What's a small change that would make working together even easier?

Your Questions:

[insert here]

7. Tracking Progress (Noticing Small Wins & Reinforcing Success)

- What's something that's already improved, even in a small way?
- What's one thing we've learned so far that's been useful?
- What signs do we have that we're moving in the right direction?
- What's one success we can celebrate today?
- What would tell us we've made even more progress next week?

Your Questions:

[insert here]

8. Closing on a High Note (Leaving People Feeling Positive & Motivated)

- What's been most useful from this conversation?
- What's one thing you're taking away from today?
- What's one thing we'll do differently from now on?
- What's the best way to keep up this momentum?
- What's a sign that we'll know we're really making an impact?

Your Questions:

[insert here]

How This Works in Any Situation

With a colleague or employee → 'What's already working well, and what's the next step?

With your team → 'If we were already making progress, what would be different?

With yourself → 'What's one small action I could take today?

With a friend or family member → 'What's something good that happened today?

In goal-setting → 'If we achieved this, what would it look like?

In problem-solving → 'What's an opportunity in this situation?

Crib Sheet

Your Personal Go-To Solutions Focused Questions

(Write down the questions that resonate most with you. Add any new ones that fit your communication style.)

My top 3 go-to solutions-focused questions:

1.

2.

3.

Additional questions I find useful in my role/context:

1.

2.

3.

Tip: The more you practice using solutions-focused questions, the more naturally they will shape your communication.

Reframing Response Bank

How to Use This Resource

The way we frame a challenge shapes how we think, communicate, and act. Negative framing reinforces roadblocks, while reframing creates clarity, momentum, and solutions.

This resource provides go-to reframes for common negative statements, helping individuals and teams:

- Shift from barriers to opportunities.
- Encourage positive, action-oriented problem-solving.
- Improve communication by fostering more constructive dialogue.

Tip: The following table provides pre-built reframes, followed by a crib sheet where you can capture your preferred reframes.

Negative Statement	Reframe
'This is impossible.'	'What would make this possible, even in a small way?'
'We can't do that.'	'What's another way we could approach this?'
'We've always done it this way.'	'What's one thing we could experiment with to improve it?'
'I don't know what to do.'	'If you did know, what might your first step be?'
'I'm not sure this will work.'	'What would give us more confidence in this approach?'
'I'm overwhelmed.'	'If we broke this into steps, what would the first step be?'
'I'm worried we'll fail.'	'What's the best outcome we could create, and what would help us get there?'
'I don't have enough experience for this.'	'What strengths or skills do I already have that I can use?'
'This is too complicated.'	'What's the simplest way we could start?'
'I can't control this.'	'What's within my control that I can focus on?'
'I don't have time for this.'	'What's one small action I could take right now?'
'This isn't my job.'	'How could I contribute in a way that supports the bigger goal?'
'We don't have enough resources.'	'What's the best way to make progress with what we do have?'
'People never listen to me.'	'What's one way I can communicate this message differently?'
'That team never collaborates with us.'	'What's one action we could take to build stronger connections?'
'There's no point in trying.'	'What's one small win we could aim for?'

Negative Statement	Reframe
'I'm not creative enough to solve this.'	'What ideas have worked before that we could build on?'
'No one else seems to care.'	'Who has shown interest before, and how can we build on that?'
'It's always been this way.'	'If we could design this from scratch, what would we do differently?'
'This will never change.'	'What's one thing we could shift today that moves us in the right direction?'
'I'm bad at this.'	'What's one thing I could practice to improve?'
'They'll never agree.'	'What part of this might they be open to?'
'I can't keep up.'	'What's one way I can pace myself differently?'
'Nobody ever supports me.'	'Who has helped me before, and how can I build on that?'
'I hate doing this.'	'What's one way I can make this task easier or more enjoyable?'
'It's just too risky.'	'What's the risk of doing nothing?'
'They won't like this idea.'	'How could I present it in a way that connects with their priorities?'
'We have no control over this.'	'What's the smallest action we **do** have control over?'
'It's not fair.'	'What's one way I can move forward regardless?'
'I don't have the right skills.'	'What skills do I already have that I can apply here?'

Crib Sheet

(Capture common negative phrases you hear and craft your preferred reframes.)

Common Negative Statement	My Preferred Reframe

Tip: The more you practice reframing your thinking, the easier it becomes to help others do the same.

Scaling for Success Template

How to Use This Template

Scaling a successful initiative requires more than just expansion—it's about sustaining impact, adapting effectively, and maintaining alignment with organisational goals. This template helps you identify what's working, adapt it for scale, and ensure long-term success.

Tip: Use this template for projects, initiatives, processes, or cultural shifts that you want to expand effectively.

Step 1: Identify What's Working Well

What's already successful that we want to scale?

- What specific aspects of this initiative/process are working best?
- What measurable impact or benefits have we seen so far?
- What feedback or insights confirm its success?

Key Success Factors:

1.

2.

3.

Step 2: Define the Core Principles

What must remain consistent as we scale?

- What are the non-negotiables that must stay intact?
- What elements make this effective (mindset, behaviours, tools, or structures)?
- How can we keep the integrity of the approach while allowing flexibility?

Core Elements to Retain:

1.

2.

3.

Step 3: Explore Adaptation for Scale

How do we tailor this for different teams, locations, or contexts?

- What adjustments might be needed for different environments?
- What potential barriers or challenges could arise, and how can we overcome them?
- How can we maintain engagement and ownership at all levels?

Key Adaptations for Scale:

1.

2.

3.

Step 4: Build a Scalable Implementation Plan

What's the roadmap for scaling this successfully?
- What are the phases of scaling (pilot, full rollout, refinement)?
- Who needs to be involved at each stage?
- What training, resources, or support will be required?
- How will we ensure clear communication throughout the process?

Scalability Roadmap:

1.

2.

3.

Step 5: Measuring & Sustaining Success

How will we track progress and ensure long-term impact?
- What indicators will show that scaling is working?
- How will we capture feedback and make adjustments?

What mechanisms will ensure this remains a sustainable practice?

Success Indicators & Sustainability Plan:

1.

2.

3.

Crib Sheet: Your Scaling Strategy Reference

Scaling Challenge	Preferred Strategy or Solution

Tip: The more you refine your scaling approach, the more adaptable and impactful your initiatives will become.

Further Reading

If you're interested in exploring the ideas behind Positive Work Ways in more depth, the following books offer a helpful starting point. They each provide accessible insights into the core fields that have informed this approach, including neuroscience, positive psychology, and solutions-focused thinking.

Flourish: Martin Seligman

A compelling read from one of the founding figures in positive psychology, exploring how people and institutions can thrive

Positive Psychology: The Basics: Rona Hart

A useful foundation for understanding the key theories and research behind positive psychology.

Positively Speaking: The Art of Constructive Conversations with a Solutions Focus: Paul Z. Jackson & Janine Waldman

A practical guide to having more effective conversations by focusing on what's working and what's possible.

Solutions Focus Working: Mark McKergow

A concise and practical resource on applying solutions-focused principles in organisational and team settings.

The Brain Book: Rita Carter

A visually engaging and informative overview of the brain and its functions, covering both structure and behaviour.

Neuroscience for Dummies: Frank Amthor

A highly accessible introduction to how the brain works, ideal for those without a scientific background.

Acknowledgements

This book wouldn't exist without the people, experiences, and conversations that shaped it.

To the friends and family who encouraged this project (even when it took over everything), thank you for your patience, belief, and well-timed nudges to keep going.

To the organisations, teams, and leaders I've worked with over the years — thank you for the opportunities, challenges and the willingness to explore new ways of working. Much of what's in these pages has been tested, questioned, and refined alongside you.

To those who introduced me to the world of therapy, positive psychology, and solutions-focused thinking, thank you for lighting the spark. What started as a simple analogy during training became a lifelong fascination with how people think, feel, and work — and how organisations can use that knowledge to do better by their people.

And to you, the reader, thank you for picking up this book. I hope it helps you think differently, lead more purposefully, and influence the culture around you in ways that ripple far beyond the workplace.

Conclusion

'Every adventure requires a first step.'
— Lewis Carroll

What If?

What if organisations weren't just drivers of performance, but creators of ripples?

What if the way we work shaped not only culture, but communities?

What if organisations held the key to stronger families, safer workplaces, and healthier societies?

What if that kind of change didn't need a grand initiative — just small, consistent shifts?

What if it started with one leader? One team? One person? One moment?

What if it started with you?

Because every ripple, every shift, every change...

starts with one simple question…

What's your Pharmacist doing?

About the Author

With a background in occupational health and safety and a long-standing interest in psychology, Louise has spent her career exploring how organisations can work better — not just in terms of productivity, but in how people think, feel, and relate to one another.

Alongside her full-time work, she also qualified as a solutions-focused therapist — but chose not to practice clinically. Supporting people one-to-one, after the crisis had already hit, didn't feel enough. She became increasingly focused on prevention, and on the potential to create wider impact through the workplace, recognising that organisations are simply the sum of their people, and culture reflects collective brain state.

It was during her therapy training that she first came across a simple brain analogy designed to help people make sense of their own reactions. It proved a powerful tool — not just for awareness, but for action. That same analogy would later form the foundation for Positive Work Ways: a workplace-focused model that helps individuals and organisations shift behaviour, influence culture, and improve outcomes by working with the brain, not against it.

Louise went on to complete a Master's degree in the Psychology and Neuroscience of Mental Health, which deepened her interest further, particularly in how positive psychology and solutions-focused approaches can be combined to support more proactive and practical change in the workplace.

Today, she works with businesses to help them build healthier, safer, more productive cultures — using practical, evidence-informed tools that influence brain state and shape behaviour across teams, systems, and leadership.

Contact & Further Support

If you'd like to explore how Positive Work Ways could support your organisation — or if you're looking for additional resources, templates, or consultancy support — you can get in touch or find out more at:

🌐 www.positiveworkways.com

✉ support@positiveworkways.com

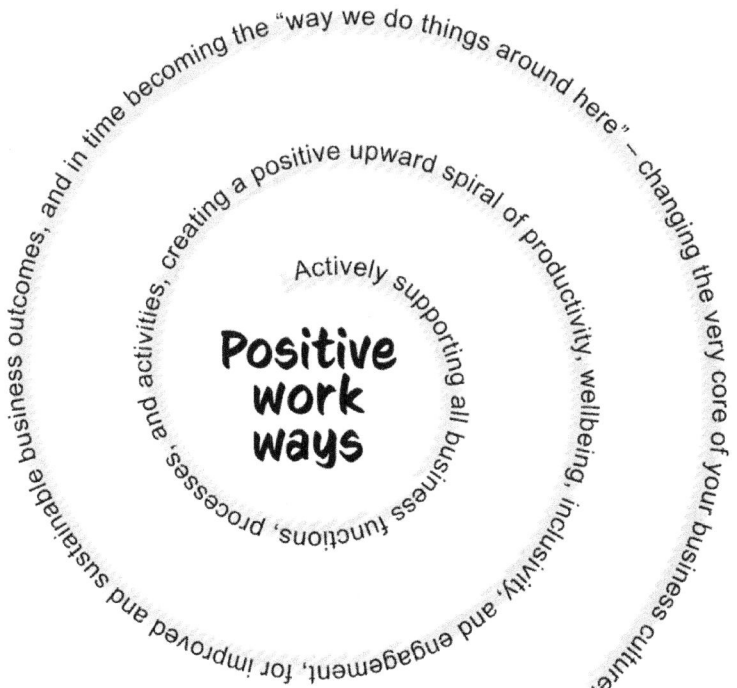

Printed in Dunstable, United Kingdom